BUTTONED UP

Buttoned Up

Clothing, Conformity, and
White-Collar Masculinity

Erynn Masi de Casanova

ILR PRESS
AN IMPRINT OF
CORNELL UNIVERSITY PRESS
ITHACA AND LONDON

First published 2015 by Cornell University Press
First printing, Cornell Paperbacks, 2015
Printed in the United States of America

Library of Congress Cataloging-in-Publication Data

Casanova, Erynn Masi de, 1977– author.
   Buttoned up : clothing, conformity, and white-collar masculinity / Erynn Masi de Casanova.
      pages cm
   Includes bibliographical references and index.
   ISBN 978-0-8014-5418-9 (cloth : alk. paper) —
   ISBN 978-1-5017-0049-1 (pbk. : alk. paper)
   1. Clothing and dress—Social aspects—United States. 2. Sex role—United States—History—20th century. 3. Men—United States—Social life and customs. 4. White collar workers—United States. 5. Men's clothing—United States. I. Title.
   GT615.C37   2015
   391.00973—dc23   2015010594

Cornell University Press strives to use environmentally responsible suppliers and materials to the fullest extent possible in the publishing of its books. Such materials include vegetable-based, low-VOC inks and acid-free papers that are recycled, totally chlorine-free, or partly composed of nonwood fibers. For further information, visit our website at www.cornellpress.cornell.edu.

Cloth printing   10 9 8 7 6 5 4 3 2 1
Paperback printing   10 9 8 7 6 5 4 3 2 1

For my parents, with love and appreciation

Contents

Photo gallery follows page 90.

BUTTONED UP

Introduction

> **White-collar people's claims to prestige are expressed, as their label implies, by their style of appearance.**
>
> —C. Wright Mills, *White Collar: The American Middle Classes*

> **I remember when there were "Occupy Wall Street" people down here, and . . . you just walked right through police barricades if you were wearing a suit. They were actually stopping other people.**
>
> —Barney Nicks, finance professional

In the 1950s, corporate America grew rapidly in size and influence, giving birth to iconic depictions of white-collar workers. Social critiques of this mass employment sector included *White Collar* by C. Wright Mills (1951), *The Organization Man* by William H. Whyte (1956), and novels such as Sloan Wilson's *The Man in the Gray Flannel Suit* (1955). When these books were written, the businessman—he was invariably a man in those days—was already firmly linked to Americans' sense of national identity. For many, he was an aspirational figure. For others, he represented coerced conformity and homogenization. Either way, he was a recognizable cultural type. Despite passing references to dress and the common use of an item of clothing, the white collar, to stand in for a whole segment of the American workforce, twentieth-century scholarship on these workers downplayed the body and appearance. Aside from the quote above, clothing is barely mentioned in *White Collar*, and it is also missing from *The Organization Man*.

Born to children of the 1950s, I'm not sure I've ever seen a flannel suit. Nevertheless, in my lifetime, popular culture has glorified, lampooned, and sensationalized white-collar men's work lives through memorable films and television programs such as *Wall Street* (1987), *Office Space* (1999), *The Office* (2005–13), *Mad Men* (2007–15), and *The Wolf of Wall Street* (2013). With some exceptions, post-1950s mainstream social science has largely ignored the world of white-collar work and the identities of the people who perform this work.[1] We know more about fictional businessmen than we do about flesh-and-blood men making their living in the U.S. corporate world today.

Pop culture portrayals from the last few decades attend to, and even fetishize, the dress decisions of white-collar workers. It's hard to imagine the film *Wall Street* (still informally required viewing for young men entering finance) without Gordon Gekko's suspenders, or the cable TV hit *Mad Men* without Don Draper's pocket square. These white-collar icons' bodies are hypervisible, sometimes conveying nostalgia for the midcentury businessman's status and style. However, scholarly research has been slow to systematically explore the role of bodies and embodiment in today's corporate work world.[2]

Like the man in the gray flannel suit, today's businessman has been criticized—for example, by the Occupy movement—as a symbol of the establishment and of unchecked greed. Yet social scientists have not often consulted him about how he views himself.

The New White Collar

Why revisit the issue of white-collar workers' identities, mostly absent from the sociological research agenda for decades, at this historical moment?

First, the world of work and the nature of employment arrangements have changed. For a multitude of reasons—recession, automation, downsizing, outsourcing—full-time employment is elusive for many Americans, and formal white-collar work has become less stable and predictable.[3] This march toward more precarious employment, which began in roughly the mid-1970s when neoliberal economic policies were introduced on a large scale, has continued even during economic boom periods.[4] When sociologist C. Wright Mills published *White Collar* in 1951, people might have only one job interview in their whole lives, staying with the same company for their entire career. Today, turnover in the corporate workforce is expected. White-collar workers often understand that the next round of layoffs may be right around the corner, or they may be looking to jump to a new company that offers more opportunities. This increasing mobility and instability raise the stakes for appearance in employment interactions. People will likely have several job interviews throughout their lives, with some feeling that they are perpetually on the job market.

Second, men's bodies and appearance are increasingly subject to social scrutiny and presented in mainstream popular culture as sex objects (in ways previously associated with women's bodies).[5] This new visibility heightens pressures on men to maintain a socially acceptable physical appearance, including in work settings. The corporate world is still a male-dominated space, and much of the research on dressing for work focuses on women trying to fit in. Because men have often been seen as the default white-collar employees, their experiences of their bodies in the workplace are overlooked. Contemporary scholars' reluctance to analyze the role of male bodies and embodiment in employment is surprising, given the growing visibility of men's bodies in U.S. society and the new expectations that this visibility places on individual men.

We cannot fully understand the contemporary corporate firm without investigating workers' bodies as sites of control, resistance, and identification. Likewise, we cannot conceive of the body in contemporary society without acknowledging the importance of the workplace and other organizations in the fashioning and display of masculine and feminine bodies.[6] As corporate dress codes relax, there is more room for individual choice in work wear, and employees must decide how much to conform or stand out. To many of the men I interviewed for this book, greater dress freedom means greater risk of making mistakes. Most favor blending in, accepting the rules employers lay down for dress, and dressing in relatively conservative, traditionally masculine styles.[7]

The Book's Aims and Claims

To understand what it means to wear the white collar today, I interviewed dozens of men employed in three U.S. cities: Cincinnati, New York, and San Francisco. From my analysis of their accounts, I argue that *white-collar men accept conformity and constraint in their work clothing because doing so helps them maintain their privileged status.* The men I studied are privileged in many ways, because of their gender, social class, occupation, and in some cases race, nationality, and sexuality. Though they might not use these terms, most of the men who participated in this research engage in what I call a *strategic embrace of conformity* in their workplace self-presentation because it ensures their continued access to this privilege.

C. Wright Mills and his peers in the 1950s were already characterizing white-collar men as corporate drones without a shred of individuality and critiquing the conformity that business organizations promoted. So why is white-collar men's conformity to corporate dress standards several decades later noteworthy? I should clarify that, unlike Mills, I see these men as strategic actors. For that reason alone, their decisions about how to present their bodies at work, and their motivations, are of sociological interest.

Men's conformity is also worth exploring because it contradicts what we might expect. Today's business dress codes have largely shifted from requiring suits to allowing "business casual" attire. Business casual is a less regimented style of dress, which should mean more, not fewer, options for white-collar men. In addition, the new language of "career management" places the responsibility for financial and job success squarely on the shoulders of individuals and encourages professionals to build their own personal brand and make that brand work for them. These discourses emphasize the individual's decisions over blind allegiance to the company. The rise of the "metrosexual" phenomenon and the fading of traditional masculine disdain for prioritizing clothes and appearance would also suggest that today men can afford greater sartorial risks. Together, these developments would lead us to expect an explosion in creativity, self-expression, and individual distinction in men's work dress. I found that just the opposite is true: across occupations and company types, men are embracing conformity, toeing the line, choosing to blend in rather than stand out.

Where does this conformity come from? How does today's work world differ from that of the businessman described in the sociological tomes of yesteryear? Part of the motivation to conform stems directly from the economic context I described above. The absence of job security makes people who are fortunate enough to be employed avoid risk. They keep their heads down in the hopes of keeping their jobs. Standing out is seen as dangerous in workplaces that are constantly looking to downsize. For U.S. men, *not* standing out aligns them with the dictates of traditional (white, middle-class, heterosexual) masculine embodiment, making it an appealing path. In today's service-oriented economy, the metrics for job productivity are not always clear. For many occupations, there is no objective way to measure how well or poorly an employee is doing. In such an environment, looking competent, professional, and successful takes on more weight. Another reason men conform to clothing standards that are sometimes even more conservative than what their employers' dress codes require is that choice can be paralyzing. The shift to a business casual dress that is sometimes not as well defined as business formal dress (suits and ties) increases the options potentially available to white-collar men. However, greater choice leads to greater fear of making a mistake. Ironically, this expansion of dress options at the macro level leads many individual men to limit themselves not only to what the dress code prescribes but to a small range of clothing within that dress code.

In a society marked by gender inequality, fashion and an interest in dress are associated with women (and gay men, who represent what scholars call "subordinated masculinities"). Collectively, women and gay men occupy social statuses lower than that of heterosexual men, so there are no obvious social or economic payoffs to most men for presenting a fashionable appearance.

I've sketched a broad outline here, but the book shows some variation in men's decisions about how to dress their bodies for work. Region matters, so the standards and strategies employed in New York City vary significantly from those found in Cincinnati; and yes, San Francisco is on the frontier of casual work wear. Race, ethnicity, and nationality also influenced men's dress philosophies and practices. Sexual orientation, whether men identified as gay or straight, mattered less than I expected it would, but there were some meaningful differences in how these two groups of men talked about dress. In general, though, very few research participants felt that corporate dress codes were preventing them from expressing themselves through dress. And even some who did voice this sentiment have made peace with the situation, viewing it as the cost of doing business.

What's in the Book

Using dress and the body as an entry point into exploring men's work identities, I examine the question of what it means to wear the white collar from several angles. Chapter 1 explores how company dress codes and regional and local cultures serve as the constraints for men's work dress. Chapter 2 also investigates where ideas and norms of dress come from, focusing on what I call *dress socialization* to discuss the continuing significance of participants' family background and upbringing. Chapter 3 offers evidence for my argument that men strategically embrace conformity, endeavoring to answer the question of whether the white-collar work dress of today's businessmen is a uniform. Subsequent chapters delve into the complexities of gender performance and sexuality, arguing that white-collar masculinity cannot be understood without looking at both marginalized masculinities and femininity. Chapter 4 uses the metrosexual phenomenon to investigate how performances of masculinity are expanding even as homophobia continues. Chapter 5 foregrounds cross-gender relationships to show how men view women coworkers differently than they view wives and girlfriends. Men compare their bodies with the bodies of other men and with those of women, a theme that is further elaborated in chapter 6, on fashion. This chapter also takes on men's body ideals and their struggles with weight and other physical features. Chapter 7 examines what it means to embody the role of the boss in business organizations, which are usually characterized by rigid hierarchies. Between thematic chapters, I include vignettes that zoom in on particular men's stories, themes that cut across chapters and groups of men, or material objects that take on special meaning in the white-collar work world.

The photographs for the book were taken in the three cities studied in the fall of 2014. Casey James Wilson made the images for Cincinnati, Pamela Casanova Lorca for New York City, and Henry Casanova for San Francisco. I appreciate their willingness to prowl the streets for examples of business formal, business casual, and casual work dress, giving the street style bloggers a run for their money. These photos represent the range of dress that my interviewees wore to work and to our interviews (only the popular business casual staple of polo shirt plus khaki pants is missing from this visual compilation). Research participants' quotes serve as the captions for these illustrations.

It is easy to look at blue-collar men—mechanics or construction workers—and see how their bodies matter on the job. Women workers, no matter what their occupation, are often seen as bodies first, and in many workplaces, as bodies out of place. In this book, I show how white-collar men are also using their bodies at work. Although they are moving investments rather than I-beams, fixing copy rather than carburetors, their experiences of work in the twenty-first century demand that we account for their embodiment.

PLAYING BY THE RULES

Dress Codes in Corporate Workplaces

What are white-collar men wearing to work? Even if you are a man toiling daily in the hierarchical honeycomb that is corporate America, you may have trouble answering this question. Uncertainty about what constitutes white-collar work dress for men is a relatively new development.[1] A half dozen decades ago, for example, there was a clear answer. White-collar men wore suits and ties to work, and usually hats, until they crossed the threshold of their office buildings. Period. They also wore white shirts, as indicated by the term "white-collar," in which an item of clothing stands in for a person and an entire class of workers.

Today's situation is a radical departure from the time when suits dominated corporate work clothing throughout the United States. Harmonized dress for men who worked in offices was part of a larger context of social and occupational conformity, lamented by sociologists and cultural critics including C. Wright Mills in *White Collar: The American Middle Classes* (1951), William H. Whyte in *The Organization Man* (1956), and Sloan Wilson in his 1955 bestselling novel *The Man in the Gray Flannel Suit*.[2] Of these three writers, Wilson was the most attentive to dress, perhaps because of the need to create characters whom readers could visualize. Nine sentences into his sociological novel, Wilson describes his protagonist as "tired and worried" because he "had just spent seventy dollars on a new suit he felt he needed to dress properly for his business." Nowadays, most suits cost much more than $70, but fewer white-collar men have to wear them to work. While I argue in this book that white-collar men's appearance at work doesn't matter less than it did in the mid-twentieth century—in fact, many of my research participants believe it matters more—there has been an undeniable trend toward more casual dress in offices throughout the United States.[3]

White-collar men I interviewed were generally aware of this movement to-ward casualdom, as Pete Costa, a white thirty-five-year-old working in corporate retail, indicated: "I think as time goes on, people dress in their corporate environ-ment a lot more progressive . . . especially here in San Francisco. . . . I really see a lot of companies encouraging you to be yourself and not be[ing] so stern and conservative with the dress code."[4]

Research participants agreed that a shift in workplace clothing norms had taken place. Ron Varick, a Cincinnati interviewee in his midfifties, described dress standards as "deteriorating" during his time in the corporate world. According to Ron, when the business casual phenomenon began, it really meant only that you didn't have to wear a tie with your suit. And then,

> It evolved from there, and it became much more casual, and you know, to where we are today, which is, most everything, every place is business casual. . . . I think it's kind of the trend. . . . I don't think we're going back to anything else.

Ron's opinion that less formal dress codes are here to stay was shared by most men I spoke with, although his negative opinion of this development was not. Nearly all interviewees encountered rules of dressing for work that were ambiguous or subject to change. How they adapted to these expectations is an important part of the stories they tell about themselves as workers.

Casualizing Corporate Dress

The first pebble in the avalanche that toppled the suit as the everyday dress of the white-collar warrior was the introduction of Casual Fridays. No one seems to know exactly when that pebble slid down the mountain, although it is rumored that the idea began in the 1940s or 1950s with "Aloha Fridays," in which Hawaiian employers allowed workers to wear sportswear (like the iconic floral print shirt) to work on Fridays during the warmest periods of the year.[5] Casual Friday as an institutionalized dress-down imperative was quite common by the late 1980s and gained popularity throughout the 1990s in the U.S. corporate workplace.[6] Like scholars and cultural critics, the men in this book had their own theories about the origins and purposes of Casual Friday. Timothy Stein, a white thirty-something who worked in finance in Manhattan, told me that in the summer, he would wear a suit sans tie Monday through Thursday, and "then wear casual clothes on Friday . . . [and] the reason for that rule is of course because people are running out during the summer to weekend homes." Timothy mentioned that he usually spent summer weekends in a rental on Fire Island.

The so-called dot-com era of technology-business development in the 1990s seemed to popularize the use of more casual clothing not only on Fridays but throughout the week.[7] Among the seventy working men I interviewed, approximately forty (57%) worked in offices with business casual dress norms. Another

24 percent referred to their work dress code as casual (generally meaning that jeans and, much more rarely, shorts were acceptable), and 19 percent said that they were expected to wear a suit and tie on a normal weekday. There was some reprieve on Fridays for many of the men, regardless of the dress code at their workplace: thirty-two of the seventy employed interviewees said their office observed Casual Fridays. Five men, all employed in casual-dress workplaces in the San Francisco area, described twists on Casual Friday, including "fun Friday," at which zany outfits were encouraged; "fancy Friday," involving dressing up in a tie and perhaps a suit; and even "theme Fridays" that had men wearing kilts to work. One information technology (IT) professional in Cincinnati took advantage of dress-down Fridays at his usually business casual office to wear a chain-mail shirt (over a T-shirt or undershirt) that he had specially purchased for the occasion. He appreciated the levity that his unconventional fashion choice injected into the end of the workweek. "I'll walk by someone's office and just hear someone crack up," he said, laughing: "Chain-mail Friday."

Casual Friday is just the tip of the iceberg, one aspect of the less formal orientation of U.S. corporate dress today as compared with dress of previous eras. Business casual (a term that is open to interpretation, as we will see) was the predominant dress standard for the white-collar interviewees across all three study sites. Business casual dress codes were most common in Cincinnati (65% of interviewees' workplaces), followed by San Francisco (58%) and then New York City (48%). New York participants dominated the "business formal" category (usually meaning suits and ties), with nearly a third of those interviewees wearing this level of dress. Workplaces allowing casual dress (including jeans) for normal weekdays employed 31 percent of the San Francisco interviewees. It is striking that 62 percent of the men who wore suits on a daily basis worked in New York City, home to the most formal of the three local corporate dress cultures.

For those men who began their work lives wearing suits and ties every day, the switch to business casual required a recalibration of their wardrobe, their expectations, and their embodiment (the way they experienced or felt about their bodies). Ed Hatcher, a white man who was sixty-three when I interviewed him in Cincinnati, had entered the U.S. workforce when suits were the de facto uniform of business. He told me, "The initial switch over to casual, that ain't easy." Practically speaking, he said, "I didn't have a closet full of business casual clothes, I had a ton of suits, right?" "It was an adjustment," Ed said, but "I had to make the change." Ron, though younger than Ed, referenced a similar process of adaptation, saying, "I came kicking and screaming into this [business casual] environment." Jordan Simms, a white thirty-seven-year-old working in human resources in Cincinnati, described it this way: "As time has gone by, my perception of what looks professional has changed." Indicating the ensemble of khaki pants and button-down shirt that he was wearing during our interview, he said, "Ten years ago I would have thought, 'Why would you wear that to work? That seems so unprofessional.'" In contrast, Carlos Calle, a forty-year-old Latino executive in the San Francisco area, described a less fraught transition from a more formal dress environment to his current job's business casual standard: "I said, 'okay, no problem.'"

Despite their ubiquity, business casual dress codes have not reigned continuously since becoming more common a few decades ago. Several interviewees told stories of companies moving from business or business formal (suits every day) to business casual and then reverting back to the more formal dress regime. Four men tied these switchbacks directly to economic crises. One man credited the start of the economic crisis in 2007–8 with his company's decision to temporarily suspend the practice of dressing down on Fridays. Another, Carl Adelman, who ran the New York office of a national recruiting firm, noted that he returned his employees to a more formal dress standard when the crisis hit, as a sort of psychological boost: "When the economy softened, then we were looking for all kinds of reasons to get things getting better [improve business]. We looked at that as one reason. Let's get everyone a little more . . . bounce in their step." San Francisco interviewee Tony Hirsch, who was vice president at a Fortune 500 company, elaborated a theory of the effects of economic conditions on organizations' dress codes, claiming, "There is a correlation between the economy and dress." "In the 1990s boom years," said Tony, who had been in the corporate world for nearly three decades, "people were dressing very casually. Then the crisis hit, and people started dressing up." These subjective explanations for change propose intriguing connections between economic fortunes and dress rules.[8] Given their experiences in recent crisis periods, these white-collar men believed that economic uncertainty and instability, and concomitant worries over job security, led to the (often temporary) adoption of more formal dress. Perhaps in times of crisis, men were compelled to focus on their physical appearance, one thing that they could control. Whether or not their narratives are accurate representations of historical events, participants' lay understandings of the impact of economic downturns on corporate dress codes show that they are thinking about work clothing in the context of the big picture—what's happening at the company level and beyond.

Despite the trend toward more casual clothing at work, in most of corporate America (with the exception of some technology and creative companies), the expected dress for a job interview is business formal—a suit and tie. This unspoken rule requires some finagling if men want to interview for a new job while employed at another firm and also raises unwarranted suspicions. Brad Jennings, who identifies as half Native American and half "mostly Irish, I guess," is a high-level executive working in San Francisco. He recounted an incident that many interviewees echoed in their comments:

> One day I came in and I was wearing a suit; and I came in late in the day, like around 11 [a.m.] or something; I forget what I was doing that day. . . . [And my coworker] says this to me, "We're all talking," you know, "we all wanna know, were you out interviewing?" And I said, "No! . . . Of course not." And then I looked at that tie, and I knew exactly where that was coming from.

Brad's elite position in the company hierarchy did not protect him from scrutiny when he was out of the typical business casual dress code, although he mentioned that the person asking him this question was a friend with whom he had worked for many years, saying, "Only he can ask me this." Lower-level employees also recalled being interrogated, sometimes jokingly, when they were seen as over-dressed for everyday work activities. Some were asked whether they had a date after work, were going to interview for another job, or had a big meeting. Louis Katz, a New Yorker in advertising, actually was in the market for new employment when we spoke but was careful not to let his dress betray him. "I have been looking," he confided, saying, "I just bring the tie in my bag and put it on when I get outside" to avoid prying colleagues. Thus the mismatch between expected interview attire and everyday work wear in the white-collar world—combined with the tendency for workers to move from job to job rather than spending their entire career at one company—creates assumptions and questions that must be managed by the person who is dressing more formally than the norm.[9] However, men who *consistently* dress up in a business casual environment are often seen by my interviewees as having a personality quirk rather than being on the hunt for a new job.

So suits are worn for interviews, but not for day-to-day work activities, in many companies. This paradox highlights the symbolic role of the suit as a marker of readiness for white-collar employment (or what has been called "employability").[10] Even if the organization's leaders don't require you to wear a suit, they want to see that you can. The suit is thus a visual indicator of professional potential in most white-collar occupations.[11] It is the epitome of prototypical business masculinity. During the "magnified moment" of an employment interview, the most traditional business dress is worn.[12] Both managers and workers point to the interview as a concrete event in which appearance matters more than almost any other time in the relationship between man and organization. Thus we can't be too quick to dismiss the suit as irrelevant for men working in business casual dress systems.

What Determines Dress Codes?

Three categories of dress codes encompass nearly all of the possible permutations that were represented among the men in this study: business formal, business casual, and casual. Because of the diversity of this sample (see appendix), it is safe to say that these three dress systems represent most of what is happening in corporate Americans' work clothing. What factors govern whether a company will require its employees to don suits rather than khakis or whether the company has any official dress standards at all? According to the interviewees, some of whom have a role in deciding company dress codes, two characteristics of the firm or office are important in shaping dress rules, or lack of rules. The first is the region, city, or even neighborhood in which the office is located. The second is "company culture," whose definition is quite nebulous. Company culture is seen as being tied to sector or industry but also as varying within employment sectors, as I'll discuss.

One reason I interviewed white-collar men in three different U.S. urban centers was that I suspected that the region in which a city was located—and indeed, the city itself—would influence the dress codes under which men labored. By examining men's experiences of dressing for work in the Midwest, East Coast, and West Coast, I aimed to understand how geographic location mattered for individual and collective ideals and practices. Cities have distinct "local urban cultures" based on "collective representations" of the city's character and history.[13] These unique identities are expressed and maintained through what I call *local dress cultures*. I was struck by how many of the New York interviewees described their city as "stylish" or "fashion(able)," how many of those in Cincinnati described it as "conservative," and how many in the San Francisco area called the region "laid-back." These stereotypes generally matched interviewees' accounts of work dress. Stylish New York was the most likely to evince business dress that was "formal" (another term New Yorkers often used to describe the local dress culture).[14] Cincinnati white-collar workers were most likely to wear business casual attire, which is conservative in the sense of being neither dressy nor completely informal; this dress is middle-of-the-road, as was the image of the city that emerged in interviewees' accounts. San Francisco, consistently labeled laid-back, had a higher percentage of men working under casual dress regimes than did either of the other two cities. Astute analysts of their own social locations, participants saw region and city as important factors in corporate dress codes. Here are three typical descriptions, from interviewees in each of the cities, of the locality-dress link:

> I think Cincinnati is conservative, but there's only so many companies that you'll see—you know, I can think of a handful, that folks are suited up.

> Attire is important up here. I mean image is—it's New York—image is
> everything. . . . It's just, you have to dress stylish.

> San Francisco in general is pretty casual, so in no environment have
> I seen men try to dress in suits, except for like maybe the executive di-
> rector of my former company.

I was surprised that even smaller units of geography—for example, specific
neighborhoods or suburbs—seemed meaningful. The San Francisco Bay area
has wild variations in hyperlocal weather patterns, known as "microclimates,"
and these differences are reflected in style. For example, blazers would be more
typical in "the City" (San Francisco proper), where it is often chilly and foggy—a
pragmatic as well as aesthetic choice. Midtown Manhattan, home to many large
corporate and financial employers, was seen as the most likely place in town to
encounter men in suits; according to one participant, Wall Street is now located
in Midtown. In Cincinnati, those who worked downtown reported more pressure to dress well and said they saw more formal dress than did men working in
other parts of the metropolitan area.

Location may matter in determining dress standards, but research participants also talked frequently of company culture. They varied in their interpretations of the level at which culture operates: some meant the culture of their
particular office, while others talked about the company (which may have multiple locations) or the occupational sector (which they sometimes called "the
field").[15] Scholars have shown that organizational culture, defined as "the norms
for appropriate behavior . . . [and] the values espoused and adhered to by a majority of the organization's members," impacts leaders' and employees' ideals and
practices in concrete ways.[16] In describing the corporate cultures in which they
worked, men used adjectives such as "conservative," "lax," "rigid," "competitive"
(common in sales environments), "British," and "creative." John Wentz, whom
I chatted with in Berkeley on a warm Saturday morning, wore an untucked, plaid,
short-sleeve button-down shirt with jeans, an unzipped hoodie (hooded sweatshirt), and black Puma sneakers of the style often worn by skateboarders. He told
me that what he was wearing for weekend relaxation would also be acceptable
for a workday at his large tech firm: "The type of work that I do, it's much more
about what you're doing than who you are, what you are dressed [in]." This was
a typical description of dress for people who worked in more technical positions
or organizations.[17] According to John, "Some of the real geniuses I work with,
they dress in, you know, the typical absent professor style." On the other end of
the spectrum was the formal-dress New York office in which men risked being
publicly shamed by a boss who was famous for ripping pockets off shirts. Ted
Demetriou, who worked in the Cincinnati branch of an international advertising

company, described his colleagues as creative and casual dressers, part of a relaxed and even fun office culture: "We work in the same building as a bank. So when we walk into the elevator together, they automatically hit [the button for] our floor. Because they know we're not going anywhere else. . . . They're wearing either suits or dress slacks and they know we're going only to one place." Ted used this anecdote to distinguish his company culture from others.

The perceived existence of company cultures, nested within sector-wide norms (though there are always outliers), has implications for job interviews. When I asked Brad, the San Francisco-based executive, what advice he would give to a young college graduate trying to find employment, he invoked company cultures:

> I would definitely say think about your audience. If you're going into a business-like environment, like a bank or a retailer or some corporate office, then you gotta wear a suit, you gotta wear a tie. Um, now if you're going to interview at Google, my recommendation would be [to do] research, because I don't know how you would want to dress for an interview at Google. Would the people of Google expect this?

When I asked Jonathan Santos, a forty-eight-year-old working at a tech firm just outside San Francisco, whether it is a mistake to wear a suit to a job interview at his company, he said definitively, "In this culture it is." Contrast this with Ron from Cincinnati, who said, "I think everybody has come to recognize there's a certain dress required at job interviews regardless of what the clothing culture is" in a particular company. That required dress, in Ron's view, was a suit. Men from all three cities recalled buying one or more "interview suits" upon graduating from college.

The ultimate convergence of these two factors, location and company culture, is seen in stereotypes about Silicon Valley, the area at the south end of San Francisco Bay known as a hub of technological innovation. Silicon Valley-based firms are seen in popular culture and scholarly research as propagating a casual, creative, and fun work environment and rejecting old-school business models and traditions (including a particular type of corporate masculine self-presentation), which spills over into dress.[18] San Francisco interviewees often referenced the influence of the tech sector and Silicon Valley when explaining their area's relaxed corporate dress codes, which usually topped out at business casual.

Defining Professional Dress

When describing the obligations of midlevel managers in post–World War II America, the sociologist C. Wright Mills wrote, "Groom your personality and control your appearance; make business a profession."[19] The men profiled in my book used the word "professional" to describe how they and their white-collar colleagues should, and do, dress. In our conversations, I pressed them to define terms such as "professional" that seem obvious and commonsensical to insiders.[20] For Daniel, professional dress meant "Sunday best, minus the tie," whereas Ryan Carter, another Cincinnati participant, used the words "crisp and clean." Wilson Turner, who ran a recruiting office in San Francisco, defined professional as "smart, suited, and booted," meaning that you had on a "tie, jacket, trousers." Wilson, who had grown up in the United Kingdom, said that professional dress also required that you "polish your shoes, cut your nails, you've had a shave." Caleb Green, a software consultant based in San Francisco, defined the professional look as "very sharp" and said his advice to a younger white-collar man would be "Dress nicer, work less." He was one of many to speak of the importance of others' judgments of one's appearance: if you are "very well kept and well dressed, to some extent, people assume you are with it."

Given the variety of dress codes, what it means to dress professionally depends somewhat on the rules and the company culture. Bryan Lee, who worked in corporate real estate in New York, put it this way: "What's *appropriate* and professional, I think . . . varies, depending on the kind of work that you do." "Professional" was a universal buzzword among the research participants to describe what white-collar men (and women) should wear to work, and for nearly a third of them, the word invoked behavioral as well as sartorial expectations.[21] Many agreed that the impression they made on colleagues, management, and clients mattered, and that these people would make assumptions about their professionalism based on their dress. Andy Lipmann was an architect I interviewed in Brooklyn, where he lived and worked. As we chatted about professional dress and its effect on others, he stated that "as an architect, you have to look professional, but yet creative and stylish. . . . If you look like a frumpy architect, it just kind of shows that you aren't going to be a very good one." For Andy, part of dressing professionally was to be both "fashionable" and "classic," qualities that clients sought in their new buildings.[22]

In general, engineers and people with more technical jobs were seen—and saw themselves—as having more leeway in their interpretations of professional work clothing. Yet Richard Schneider, a twenty-seven-year-old IT professional in Cincinnati, explained that dressing up could improve his ability to finish tasks. "I learned that back when I was installing computers at a hospital," where if he showed up wearing a tie and a "nice shirt," it was "really easy to tell a doctor" to step away from his or her computer for a while so that Richard could perform upgrades or install software. If he came in dressed more casually, recounted Richard, the doctors would say "Aw, well, I'm busy," which delayed his work. Beyond "looking the part" (as Andy put it), dressing professionally could affect a man's state of mind. Travis Jones, a forty-year-old advertising manager in New York who identified as Afro-Caribbean, implied that the impression made on others in the work world might matter less than the feeling that came from being dressed properly: "It's their behavior that is partially impacted by the suit that they have on, that exudes the confidence." Since Caleb worked for a tech company, he could have probably dressed down for work, but he chose what he considered professional rather than casual dress because it made him *feel* like he was working: "I like stepping into that kinda work role when I put on my work clothes."

For the men I spoke with, professionalism went beyond dress and behavior to include other aspects of appearance, such as grooming. Joseph Davis, a thirty-two-year-old African American man working in Cincinnati, emphasized this aspect of self-presentation. "Make sure your hair is cut and you're not looking straggly, or shave or whatever, you know, *something*," he said, chuckling. "I think you should pay more attention to those things versus the pair of dress pants you got on." Many men agreed that facial hair of any kind was frowned on in their companies (even, or perhaps especially, "that half-assed stubble stuff," in one participant's memorable words). Dave Baker, who at twenty-four was one of the youngest employees at a Cincinnati financial consulting firm, tied together these ideas of appearance, behavior, and impressing others: "It's incredibly important in my position, especially being a younger guy . . . to come off as very, very well groomed; very, very in the know; very, very articulate and professional." He felt this professional aura was especially crucial since people trusted him with their finances. As another interviewee in finance put it, "You want a person to look a certain way if they're handling your money." (I'll expand on the idea of dressing for clients later.)

The professional-dress-equals-professional-actions logic implies that dress that is casual to the point of not being professional leads to less professional behavior. Many men concurred with Daniel that "when you're dressed professionally, it sends a clear message that you're a professional person." Casual dress was seen as conveying either a mixed or a negative message. Jon Harper's prep school had groomed him for the white-collar workforce by having Casual Fridays, during which students did not have to wear their ties and blazers. Years later, Jon viewed casual dress as affecting employees' mental ability to work: "If you break the routine of what you do every day . . . that one day [of dressing down] affects your behavior . . . maybe more so for younger people, [who] might not be as focused." Although he worked at a real estate company with formal business dress and business casual Fridays, Jon surmised that "if I went to work tomorrow with a T-shirt and shorts, I'd probably behave a little differently," and he saw potential negative consequences. The following snippet of my conversation with Luke Gottlieb, a white thirty-four-year-old managing a team of recruiters in a Manhattan office that was business formal four days a week and business casual on Fridays, typifies this view:

> *Luke*: I would almost prefer to be formal on Fridays because I feel like people are more productive when they have to wear a suit. . . . I know for a fact on a Wednesday, if my guys can secure a meeting on Friday or Monday, they'll opt to do it Monday 'cause they won't want to wear a suit on Friday. But the reality is, somebody else can get the meeting on Friday and get the job and make money. So I would prefer it to be that way. . . . Maybe I'm wrong, but in my opinion I think it would increase productivity, profitability.
>
> *Erynn*: So you think that maybe people, the way that they're dressed can affect like how they're behaving? How they're working?
>
> *Luke*: Oh yeah. Absolutely. Hundred percent. Yeah. . . . That's going to transcend across to your attitude. . . . I mean this is a performance-based environment. . . . You want people driving performance as much as they can.

On the other hand, some research participants felt that casual dress affected their behavior and productivity in a positive way and that professionalism was not necessarily tied to dressing up. Brad, whose office allows jeans on Fridays, typified this sentiment: "I feel like I can operate better when I don't have the restriction of the tie, I really do." On Fridays, just putting on his jeans made him feel "a little looser, a little freer" and "a little more productive, strangely." Men agreed that different levels of dress on the job can alter the flow and effectiveness of one's work; they differed on their views of the specific consequences.

Men held a range of opinions on Casual Fridays, from those who said they despised it to those who loved it and every sentiment in between. Jim Shaw, a fifty-two-year-old executive in Cincinnati who in general favored more formal dress codes, said, "I think having a Casual Friday is a fine thing. Do you know what I mean, it's a nice break." Ed, who was a couple years from retirement, was a fan of his employer's "Jeans Fridays." As we chatted in a small meeting room in his company's downtown office, he said, "I like wearing denim for two reasons. It's comfortable, and on the days I'm wearing denim . . . I don't have to get a pair of pants dry-cleaned. . . . It saves me money, as crazy as that sounds, not a lot, but enough for lunch." In his sales job for a San Francisco-area technology company, Clark Landon, a white man in his early fifties, didn't have a strict dress code or an institutionalized Casual Friday; yet he dressed more casually on that day. On Fridays, he said, it "psychologically feels like there's more freedom to color outside the lines."[23] Thus the Casual Friday trend affects even offices without rigid dress codes.

The split was about even between men who liked Casual Friday and those who disliked it. Some men were especially opposed, and several told me that they just didn't participate, instead wearing their Monday-through-Thursday attire on Fridays. Tom Marino, a white thirty-six-year-old whom I interviewed in a microscopic park near his office in lower Manhattan, just didn't see the point in dressing down from his usual business casual clothing:

> I started to realize that, like, jeans are not any more comfortable than these slacks. So why do I really need to wear 'em? And in warmer weather, they're heavier. So I have worn jeans to the office on casual days, but, um . . . I probably wouldn't do it now given the chance. 'Cause I—you know, these [indicates his dress pants] are as comfortable, if not more, than my jeans.

Daniel was similarly indifferent to dressing down: "Casual Fridays could come or go for me; I really don't care. . . . I'm just like, I don't really get it, to be honest. It doesn't much matter to me." Carlos chose not to participate in Casual Friday for another reason: he thought that wearing casual clothing was too revealing of his nonwork persona. Unlike using jeans outside of work, wearing denim in the office may raise personal issues: "Are you wearing trendy jeans, or expensive jeans, or two-hundred-dollar pairs of jeans, or way-too-tight jeans?" Carlos was "uncomfortable" with wearing jeans to work, as they presented "all these other things that you have to deal with." For this reason, when his coworkers jokingly asked him on Fridays, "You own any jeans?" Carlos would reply, "Yes, I do. I just—you don't need to see them."

Though companies may have cultures that are somewhat coherent, dress codes can vary within a single firm. Different units or floors in the same building could have different norms. Sometimes these internal disparities are related directly to the manager or boss overseeing a group of employees (see chapter 7). Distinct dress styles within a company or site can also have to do with individuals' roles: expectations for engineers and IT staff tend to be much less formal, regardless of official dress codes. In advertising or other creative fields, similar slack is cut for designers who work primarily in the studio.

The existence of multiple dress codes within companies is something I discovered because I focused on men's individual accounts of dressing for work, rather than trying to outline corporate dress codes and practices in general. These striated dress norms within organizations make it impossible to say, "At Company A, men wear this" or even "in the Main Street office, employees dress this way." Since dress norms often vary across levels and job functions within a company, it is difficult to speak generally about entire segments of the workforce. What I can and do explore are the similarities and differences—the patterns—in the ways that white-collar men speak about dressing for work, and the constraints and pressures that they face. Men's narratives about self-presentation in the white-collar workplace are fascinating precisely because they highlight the complexities of intraoffice interactions, the tension between conformity and individuality, and the strategic decisions that go into wearing the white collar.

Suiting Up

In *White Collar*, C. Wright Mills wrote, "The stylization of their [white-collar employees'] appearance, in particular the fact that most white-collar jobs have permitted the wearing of street clothes on the job, has also figured in their prestige claims."[24] Reading this today, we may laugh at Mills's use of the term "street clothes" to describe a suit and tie. To many Americans, suits now signal work or special occasions (weddings, funerals) rather than recreational activities that take men into the "street." Many white-collar men who can wear "street clothes on the job" are wearing not suits but more casual gear. I've outlined three main categories of work dress codes: business formal, business casual, and casual. Yet a meaningful split emerged between jobs that require men to wear suits to work most days and those that do not. What I didn't predict before conducting the interviews was the sharp divide between those who are fond of suits and those who, for a range of reasons, find them anathema. It is difficult to ascribe causes to these different opinions; however, social class, job history, local dress cultures, and general orientations toward or away from fashion seem to matter. For the men I spoke with, the suit—and business formal dress rules more generally—represented a particular type of white-collar person. The "suit" might be a person they wanted to embody, or a figure that they distrusted or despised.[25]

Fifteen of seventy-one interviewees, when asked to describe professional dress, stated that dressing professionally meant wearing suits.[26] Seven men, including some of these fifteen, claimed that suits were easier to wear for work than more casual clothing. Luiz Rodrigues, a sixty-two-year-old Brazilian working in Manhattan, epitomized this sentiment: "I find the suit and tie comfortable in a sense that I don't have to choose. I don't have to find myself in between this big range of: What should I use? Khakis? Or jeans? Or actual formal trousers? Or . . . ? The suit: you're there. Wherever you go, you're ready to go anywhere." Other interviewees described feeling "at home in a suit" or being "a suit kind of person." Most suit wearers described them as easier because they involved fewer choices and less complicated color matching than business casual or casual wear. Even some participants who didn't wear suits—such as Patrick Flowers, who worked in lower Manhattan in a business-casual work environment—recognized this benefit. Yet in the same breath, he complained about the way that requiring suits constrains workers' choices: "I mean, the advantages to [wearing suits] are, nobody expects you to have, you know, 365 different suits. And so, it simplifies a little bit your decisions. It's like, okay, you know, I have no freedom, but at least I don't have to make a choice." Patrick's explanation is reminiscent of sociologist Georg Simmel's argument that in the act of dressing like others, "the individual is freed from the worry of choosing and appears simply as a creature of the group, as a vessel of the social contents."[27] I found that, as recent scholarship on dress suggests, greater freedom in clothing choice also implies greater risk of erring in one's choices.[28]

Many participants thought putting on a suit was simple, whereas business casual involved more thoughtful calculations about both the level of dress and how to combine colors and patterns. Ed, who recounted his begrudging adaptation to business casual, told me matter-of-factly that for most of his career, "I didn't feel like I was at work if I didn't have a suit on." Graham Houston, the top man at a Cincinnati advertising firm, dressed more formally than the other people in his office because it just felt right. "People see me in a suit every day," he told me as we chatted in his glass-walled office, "three-piece, with a tie, um, that's how I think about going to work. . . . There's something about putting a tie on when you go to work." Some men got satisfaction from embodying white-collar status by wearing a suit. Luke told me that as he considered career options in college, he explicitly thought, "I want to have a job where I'm wearing a suit." The suit represents something aspired to, achieved, and accomplished, especially for men raised in working-class or poor families (see chapter 2).

The suit is a powerful symbol of professionalism[29] that can be used strategically to counter possible negative associations with certain types of work, as Nigel Peters, who worked at a corporate recruiting firm, explained:

> We work in sales, and there's so many like sleazy salespeople, cheesy salespeople, so you know, we want—even though we are salespeople—we want to come across as business people as well. . . . That's what I mean probably by "professional." So, you know, not sort of, slicked-back hair . . . looking like a sort of secondhand car salesman . . . not being too brash and loud. You know, being somewhere in the middle. . . . "They're wearing suits, so they must know what they're talking about," that kind of thing.

Dressing professionally can thus be seen as a tool for overcoming occupational stigma, embodying one's middle-class status through tasteful clothing, and, in the case of Nigel and colleagues, making the sale. Nigel's use of the words "brash and loud" to describe undesirable dress also seems to connote actions and ways of speaking that should be avoided.

When asked, a dozen men who didn't have to wear suits regularly at their current jobs told me that they would like to, or wouldn't mind, working at a place where suits were required daily. One of the Cincinnati interviewees wished he had the opportunity to dress more formally at work. He had attended college in Kentucky, where he enjoyed attending horse races: "I love getting dressed up . . . in a nice suit that's tailored, and nice cufflinks and a nice tie. . . . It kind of makes you feel good." Several men who would like wearing suits worried about the expense of building and dry-cleaning this work wardrobe. Domingo Sala, who worked in a business casual healthcare firm in the San Francisco area, said wearing suits to work "would be fine," because it "would be a chance to go get better stuff, and it's for work, so there's a reason why I'm doing it." He imagined a switch to business formal work dress as an excuse to go shopping for high-quality clothing; to "buy like a brickload" of new clothes and not feel guilty about the expense. Whether or not suits were "easier" than more casual work wear, as many men claimed, they involved a potentially large initial investment plus the ongoing cost of maintaining and replacing more delicate clothing.

On the other hand, sixteen interviewees stated—some adamantly—that they wouldn't want to work in suits. Five men said suits were more difficult to wear, for reasons of cost and comfort. Beyond the potential overheating caused by wearing wool or the choking sensation of a tie (which even some suit lovers complained about), some men said they wouldn't want to wear a suit because of what it meant about the company culture and the work that would be required of them. R. J. Logan, a white twenty-eight-year-old in marketing, told me, "I don't think I would work comfortably in that dynamic." Bob Liu, a fifty-three-year-old Asian architect, agreed:

> My first reaction is: I probably wouldn't go for a job like that. Uh, but I shouldn't say that in this economy [*laughs*]. . . . I *do* associate jobs that require more formal dress all the time with a more corporate environment that maybe has priorities that are different from mine. So it just seems less likely that I would work for one of those places. But, never say never.

Several men who said they wouldn't want to wear a suit every day referenced the activities they might be called on to perform (e.g., dealing with specific types of clients, presenting to large groups). For them, suits symbolized a particular kind of organizational structure and culture; wearing the garment called a suit would make them the type of people derisively called "suits." Femi Banjo, a second-generation African working in IT, revealed his opinion about "suits" (the people):

> When you're wearing a suit, like a lot of people wear suits, but they're dumb as rocks [*laughing*]. You know? I'd rather you be a slob and be technically superior, than be like, a suit and tie type, and be like [*dumb jock voice*]: What's two plus six? Is it seven? You know like, really? How'd you get this job? Why you making more money than me again?

Not wanting a business formal dress code stemmed from men's concerns about the type of people they wanted to be, be seen as, and associate with.

Rules, Repercussions, and Resistance

In *White Collar*, C. Wright Mills expressed concern about companies' extensive control over workers, including regulation of bodily appearance. He wrote sardonically that the "neglect of personal appearance on the part of the employee is a form of carelessness on the part of the business management." In capitalist organizations, workers' bodies are the object of discipline, and dress is one area in which this discipline is felt.[30] The white-collar workers in my study understand that they are, as Mills put it, "links in chains of power and obedience" within their organizations. The degree of obedience required varies from office to office. Andy described an architecture firm he had worked for that required all employees to wear a white shirt and black pants (or skirts, for women). Andy felt this was overly rigid and a reflection of the boss's personality and drab aesthetic: "The guy's a total Nazi and every building that he does is white . . . so it's like you had to fit in with the decor."

Nearly all the interviewees knew of dress regulations that were "on the books," outlined in employee manuals or other documents workers received from managers or human resources (HR) departments. However, the intricate expectations related to clothing and appearance were really learned on the job. Although some men reported being instructed on how to dress, Aiden Curry, who was about to begin working at a business casual tech company in San Francisco, said this had not happened in any of his previous jobs, and he didn't expect it to at his new office. "I think that you are pretty much expected to test it out, and give it your best guess," he said. Jeff Michaels, a New York interviewee who worked in a casual-dress office but had worn suits in previous jobs, describes how he learned the dress code: "Well, it's very weird, because you know, you have this image of working on Fifth Avenue, and you think that it's a suit and tie type of deal. And my first day, I did come in a dress shirt, a tie, and slacks, and I was the odd man out [*laughs*]."[31] While there was substantial agreement among the men on the need for "professional" dress (even in casual workplaces), eight interviewees described their jobs as having nonexistent or minimal dress codes. Nicholas Georgiou, a thirty-nine-year-old employed in a Cincinnati design firm, avowed that "dress code-wise, the only thing that I would say is official is, you can't wear shorts to work, or flip-flops. . . . Everyone's a grown-up [and] should know what's appropriate." Dress codes may apply only to certain workers. One interviewee who worked for a national retailer said, "Our store employees have a dress code . . . but we don't have one at headquarters. . . . [This can be] a source of tension" between the two groups. Although a handful of interviewees claimed to favor stricter or more formal dress codes, Jonathan saw the lack of rules as a perk: "The good side of tech business has always been no dress code."

The eight men working under minimal dress codes were in the minority, as most research participants reported that their companies had both formal policies and informal expectations that could vary depending on department or job function. The existence of rules means that dress code infractions may be punished. Ron, the human resources executive, favored more routine enforcement of his company's dress standards. But he understood that enforcement could be distasteful for both enforcer and rule breaker: "Who wants to evaluate whether that's a sneaker or a dress shoe? Who wants to be the policeman?" Ron classified having to talk with someone about their inappropriate dress or self-presentation as "one of the most difficult conversations," a "very awkward conversation."[32] Others agreed. Enforcing dress rules could take various forms: a mass e-mail from HR reminding employees of expectations, a manager requesting that an individual refrain from wearing certain items, an employee being sent home to change, joking comments from peers meant to be taken seriously, or the aforementioned pocket-ripping spectacle.

Carlos, who had worked in HR for nearly his entire career, claimed to feel comfortable calling employees to account for their dress, saying what mattered was "the approach [and] how you say it." Once people found themselves in this situation, said Carlos, they often tattled on their coworkers ("Well, so-and-so is doing . . ."). He said he would have to stay focused, asking, "Is that [how] you want to present yourself? We'll deal with the other people, thank you." When I asked one New York interviewee whether dress codes were enforced in his office, he told me no but then mused that no enforcement did not mean no consequences for dressing less professionally, as there were "opportunity costs." He and others told me that they might think twice about "pulling someone in" to a meeting with clients or managers if his or her dress was not up to snuff.

While some research participants described high levels of control over workers by management or HR, most did not experience corporate workplaces as sites of total domination. Indeed, some interview narratives featured employees resisting the dress dictated by higher-ups. Aiden said he often wore "Chuck Taylors" (Converse brand sneakers) to his previous tech job in San Francisco. He recounted a hallway encounter with the head of HR, who said, "You know, it would be good if you wore nicer shoes here. . . . What if a client comes in unexpectedly?" Aiden recalls replying, "Well, I'll keep a jacket and a nice pair of shoes in a drawer—does that work?" She agreed to this, and he was able to keep wearing his Chucks. According to Aiden, employees in smaller companies are more vulnerable to managers who personally don't like them and want to "flex the rules at them." He felt that in bigger organizations, dress codes were more likely to be enforced across the board. Aiden's talking back to human resources allowed him some control over his clothing choices.[33]

Others told stories of collective resistance to dress regulations, which could sometimes change the dress code entirely. Jack Harrison, who managed a corporate recruiting office in Cincinnati, described an instance of bottom-up pressure:

> A year or two ago, we had a town hall [meeting] and you know, one thing our um, our female population wanted to do away with is having to wear hose, whether it was Monday through Thursday, or Friday, whether they were wearing pants or a skirt, to be able to do away with that. And we actually did end up amending our . . . dress code.

An interviewee from a New York recruiting firm that previously required suits for all male employees recounted that the back-office staffers complained about the expenditure required and were then permitted to wear business casual dress. This was justified by their non-client-facing position in the organization. Dinesh Devi, from the Cincinnati sample, discussed gradual changes over time that transformed his company's dress from business casual to casual. His office (like those of several other participants) occasionally held "dress-down" or "jeans" days to raise money for charity. Employees could pay a couple bucks and get to dress down for the day. Their enthusiasm led the office managers to allow a dress-down week for a $10 donation. Dinesh said, "We went from dress-down days, to dress-down weeks, to dress-down season," in which a $50 donation got an employee casual dress privileges for the entire summer. When the bosses saw that nearly everyone was donating $50, they decided to officially change the dress code to casual and simply make a sizable donation to charity in the company's name each year. The people had spoken.

Sometimes resisting the dress code is a way of blowing off steam, displaying frustration with top-down regulations. Fabricio Silva, originally from Argentina, worked in public relations in New York. Fabricio was not opposed to dress codes; in fact, back in Buenos Aires, he volunteered to develop the guidelines for his entire office. But when his Manhattan firm switched from suits to business casual a few years back, he and the members of his work group responded in silent, symbolic protest. The announcement of the new dress standards was made on Tuesday, and on Wednesday morning,

> we all came with suits and ties. None of us had *spoken* about it. It wasn't like we coordinated. It wasn't like on purpose. But *everyone* naturally the following day chose to dress formal. . . . There was a statement like, you know, this is what we are and the office is moving into a more kind of like creative/advertising/being cool kind of thing, and we're not—We're creative people in a different way [*deep inhale*]. But, that's not *us*. So I think as a group, unconsciously, it was a way of like getting the statement out. This is who we are.

Fabricio's example highlights the group members' collective resistance to the new rules, and the way they asserted their identity as professionals ("creative people in a different way") by wearing formal dress. Andy, whose "total Nazi" boss demanded only black-and-white clothing, recounted how he and "the young punks in the back" of the office wore short sleeves, brightly colored shirts, and more casual pants, flouting the dress code. "I felt like I was justified," he said. "I was such a diligent guy in the office . . . that was my own real way of like flipping them off." Because Andy did important tasks, often working on weekends, he said with a chuckle, "They needed me . . . so they kind of had to just deal with it." His commitment to the work may explain why Andy never got reprimanded for being dressed differently. While these acts of resistance did not lead to new dress codes in Fabricio's or Andy's offices, they were meaningful to them and their coworkers.

Many participants described dress as a highly "personal" issue in the workplace; perhaps this is why employees are able to exercise some agency in this area and why it is so difficult to sanction dress violations and even harder to fire someone for not complying. Here corporate work diverges from lower-wage service occupations, in which being out of dress code could lead directly to disciplinary action and even termination of employment. It is probable that the sea change in corporate America's dress codes, ensconcing business casual as the standard, has empowered some workers to ask for dress rules that they see as reasonable or to test the boundaries of acceptable dress. More commonly, though, men described not resisting but conforming to what they believed the expectations to be.

Selling Yourself

In the chapter of *White Collar* entitled "The Great Salesroom" (spoiler alert: the great salesroom is U.S. society), Mills anticipated current scholarship on the commodification of emotions, which transforms personality and feeling into a performance that overspills the boundaries of the workplace.[34] There is a corporeal dimension to these performances. Research on the role of bodies in paid work often focuses on service workers, whose "emotional labor" is a job requirement, or sex workers, who literally sell their embodied services and use of their bodies to customers.[35] It makes sense to address the body and bodily experience in work that is physically demanding, such as domestic work or being a nightclub bouncer.[36] People assume that blue-collar workers use their bodies on the job but that white-collar workers use their brains; white-collar labor is seen as cerebral and disembodied.[37] My analysis of the reports of white-collar men from across the United States is a first step toward dispelling this erroneous notion.

Like interviewing for a job, meeting with clients is another magnified moment in which appearance and dress take on heightened importance and are seen as influencing interpersonal interactions.[38] The men I spoke with have mixed feelings about clients; as one put it, "We have a line around here that says this is the greatest business in the world, except for one thing: the clients!" A few interviewees mentioned the oft-heard idea that in the business world, regardless of the task or setting, employees are "selling themselves" and that the patterns of self-selling that they establish over time develop into their brand. When I asked Carlos why dress mattered in his work, he said, "I think it's part of your personal brand. Every single company's so focused on the company brand and reputations; it is the same thing on a personal level." Whether or not you are selling a product, you are selling yourself constantly in white-collar work: to higher-ups, including your boss, and to clients. Vijay Singh, a thirty-one-year-old corporate recruiter, explained:

> If you're a person who's helping to market an iPad, you're actually marketing the device [*knocks on table*]. The device is what's selling. Right? Ultimately when you're more in a services function, you're selling yourself. And part of selling yourself is selling . . . how clearly you communicate, and, yeah, how you look. . . . If you look sloppy, it's immediately gonna diminish . . . your basic credibility. But, I think you definitely need to kind of know your audience and know the situation.

Carlos and Vijay were not the only research participants to talk about white-collar employees as developing an individual brand in the workplace or selling themselves to various audiences.

How do you dress to meet with clients? Employers' rules may provide some guidance, but you may have to make some judgment calls, based on experience and received wisdom. Some interviewees valued dressing "better" or being more "dressed up" than their clients. Vijay talked about dressing nicely for client meetings as a way of getting "a leg up," saying that it was "always better to be dressed better than the person [client], or just more formally." Trevor Robins, who at age fifty-nine had been an architect all his professional life, agreed: "I think people [clients] who might dress more casually . . . don't expect *me* to be dressed casually." For Trevor, it's fine to be dressier than the client, "so I'm not offending anybody"; he saw this as a gesture of respect. A few men talked about having "lucky" suits, or outfits they felt particularly confident in, for making presentations or talking to clients.[39] Nigel, for example, said, "I have my more expensive [Hugo] Boss suits for client meetings. . . . I definitely have—I have four or five sort of 'Project Pitch Suits.'" These men argued that wearing something you feel you look good in affects how you feel about yourself and your ability to sell yourself or your services to clients.[40] External appearance is seen as a reflection of internal abilities but also shapes your performance of those abilities.

Some of those who claimed to aim for a higher level of dress than clients wore also talked about adjusting their dress according to who the client was. One interviewee whose company worked mostly with university clients said that when a client visited the office, all the staff wore the school's colors; clients loved it. Others commonly associated particular clients with one type of dress: "Citibank used to be one of our big clients," said one man, "and when those people came [to the office], they were *very* conservative." In general, banking and finance companies, with few exceptions, were seen as having the most conservative and formal dress codes,[41] which some other businesses' representatives tried to follow for client meetings. Sometimes clients educate their service providers on what's expected, as when an advertising sales representative was told to "just wear jeans" next time he went to a particular client's office on a Friday.

Barney Nicks, a financial planner, was even sensitive to indirect signals about dress. He dressed down or even "a little bit badly" for meetings with accountants, who had skills similar to his but "on average make about one-tenth of what we do." Barney's elite clients had concerns about being taken advantage of: "If a client is very wealthy, they will tend to actually not want us . . . as dressed up as someone who is slightly less wealthy. . . . Their concern is that they're overpaying . . . and that's something that a lot of high-income people are more sensitive to." Gesturing toward his office's sweeping views of San Francisco Bay, Barney told me that he drew the shades when some of these penny-pinching rich clients visited him so they wouldn't start wondering about the rent he was paying for with their fees.

Although no interviewees pointed to negative outcomes of dressing inappropriately for a client meeting, some remembered feeling embarrassed when this happened, as with the tech professional who was called into a meeting with some Sony executives while wearing a "pretty ratty" T-shirt. "I felt awkward and wasn't one of the serious players" in the meeting, he told me, stating that after this he stopped wearing T-shirts to work. Timothy, who worked for a hedge fund, vividly recalled wearing a dress shirt with French cuffs and cufflinks to meet with representatives from a mining company in Canada, where he felt "silly" and "overdressed"; he told me he now avoids wearing that shirt.

Salesmen agreed that, given the possibility that each pitch might not result in a new account, dress was at least one element of the equation that they could completely control. As Pierre Molyneux put it, echoing others, "When I'm meeting outside [the office] with someone, I always put all the chance on my side." He said he wouldn't make the sale simply because he was "wearing the right stuff," but "at least I won't make any mistake with this [dress]." In Pierre's formulation, the worker does not dress a particular way because of direct control by the employer but rather exercises self-control that may materially benefit both him and the employer.

Some interviewees painted meeting with clients as a clash of dress cultures. Brett Mason, who worked for a Manhattan branding agency, said that clients expected creative professionals like him to dress a bit differently than the typical white-collar person: "We need to have the appearance of not only being a creative person, but someone who's stylish and knows . . . what's going on in society, because our job, so much is about reflecting what's going on in society and pushing the society forward with bringing new, innovative things to market." Other "creatives" (folks in advertising, marketing, and design occupations) agreed with Brett that their clients expected a different kind of professional dress from them.[42] One said that if he were to wear suits and ties to meetings, it would not "give the right message to clients." The tech field is similarly seen as an outlier. When John worked at a start-up in San Francisco, he witnessed "a dichotomy between some of the people we were meeting with, who wore (sometimes) suits, and . . . we sort of had this image of like the 'young tech kids' . . . khaki pants and a button-down [shirt]." Stereotypes that white-collar workers hold about those they might encounter in the business world thus enable some variety in dress styles to exist. In some cases, a clash of dress norms is seen as desirable. For instance, meetings may give clients a break from their typical dress routine; one architect opined that sometimes his clients "set meetings with us so that they can take their tie off, and just, you know, relax. . . . 'The architects are coming in, so . . .'" The client meeting is a place where participants use dress strategically to try to achieve favorable interactions that make money for their companies, and by extension, themselves.

It is ironic that despite the widespread language about creating a personal brand and selling yourself, most participants did not take risks with their work dress. Selling yourself, then, was not about standing out or presenting an image that was uniquely *you*; it was about conforming to clients' expectations and in some cases mimicking their self-presentation and dress. The personal brand is not that personal for these men. The self they are selling is a particular version of corporate subjectivity that connotes competence rather than originality.

Corporate Dress Norms: What Do We Know for Sure?

Men's accounts of what they wear to work in white-collar jobs set the stage for a more in-depth exploration of the meanings of their dress decisions, which exemplify what social scientists call "impression management."[43] I found quite similar ideas about the importance of appearance in white-collar work, and emphasis on professionalism in dress and manner, among many of my interviewees, regardless of their specific job, racial or ethnic identity, age, or country of birth. This could be evidence of what the sociologist R. W. Connell termed "transnational business masculinity"; in an era of capitalist globalization, power becomes concentrated in the hands of managers (mostly men), who "self-consciously manage their bodies and emotions as well as [their] money."[44] Or it could be seen as indicating continuity with the white-collar world immortalized in the now-classic writings of Mills, Whyte, and other thinkers of the 1950s. The office is a place where men (and women) see each other and are seen,[45] and where assumptions about abilities are often based on appearance. The men I interviewed said that they had to look presentable and conform to a particular "professional" appearance at all times, as they never knew who might be watching and evaluating them. The external supposedly signaled internal qualities such as competence and commitment while also indicating a privileged position vis-à-vis workers in less prestigious occupations.

My interviews point to some diversity in work dress standards, but clear patterns emerge. Over the past several decades, the white-collar work world has become less formal. Research participants tended to categorize their work dress regimes as (1) mostly business formal, with suits worn most days, (2) mostly business casual, or (3) completely casual. While business casual was the most common dress standard across all three research sites, New Yorkers were the most likely to experience business formal dress codes, and San Franciscans were the most likely to have casual-dress workplaces. Thus, region and local dress cultures matter for what white-collar men are expected to wear to work. The trouble with business casual is that, in the words of one interviewee, it is "open to inter-pretation." Many men lamented that they weren't exactly sure what counted as business casual, and several claimed this ambiguity made business formal dress codes easier to follow, requiring less thought. More flexibility in dress resulted, on the one hand, in greater fear of making a mistake: these men wanted to en-gage in more conformity, not less. On the other hand, dress codes are often not explicitly enforced ("No one wants to be the style police"), and some employees complain about and resist dress rules that they see as "overkill." Sometimes this pressure was effective, and dress codes were changed. But since dress and appear-ance figure into evaluations related to hiring and promotion, there may be an "opportunity cost" to dressing in a manner that is perceived as unprofessional, even if a worker is not technically breaking the rules.

While most men in this study (and in corporate America more broadly) do not wear suits to work every day, suits still carry tremendous symbolic value. As other researchers have shown, in the United States a man wearing a suit connotes power, authority, and capability.[46] This is certainly part of the reason that suits are still the default dress for interviews and important meetings or events. Even though most participants were not in business formal office environments, they all had opinions on suits and cited reasons they would or would not want to wear them daily. For some, it didn't feel like work unless they were in a suit, and the start of nonwork time wasn't official until the suit came off. Others saw the suit as an uncomfortable item of clothing representing an equally stifling work climate.

Across jobs, many men talked about the role of appearance in "selling your-self." They thought carefully about how to dress for internal and external clients, seeing this as the one aspect of these encounters that they could fully control. For those in client-facing positions, the imagined client became, to use the terms of social psychologist G. H. Mead, the "generalized other," whose imagined judg-ments were internalized and used by the men to regulate their behavior and con-form to dress expectations.

My task in this chapter was to describe, using the men's own words, today's white-collar dress norms as they are institutionalized through written and un-written codes and rules, and to show how dress codes matter to employees. These are the parameters within which men make decisions about how to present themselves in the corporate world and about their identities as workers and men, decisions related to changing views of masculinity and changing conditions of employment.

TRADING PLACES

Jim Shaw, a heavyset white man in his early fifties, wore delicate glasses, kept what was left of his white hair cut short, and aptly described himself as "soft-spoken" yet "direct" and "inquisitive." Al Elkin, half a dozen years younger, was also a "white guy"; his personality was more boisterous, his hair thicker and darker. Jim grew up in the Northeast and worked in New York City for many years before transferring to a job in his company's Cincinnati office. Al grew up and attended college in Cincinnati, bouncing around to a few different U.S. cities before ending up in a spacious Manhattan office with a prime view. Both were human resources executives who spent their days dealing—as Al put it—with "people problems."

Jim was from a blue-collar family, learning everything he knew about dressing for white-collar work in spite of, rather than from, his father's example. Al's family was solidly middle class: he was proud to belong to the third generation of Elkin men to wear Brooks Brothers suits to work. While Jim admitted to a brief adolescent dalliance in countercultural fashion trends, both he and Al classified their work dress styles as conservative. Both recalled buying suits at the beginning of their careers in corporate America, before companies started switching over to business casual en masse. "When I graduated college," Jim reminisced, "I bought a whole bunch of suits . . . to start the interviewing process." These interview suits were meaningful to Jim, as they represented the start of a new life and the possibility of moving up the socioeconomic ladder. He didn't think he was unique in this regard; he claimed that when recent college graduates—whom he could now call "young kids" by virtue of his age and senior position—have to put on a suit for interviews or for their new job, "that *changes them*." Al also valued the chance to build his suit wardrobe as a young corporate worker. "I do remember those suits," Al said. "I wanted to have *five suits*—one for every day of the week. . . . That was one of my primary goals." He still remembered the way he felt when he was able to purchase that fifth suit with his earnings.

In a way, Jim and Al traded places. An East Coast guy who had built a successful career in Manhattan, Jim moved to Cincinnati a couple years before I interviewed him. Al, a Cincinnati native, had been working in New York City for about a decade when we met. Jim and Al were aware of, and spoke vividly about, the divergences in these two local dress cultures they knew well. They were strategic in adapting their appearances for their new professional environs.

"There is probably no place as conservative as Cincinnati on the planet," Al proclaimed. As Jim clarified, when people say (as they did in interviews for this book) that Cincinnati is conservative in its work dress, "conservative doesn't necessarily mean wearing a suit, it's just more casual." Living in the Midwest, Jim told me, "I can tell when somebody's not from here, or they're a businessman on a visit, or if you're down in the lobby and see people coming in dressed like they're in New York, you can tell they're a vendor or something like that." He went on to say that even when men in Cincinnati wear suits, "there's a casualness about the suit; it's not as crisp."

The Big Apple was a different story. According to Al, the transplanted Cincinnatian, "if you go to Grand Central or you go to Penn Station [train stations in midtown Manhattan] . . . you will see the preponderance of people who *really wear suits*." It wasn't that every man on (or below) the street was sporting a business suit, "but there's a significant number of people who wear the traditional style." Jim agreed, stating that in New York, even if a company has a casual or business casual dress code, at least some people will be wearing suits: "I think people in New York have an expectation that others would want them to rise above the policy." Like Al, Jim referenced the public visibility of formal business clothing in New York, saying "just walking around the streets, you see more people in suits, and it seems more comfortable."

So they changed their tactics when they moved.

> *Al*: When I used to dress casual [in the New York office], I was stopped at one point by a vice president who pointed out that I dressed more casual than most people, which was a symbol to me that meant I'd got too far. . . . The other interesting thing was my kids did not understand the difference between what I wore to work Monday through Friday and what I wore on weekends. I had a difficult time explaining to my kids what I was doing during the week because they didn't understand it. So, those things led me back to wearing a suit, and I've been doing it for a number of years now, seven, eight years. . . . When I wear a suit, the recognition I get and the way I'm treated when I'm in a suit versus casual is entirely different.

> *Jim*: I'll tell you a story! I'm old school. I went to a meeting with someone much higher than me and I have a tendency and I have sort of a cultural bias that when you meet with certain levels of the organization, you wear a suit. It's just the way I am. I wore a suit. I was the only one in the meeting with a suit. And the person I was meeting with, who is clearly up there [in status], turned to me and said, "Jim, what the hell are you doing wearing a suit?!" And I said, "Well, I do it out of respect." I was truthful. You shouldn't [do what I did],

because you should wear—you should dress according to the culture of your environment. And he actually said to me, it's wrong to do that. He was very nice, I mean, he was sweet about it. And I joked about it. . . . But, really, that's the way, that's the expectation. So, but it's very different than my traditional thinking.

Al: I believe that we are a conservative company. . . . And there is a look that we have, and we should present that every day. We're a business. And I choose to wear a suit and tie because I believe it's a uniform, and I believe it exhibits an amount of discipline and also garners a great deal of respect. . . . Some of these people [I work with] are much more into the casual environment—and I used to participate in the casual environment—But I believe—I learned quickly that it sends a mixed message. You garner much greater support and confidence in how you dress. It's the first thing people see: appearance. And that's what they judge you on. And people mix up the casualness with the professional expectations. So, a suit is a uniform that demonstrates confidence, respect, and a formality. So, the short end of the question is: I wear the suit four to five days a week.

Jim: I believe that people had a perception when I came here, because I'm a New Yorker. And I am intim—I can be intimidating, and stuff like this, which I never understood. But people become intimidated by me. I believe they perceived me wearing, dressing in that business attire, carried with me that New York "thing" and that they needed me to dress more casual to make me more approachable. And that's why people talked about it. And Bob [a colleague] really wanted me to get away from that thing. Because there's a perception [here] when you're from the East or New York, that you're nasty. And they perceive the clothing you wear to facilitate getting rid of that perception.

The motivations each man explicitly gave for adapting his dress were not identical—though both were fathers, only Al mentioned wanting to model formal work dress for his children—but they both referenced the importance of place and their hoped-for outcomes. Conservative Cincinnati and a business casual office required Jim the New Yorker to dress down in order for his subordinates and colleagues not to feel put off. New York, conservative in a different (more formal and buttoned-up) way, allowed Al to feel great wearing a suit even though his office dress code required only business casual. He fit in when rubbing elbows with other commuting executives in Grand Central Terminal, despite being slightly more dressed up than some of his coworkers. Jim and Al believed their dress could color their interactions with folks at the office, and they wanted to actively rather than passively shape those interactions.

Trading cities, trading dress styles—in trading places, Jim's and Al's stories show how influential company dress codes and local dress cultures are in men's decisions about what to wear to work. They also highlight the balancing of external pressures against men's personal preferences and their degree of comfort with different levels of professional dress. The way that Jim and Al dressed at work, although it changed as their working conditions and locations changed, related to the men's identities and sense of themselves as skilled and high-level corporate workers:

> *Al*: I understand people. I read people very well. And then I am able to *adapt* to that.

> *Jim*: I remember I was twenty [years old] and somebody walked into my little training room and they referred to me as Mr. Shaw. . . . And I've been a Mr. Shaw ever since. And there's something about it.

JUST LIKE DAD?

Family Relations and Class Origins in Dressing for White-Collar Work

Erynn: What kind of dresser was he [your father]?

Domingo: Oh, he thought he was like Mr. Slick.

Erynn: Oh, yeah?

Domingo: Yeah, old school slick.

Erynn: He was very interested in style?

Domingo: Yeah, I think that's where I got my match your socks to your . . . kind of thing . . . and yeah, he was very interested in going out. He was a dancer too, right, so he kind of had to look good. You know, jacket, smoker's jacket or whatever those kinds of jackets are called. . . . He would wear that all the time, and then slacks and stuff like that and, yeah, he was okay.

Erynn: Do you remember him trying to teach you lessons about dress or how to present yourself or anything like that?

Domingo: Well, I still remember him telling me [*mimics father*]: "Your socks should match your shoes [*laughs*]. Your shoes should match your shirt" [*laughs*], you know, in his accent or whatever. Yeah, yeah, that stuck with me.

Carl: My son is working . . . across the street in investment banking. He had a meeting last Friday . . . a lunch meeting—not even a formal meeting, just a lunch engagement with a contact at Goldman Sachs. And my son is interested in being in finance and banking. I picked him up in the morning and he got into my car and he wasn't wearing a suit. He was wearing a pair of slacks and an open shirt. And as he got into the car, I was just talking about, "So what do you have going on today?" And he said he had this meeting at Goldman Sachs, with this guy from Goldman. I said, "You're gonna have to cancel that. There's no way you're going to meet with this guy dressed the way you are." And he said, you know, "Why? It's Friday and it's casual; we're just going out for lunch." And the fact is, the guy from Goldman probably would have been dressed casually also. But in my mind, since it was my son's first meeting with him and a first impression for somebody who could influence his career, I felt it was very important that he make a significantly strong first impression. And I don't think an open-collared shirt and a pair of slacks would do that. I felt he needed to be buttoned up in a suit. So we debated it a little bit. I ended up winning. He called the guy at Goldman and said that he was called into a meeting; couldn't get out; could he potentially reschedule; he really wanted to meet with him; and they rescheduled it for sometime this week.

The men quoted above are very different. Domingo Sala is thirty-eight, with two preschool-aged children, and Carl Adelman is fifty-one, with three kids who are pretty much grown. After leaving the navy, Domingo finds himself near the beginning of his career in healthcare administration in the San Francisco Bay area, whereas Carl has decades of experience and runs an entire Manhattan office for a business services firm. Domingo is Filipino and Carl is white. Yet in our conversations, both of them told stories of fathers teaching their sons lessons about how to dress. Domingo always admired his father's style, even if it differed from his own. Carl was horrified that his son would consider wearing anything less than a full suit and tie for even an informal meeting with someone from Goldman Sachs, one of the most powerful forces in banking and finance. He went on to tell me that if *he* had a meeting with someone from Goldman, "I would probably wear my best suit, my best shirt, my best tie, my shined shoes, and I'd look like a million bucks, whether or not the guy I was meeting was dressed down." Carl's son—who decided to heed his father's advice—can benefit directly from Carl's professional background and familiarity with the particular dress culture of Manhattan banks. Domingo's father, an immigrant, lacked access to this kind of specialized white-collar knowledge; nevertheless, he worked to instill in his son a sense of appropriateness and style. He did this directly, by dictating rules for matching, and indirectly, by embodying the nightlife persona Domingo laughingly and lovingly calls "Mr. Slick."

Sociological research examines issues of work, gender, and family in U.S. society: the wage gap between men and women and its link to men's idealized role as breadwinners;[1] the unpaid work done by women in the home and their greater likeliness to drop out of or pull back from the paid workforce;[2] the stereotypes about women's nurturing instincts and caregiving responsibilities that have real effects on their career prospects;[3] and the struggle of both women and men to combine income-earning activities with other family responsibilities.[4] Drawing on social science research, Facebook COO Sheryl Sandberg's splashy 2013 treatise on women's work-family dilemmas, *Lean In*, shows that these issues are also part of American public discourse outside academia. Yet scholars and cultural critics have not fully explored the movement of *bodies* across the permeable border between work and home.

About 39 percent of workers in the United States occupy white-collar positions, and many in the other 61 percent aspire to these jobs.[5] People must learn how to dress somewhere, and this learning or socialization process begins at home, with parents teaching their offspring directly and indirectly.[6] We encounter parents and family before other agents of socialization, such as schools. Socialization into workplace dress norms is consequential for children's career goals and ambitions and for their future ability to fit in and adapt to the work world. But learning to dress and present the body at work is one factor in the work-family equation that's generally ignored by scholars.[7] I examine this *dress socialization*, which includes everything from teaching boys to properly knot neckties to teaching them to conform to ideals of middle-class respectability.

Work, Family, and Social Class

Interviewees highlighted the role of family in the crafting of their personal style and dress both inside and outside of work. Here I present and interpret their experiences of embodied socialization as children and parents.[8] Research on how social class is reproduced can help us make sense of these narratives of self-creation, conformity, and differentiation through dress. The French sociologist Pierre Bourdieu's famous work on class reproduction delved into the role of school, family, and other social groups in maintaining the structure of society and the divisions between social classes.[9] One of the few big-name sociologists to theorize about the role of the human body in social processes, Bourdieu is often cited in studies of the body, embodiment,[10] and fashion. Here I build on his work about the tastes that characterize different social classes to explain the formation and transmission of white-collar dress norms in families. Bourdieu's concept of cultural capital—specialized, class-based knowledge—is useful in interpreting the men's family experiences. Their parents passed on certain cultural capital to them, and those who are parents often see themselves as inculcating cultural capital in their own children (though they wouldn't use this sociological jargon). Bourdieu's idea of "habitus" refers to people's mostly unconscious orientation toward the world and enactment of class-based lifestyles. We can see in the accounts of these fathers and sons the building blocks of a contemporary white-collar habitus or image. Despite the men's emphasis on conformity, this image is more fragmented and individualized than it was in the post–World War II era of *The Man in the Gray Flannel Suit*.

Other studies of class reproduction extend and support Bourdieu's theories. Without getting bogged down in an extensive overview of this research, I'll briefly mention a few influential works. Paul Willis showed in his classic ethnography *Learning to Labor* (1981) how young men in England were socialized into working-class values, practices, and norms, especially in schools. The body is present here, as Willis documents styles of appearance favored by the "lads," as he calls them, and shows how they prize physical prowess over pencil pushing. Their bodies are shaped from a young age to be useful blue-collar tools, and the lads accept this socialization and the work lives to which it destines them. The sociologist Annette Lareau's book *Unequal Childhoods* (2003) compares the ways that middle-class, working-class, and poor parents raise their children, socializing them into different recreational activities and patterns of interaction with authority figures (e.g., doctors, teachers). Lareau does not address bodies, dress, or style in detail. Julie Bettie's 2003 book *Women without Class* shows how social class identities are reproduced in a multiethnic high school. Young working-class women in Bettie's study differentiated themselves from other social groups in the school space by embodying specific (often stigmatized) styles of femininity.

I approach class socialization from a different angle. First, I am working not from theoretical propositions or in-depth participant observation but from interview accounts. I can't get in a time machine and jet back to the interviewees' childhoods to find out if their parents really raised them the way they say they did. So I am confined to presenting and analyzing the narratives men told about themselves and their upbringing. Second, I'm interested in how *adult men* conceive of the relationship between family and work dress, rather than analyzing children's experiences of socialization in real time. I am inspired by sociologists' assertion that social class is not just a function of family income but also has a cultural component and is an identity that is *performed*. These class performances always involve the body, dress, and appearance. Finally, I am interested in men's stories of class mobility as well as class reproduction.

Learning How to Dress

Many in the core group of seventy-one white-collar men expressed a belief that their parents (and other members of what we sociologists would call their "family of origin") affected their views on dress. Interviewee accounts emphasized how parents explicitly or implicitly socialized them into standards of dress and appearance that can best be described as respectable, professional (in the case of work dress), and middle-class. As I'll discuss, some of the men claimed to have learned these dress norms not from, but in spite of, their parents, especially fathers. But many participants remembered receiving from an early age the message that being presentable and dressing appropriately was important and expected in locations such as school, church, and work. The predominant middle-class orientation toward dress—that is, the devaluation of lower-class or street style and the simultaneous shunning of overly luxurious clothing—held true even for families that were wealthier or poorer than the average U.S. family.

Father Knows Best

For men, "fathers play a symbolic role in our [men's] transition into the masculine world, [and] they become a focus for all the promises and status symbols we learn to expect will be ours."[11] Curious about whether and how ideas about dress and appearance get passed down, I asked men to describe their fathers' dress style and whether they felt their own dress practices had been influenced by their dads. Of particular interest in the context of class reproduction, several men described their fathers as embodying white-collar or professional dress standards. It's as if people who grew up in the United States over a certain time period—and some who grew up elsewhere—have a picture in their mind of the businessman, the professional man. When they call up the image of their father, it matches this image of the businessman. R. J. Logan, a white twentysomething, equated his father with white-collar dress. As we chatted in a faux-gritty Manhattan café, he said, "He's suits and ties . . . very, very corporate." R. J.'s dad, who worked for a "large, international-type company," didn't just wear, but seemed to become, the suit and tie by embodying the corporate ideal of self-presentation so perfectly. Another New York interviewee, Vijay Singh, remarked that his father's work dress was also his weekend dress: "He worked for the United Nations, you know, so it was business [dress], I guess every single day. . . . But he *always* wore a suit. Even when he would go out to like a friend's place, you know, for dinners. . . . It just was his style." Sixty-two-year-old Luiz Rodrigues, who grew up in Brazil and now lives and works in New York, painted a similar portrait of his father, a university professor, marveling that he was "able to do landscaping or take care of flowers wearing a tie." This is a portrait of not only a certain type of work dress but perhaps also a level of formality associated with bygone eras. Vijay's and Luiz's accounts were echoed by Nigel Peters, a British executive in New York: "He [my father] wore a suit every day. And in fact he would probably wear a tie at the weekend." Nigel recalled his father routinely wearing a suit to church or for "Sunday lunch." He embodied this professional image so perfectly that Nigel claimed, "I've never seen my father in a pair of jeans in his life." These descriptions depict a man who is dedicated to his work, or at least to dress that represents such dedication and telegraphs middle- or upper-class status.

Al Elkin, who was in his mid-forties and worked for a corporate retailer in New York, traced this incarnation of professional dress back two generations, saying, "My father and grandfather wore Brooks Brothers and they wore suits every day. And so it was a uniform. And that's how it was explained to me, that when you get in business, *this is* your uniform." The Elkin men had worn suits to work, expressly preparing young Al to follow in their footsteps by using the nonoptional language of "uniform" to describe work clothing.[12] Sean Albertson grew up in Northern California, where he still lives and works in sales for a Fortune 500 company. His father went "out of the house every morning in a suit and tie and . . . instilled in me to, you know, look professional, polished and—he was in sales as well—he would come across as . . . a professional" who took his job seriously.[13]

For some men (remember Domingo?), Dad was a sort of style icon, a role model to be admired and possibly emulated. Dinesh Devi, a man in his midthirties working in Cincinnati, was impressed with his retired father's commitment to looking nice, saying, "He's still a really good dresser." The "still" implies that the elder Mr. Devi could get away with doing less, as he is older and out of the workforce, but that he maintains high standards for his appearance and clothing. "He's just always ironing," attests Dinesh. Louis Katz, a fifty-eight-year-old "white Jewish" man employed at a New York advertising firm, also recalled his father's stylishness and connected it directly to his own reputation for dressing well:

> When I was young, I thought he was a very snappy dresser. And um, he seemed to like *know* some things about clothes and he seemed to care about the—You know, it's like, I feel like I learned some things about clothes from him. Like I knew what glen plaid was or something or . . . I felt like I was kind of more trendy and fashionable, like in high school. I think other people considered me that.[14]

Pierre Molyneux, who worked about thirty blocks uptown from Louis, remembered borrowing his father's Hugo Boss brand shirts to wear to school as a teenager. He can't be sure, but he thinks his father was "proud" that his son copied his style and found his clothing fashionable.

Two men described themselves as actively cultivating aspects of their father's look. Jacob Burstein's father was a restaurateur whom he classified as "old-school Italian" and "a pretty snazzy dresser." He narrated a recent incident as evidence of his dad's fashionableness:

> So my dad got a pair of sunglasses. I'm like, holy shit!—where did you find—Like where did you *get* those?! Like where? Or how? I saw those in a magazine. I was like, "Oh, those are kind of cool." And then my dad like walked into brunch, you know, with them on.

Travis Jones, who works in advertising in Manhattan, admired the way his father dressed in the days before Travis was born, while living abroad. As we chatted at his dining room table one evening, Travis waxed nostalgic for a time he could not remember but that was vividly etched in his mind.

> I love looking at pictures of him of when he was younger and he was in London. 'Cause certainly there was a sensibility of how he dressed then that I'm very much attracted to and—and am sort of emulating now. I think, I see him in fitted trousers, and you know, skinny, like the whole idea of skinny jeans, skinny pants. I mean, this is the era that he lived in. Polos [shirts] that are all fitted. He looked fantastic.

Travis's father actively socialized him into a certain way of thinking about dress, telling him it was impossible to be overdressed in any social or work situation ("Everyone else is underdressed"). His stylish appearance as captured in old family photos continues to influence Travis.

This emotional connection between fathers and sons through dress lives on even after fathers have died. Aaron Levitt, a recent college graduate from Cincinnati who worked in health care, lost his father when he was in elementary school. He told me proudly, "Years after my father's passing, I still have family friends that will come up and randomly say, 'Your father was always the best-dressed man at the office.'" These patterns, most common among the men from middle-class families, show that fathers' dress can shape sons' perceptions and practices beyond the years they spend living in the same home.

Demographics and Dress

Since I don't have data from a random sample of white-collar men, I'm careful about generalizing from their responses and recollections. However, when I asked about their fathers' dress, many interviewees immediately resorted to ethnic or national-origin identifications. Jacob referred to his "old-school Italian" father, and Nigel called his dad a "very traditional, like English gentleman." Vijay explained his father's preference for formal dress by saying, "He came from India, I guess [that's why]." Michel Jean, whom I interviewed in Brooklyn, said, "My dad is—my dad is Haitian, right? So, Haitians are known for like vibrant colors and like crazy dress in some ways." In these cases, it seemed that men brought up their father's nationality or ethnicity in order to distance themselves from that identity. In other cases, men clearly placed themselves in the same ethnic or national category as their dads.

When I asked New York interviewee Luca Constantino about his father's style, he replied matter-of-factly, "Well, he's Italian," before elaborating. Though Fabricio Silva's father is Argentinian, Fabricio described him as having an "Italian glamour in the way he dresses." Phil Blum, a transplanted New Yorker and retired salesman living in the San Francisco Bay Area, described his father as the son of Eastern European Jewish immigrants who lived by the motto "Think Yiddish and dress British."[15] Phil's maternal uncles were "Jewish businessmen" who, in his opinion, dressed "not really flashy, but a little bit like gangsters." He then asked me, to illustrate his point, had I ever seen *The Sopranos*? Many of the men in my study mentioned the greater emphasis placed on men's dress and fashion in Europe and the more formal dress expectations in developing countries by comparison with the United States. This country is seen as the anomaly in its prevailing antipathy toward men's concern with dress, style, and appearance.

What are we to make of the ease with which men forged the father→dress→ethnicity link? To a certain extent, they are relying on stereotypes about immigrants and ethnic "others" that have been common in the United States for a long time. Stereotypes could act as a conversational shortcut, a useful tool in a time-limited interview. If I showed familiarity with the idea that Haitians are supposedly "crazy" dressers, then Michel could move on and get to his next point more quickly. However, as with many stereotypes, there may be some truth to these comparisons.

Appearance matters for everyone, but especially for people who have lower status (e.g., class standing), as they lack economic resources or prestigious social connections.[16] In the United States, blacks, Latinos, and some immigrants are more likely to be poor and working-class. Throughout the history of the United States, black and Latino cultures have emphasized style, dress, and appearance differently—and in some cases more strongly—than have mainstream white groups.[17] Nearly all the black men I interviewed referred to the distinctiveness of black style and the importance of dress and fashion in their communities.[18] Some of these men felt that fashions that were popular in their social circles were off-limits in the office, meaning that they kept their work and nonwork clothing separate.

In corporate work, minorities are hypervisible and thus often hold themselves, and are held by others, to a higher standard of dress formality.[19] As one African American participant put it, "Black men do have more of a conscious[ness] of how they appear than their white counterparts. . . . I think black men, especially in the professional work area . . . can identify with each other." His experience of being a minority in the corporate world differed from that of his white colleagues, in ways that he felt were consistent with the experiences of other minorities. Another black participant recalled two instances when his presence in his new workplace was questioned because he was dressed casually. The first time it happened, he recounted, "Everybody was up in arms, and like, 'who are you, what are you doing here?'" The second time, he encountered the chief executive officer (CEO) speaking with the head of sales in the hallway; when they saw him, the "conversation went dead silent; it was so silent that I heard the CEO ask the VP, 'who is that and why is he walkin' in our office?,'" only to be informed that he was the new director of marketing. "Oh," was the CEO's only reply. Interviews with black men reiterated the idea that conformity to (or exceeding) dress standards was critical to their success in corporate America, since they were already seen as different. One black interviewee told me that the white men he worked with "do the bare minimum" when it comes to dress, whereas in his family and community, "everyone matches . . . and I'm not even African American. I'm African. And even Africans match [their clothes]. If you don't match, it's like, what happened to you?"

Another demographic category seemed to matter for families' dress socialization: father's military status. Some men whose fathers had been in the service described the home as a tight ship with regard to dress expectations, and recalled specific lessons their fathers had taught them, such as the "military tuck" for shirts. An interviewee who followed several generations of his family into the army described how learning to iron proficiently at home made his transition to preparing his own uniforms—and later his corporate work clothing—easier.[20] On the other hand, one participant whose father "hated being in the military" and wearing uniforms likewise opposed uniforms and strived for individuality in his dress.

Looking in from Outside the Middle Class

While parents' insistence that their children look presentable and uphold middle-class dress standards was common across the board, some interviewees talked about growing up in working-class or poor families. These men usually did not see their fathers wearing suits or other "professional" clothing to work. Cincinnati interviewee Hans Schroeder, who grew up in Germany, recalled his father wearing blue-collar dress to work, but more formal dress in other settings, and stressing the importance of "looking sharp." Hans said his father dressed "very simple. . . . He was a handyman, so he didn't have a lot of money. But he was always on Sundays, when we went to church, with a suit and tie and his best shoes." Jordan Simms, a thirty-seven-year-old white man whom I spoke with in Cincinnati, not far from the Ohio town where he grew up, presented the following portrait of his blue-collar father:

> *Jordan*: Fashion was not a big priority and it still is not a big priority for him either. Um, he wears jeans a lot. Most of my childhood he worked for Rick's Lumber and . . . they had a uniform. They had a special shirt that he had to wear. I don't know why he did this, but he

wore that shirt seven days a week. I mean, he had a bunch of them, but even when he wasn't working that day, he was still wearing that shirt, which I always thought was [*slight pause*] really weird.

Erynn: Now I'm picturing one of these button-down, short-sleeved, with like his name on it or something. Is that—

Jordan: Yeah, it was . . .

Erynn: —what kind of shirt that it was?

Jordan: Yeah, it was that kind of shirt, yeah.

It is striking how Jordan's description of his dad wearing his work uniform shirt all the time, even outside of work, parallels the narratives of some research participants with middle-class or white-collar fathers. Just as Luiz's father could do the gardening in his tie, Jordan's father wore his work shirt everywhere. Off the job, working-class status is written on the body just as surely as middle-class or professional status is; here Bourdieu's ideas of habitus and people seeming to want the lifestyles that correspond to their class positions are brilliantly illustrated.

It seemed that most of the interviewees came from middle-class homes. I did not ask specifically about the class background of their families of origin, but for sociologists, clues about class are sprinkled throughout every conversation. Only about a quarter of the men talked about growing up in families or communities that were blue-collar, working-class, or poor. Take Andy Lipmann, a white thirty-six-year-old who hails from central Pennsylvania:

> Well, my dad worked road construction, so he wore Dickies with like a blue T-shirt, pretty much every day. You know, and mostly like a construction hat. During the winter there'd be like a heavier, uh, construction, you know, button—Ben Davis-type jacket.[21] It was like . . . for the area that I grew up in, most people's jobs were mechanics, construction, that type of stuff; so most people dressed pretty blue-collar.

Pierre, who grew up in a modestly sized city in France, told me that he was the first person in his family to wear a suit to work every day. His father, a shoemaker, "was working in shirts and jeans and everything," and Pierre recalls only rarely seeing him in a suit. San Francisco interviewee Jonathan Santos, who works at a casual-dress tech company, said his father's work was "fairly physical," so he wore clothing that "he considered expendable."[22] A couple of men remembered their fathers' uniforms; for example, one father was a police officer, and another worked for a public utility company.

Ideas about class mobility were sometimes part of family lore or autobiographical ruminations. Phil associated his father, who "grew up behind a butcher shop in the Bronx," with a style of dress that was above his station. He "liked clothes" and dressed as though he "lived on an estate." Phil's father had ascended from humble beginnings to become a suburban dentist whose children attended Ivy League colleges. Some men used their working-class or poor origins as a yardstick by which to measure their success; one was Barney Nicks, a financial planner in San Francisco. "I make considerably more money than my father did," he said proudly as we talked in the office of the firm he founded. When I asked if his father was also in finance, he answered, "No, no, he was a blue-collar guy," before repeating that he earned "considerably more money than he did, and more money than I kind of ever thought I would, at this age." For Barney, moving to white-collar—in this case, upper-middle or upper-class—status also meant surpassing his father on one of the primary metrics by which masculine performance is measured: income.

Some men who were not from blue-collar families speculated on the social mobility of colleagues from working-class backgrounds. Timothy Stein's boss at a Manhattan hedge fund was, in his words, "born to no money." Timothy, who had been raised upper-middle class from what I could tell, saw his boss's love of shopping and penchant for luxurious clothing as a direct consequence of his hardscrabble childhood. "He sees clothes as a symbol of his success," Timothy half-shouted over the din of a cramped, hectic midtown café. "If he made a good trade that day, he'll go shopping to reward himself." Timothy's analysis was that his boss had "a very short-term, rewards-focused mind." Timothy also spoke disparagingly of the floor traders in the stock exchange, whom he characterized as New Jersey Italians with overly flashy dress.[23] It is possible that men like Timothy, with more stable middle-class status, look down on people who flout middle-class dress norms (e.g., by wearing bright colors or "hideous" patterns) or who achieve middle-class resources later in life. Again, Bourdieu's concept of habitus is useful: unless you were socialized into tastes and norms of dress while very young, your aspiration to that class-signaling embodiment might be judged as lacking by those who could claim middle-class habitus from birth. Timothy was not the only interviewee who attributed coworkers' or bosses' avid pursuit of impeccable dress to their rags-to-riches biographies.

Two men used the word "poor" to describe their families—one referring to his parents and grandparents and the other to the household he grew up in. Both interviewees were Latino.[24] The career success of these men, one born in the United States and the other in Mexico, represents a rapid rise in status. Carlos Calle, one of nine children, moved to California from Mexico as a teenager. He remembers that his parents had a "very, very simple rule. . . . 'I don't care if you're gonna wear the same pair of jeans every day, you're gonna have to go wash them and bathe yourself.'" Carlos described his parents as "very strict on hygiene" and attributed this to their poverty. According to Carlos, his mother said, "Being poor doesn't give you an excuse to be filthy." He believed that this background carried over to his meticulous dress today: "It was the idea that people should not know [by looking at your dress] that you don't have any money, or you have a lot of money: it doesn't matter." Carlos told me he didn't place much importance on labels or brands for this reason. Sergio Rivera, a New York interviewee who also grew up on the West Coast, described his mother's family as being "pretty poor" and mentioned a similar emphasis on cleanliness and self-presentation. "I, as a kid, would not be allowed to go anywhere," he told me, "without having bathed, combed my hair, and you know, had ironed pants, ironed shirt, just like very old-school, traditional-type." These narratives exemplify the commitment to a particular middle-class appearance in families across the class spectrum. I don't have a large enough sample to determine whether these types of stories are more common among Latino professionals. Certainly they were not the only interviewees from working-class or lower-class backgrounds to highlight the importance of dress in their early socialization experiences, yet together their stories have a certain resonance.

What Not to Wear

At least fifteen men cited their father as a negative influence on their style of dress or as a model of what to avoid. These dads, in the opinions of their now-grown sons, were more likely to dress like the victims of the makeover crew from the television show *What Not to Wear* than like Don Draper and his natty *Mad Men* colleagues. About one-third of these men were from blue-collar backgrounds, and a few explicitly linked their fathers' occupation with inadequate dress. Jim Shaw, who worked in corporate retail in Cincinnati, described his father's work clothing this way: "Oh, he wore jeans all the time. . . . He worked for the Department of Transportation, and he was on the road crews. He was a blue-collar worker." Jim went on to describe his father's usual work wardrobe of thick khaki work pants, flannel shirts, and boots. I then asked a triple-barreled question (something I advise my students never to do in interviews): "Did he teach you anything about style or clothing or appearance?" Jim's response was a quick and definitive "absolutely not." He had to learn how to dress as he moved up from low-level service jobs to management and then executive positions. Ron Varick, another Cincinnati interviewee, recalled his father wearing a company shirt in his position at a hardware store, and when asked whether his father had taught him anything about how to dress, he echoed Jim: "No. No. Not at all." Jordan, whose father wore his work shirt seven days a week, described him as "clueless" and "not someone I wanted to emulate" in dress and appearance. These men reject their dad's work style, and, symbolically, their blue-collar occupations.

Others were less charitable in painting their fathers as negative style role models. When I asked Femi Banjo, who worked a tech job in New York, what he learned about dress from his father, he said sarcastically, "Oh, I learned how to dress like a slob . . . got that down pat." According to Femi, his father "doesn't give a flying fuck what he wears." Femi said that he and his sisters used to "hound" their father because they wanted to have friends over and felt they couldn't because he routinely wore "some tighty-whiteys [brief-style underwear] and a wife-beater [sleeveless undershirt] and, if you're lucky he'd rock a robe." When they complained, he'd remind them who paid the bills. Femi recounted, "I'd be like, 'Yo, mom, what's up?' So she bought him a robe [*laughs*]." Femi's father was from Nigeria, and like other interviewees' immigrant fathers, he emphasized the importance of appropriate self-presentation in public. Yet his über-casual stance on dressing at home made an impression on his son. Other interviewees described their dad's style—or lack of style—with phrases like "he doesn't have any aesthetic sense at all"; "he could give two shits about what he wears"; "non-fashionable to the nth degree"; and "he's still wearing the same stuff that he was wearing when I was a kid." Some verbal portraits of poorly dressing fathers, told with relish, were hard not to chuckle at. Brett Mason, a white forty-year-old who works in advertising in New York, described his dad's work dress this way:

> *Brett*: He was the quintessential PE coach. Uh, for my *entire* life until he quit his job, he wore a pair of Cardinal polyester stretch shorts with about five thousand keys on a big fat belt and a tight T-shirt and a whistle around his neck. Pretty much all the time.
>
> *Erynn*: And that's still the style he's—
>
> *Brett*: Uh, no. He kind of—Now that he's retired, he's moved on to Hawaiian T-shirts, I think. Now he channels more of a Jimmy Buffett sort of aesthetic.

Frank Miller, who was just starting his finance career in Cincinnati, had an equally humorous description of his father's dress:

> I would say 80 percent of his uh, *wardrobe* is from—I don't know if you've ever heard of it—Power House Gym. It's just a gym. He gets T-shirts at a discount there. . . . And he would wear Power House pants. He just doesn't care. He usually tucks his shirt into his underwear, and you can see it. I mean he's just very—He just doesn't care. He's just very like, you know, the person speaks for themselves rather than the clothes they wear.

Frank viewed this lack of concern with appearance as outside the bounds of acceptable middle-class dress and saw his father's behavior as "very odd, because he was an attorney." Frank expected an attorney to dress nicely both in and out of work. Perhaps the occupational and class privilege that Frank's dad enjoyed allowed him to hold the view that "the person speaks" rather than the clothes—this privilege might not be shared by folks with less prestigious jobs. One participant summed up many men's thoughts on their fathers' dress this way: "I sort of look at his clothing choices, and I'm like, yeah, I'm not so sure I would make those kinds of choices." These men saw themselves as having superior cultural capital in the area of dress when compared with their fathers, even if they did not consider themselves stylish or fashion-forward. When I analyze patterns in the interview data, there is a cluster of white-collar men who identify themselves in stark opposition to their fathers' blue-collar dress. However, they are not the only ones labeling their fathers as fashion disasters or claiming to have learned nothing from Dad about dress except how not to do it.

Many of these sons claimed that their fathers' eschewing of fashion concerns did not affect them. Paul Massey, who worked for a publisher in Cincinnati and recalled always being interested in fashion and clothing, felt differently. He described his "aesthetic interests" as something that "didn't seem proper" for a young man, that "didn't seem [*laughs*] like something my dad probably would want me to do." A couple other men who enjoyed fashion and dress felt their fathers' disapproval of this form of cultural capital, which was inconsistent with traditional masculinity. These accounts show how family ties shape the performance of masculinity. Generally, gender conformity was part of men's dress socialization, perhaps preparing them for the conformity expected in corporate America. Because of his father's stance, Paul bonded more with his mother over clothing: "If anything, I got my sense of style probably from my mom."

Mothers Matter

What role do mothers play in teaching their sons how to dress? My interview guide did not address mothers' influence, yet several men brought up their mothers as we discussed early life lessons about self-presentation. This makes sense, given the association in our society between women, fashion, and appearance, and mothers' traditional role as shoppers for the household, especially for children's clothing. Dressing your children for the public world can be a fraught and thankless task. Some of the men I interviewed expressed distaste for how their mothers performed this function, while others remembered negotiations during the clothes-shopping process:

I remember, from a really young age, like five or six, and my mom would dress me up in lederhosen for the school photos. That was not something I was keen on at all. (Caleb Green, thirty-eight, San Francisco)

You know, growing up, my mother dressed me originally. I still grieve for it, because she dressed me terribly, in retrospect. (Bryan Lee, thirty-one, New York)

I remember like, shopping for sweaters a lot . . . with my mom, because at that point sometimes she would have to pay for that, or I'd have to ask her, "Please buy me this so the girls will like me?" (Paul Massey, forty, Cincinnati)

Several men claimed their mother had shaped their style more than their father. It's difficult to know whether this was connected to her responsibility for buying clothes, the nature of the boys' relationship with each parent, or Mom's style expertise. Without explicitly being asked which parent had had a greater impact on their dress, eleven men volunteered that they learned more from their mother, and two said that their mothers and fathers had an equal influence. Several men mentioned mothers and sisters in the same breath, as if they worked together to mold the style of the men and boys in the household.

The Protestant Ethic of Dress

In *The Protestant Ethic and the Spirit of Capitalism* ([1905] 2001), Max Weber (one of the fathers of sociology) lays out the Protestant virtues of thriftiness, living parsimoniously, and saving money that formed the bedrock of early U.S.-style capitalism. I recognized these values in the accounts of a dozen of my interviewees, irrespective of religion, country of birth, or social class. I distinguished two different strands of this ethic: (1) not spending excessive amounts of money on clothing and (2) caring for one's clothing to make it last.[25] Men remembered being taught these lessons both directly and indirectly by their families. Cincinnati participant Nicholas Georgiou's Greek immigrant parents were "very practical. . . . Why spend two hundred dollars on jeans when you can spend forty on a pair of Levi's?" Timothy said he was "raised by a family that believes that . . . you are supposed to spend as little money as you can on anything, and in particular with clothes," and he also espoused this virtue. Brett talked about "the cheapness my parents instilled in me," which he claimed to be slowly leaving behind as he began buying designer jeans and other pricey clothing.

Jacob, the young New Yorker whose father shocked him by wearing stylish sunglasses to brunch, told me a comical story about the time he decided to splurge on the most expensive thing he had ever bought: a Dolce & Gabbana jacket that cost several hundred dollars (as part of an outing with a female friend that led Jacob to conclude, "Drunk shopping is the worst thing you could possibly do"). After he told me about his purchase and subsequent mortification at his poor decision making, confessing that the designer jacket still hangs unworn in his closet, Jacob and I had this exchange:

> *Jacob*: If this makes it into any book, my—my dad—You—I will—My—
> *Erynn*: But your real name won't be used.
> *Jacob*: Okay! [*Laughing*]
> *Erynn*: So he'll never know [*laughs*].
> *Jacob*: He'll—I'm sure he'll figure [it out].
> *Erynn*: [*Mock teasing*] He'll know what you did!
> [*Jacob laughs hard.*]

Jacob expressed real concern about his father's view that spending too much money on designer clothing is offensive. Those of us who were socialized to view clothing as a necessity that should require minimal economic investment have a difficult time shaking these values as adults. There also seems to be an element of traditional no-frills masculinity in the attitude Jacob (who identifies as gay) imagines his father taking toward an extravagant expense on a faddish clothing item. White, heterosexual, middle-class masculine ideals in the United States have traditionally discouraged men from drawing attention to themselves and their bodies through dress.

Parents' thriftiness—or spending constraints—led to some memorable moments for the men I spoke to. Louis recalled that "the first item I wanted really badly were Beatle boots." Despite the fact that this footwear was a must-have for certain young people in the 1960s, Louis's parents wouldn't buy them. His solution: "I tried to save up my—it took me so long to save the money out of my allowance," which was "so tiny." He finally saved the money and didn't care that the boots "were completely out of fashion" by the time he had accumulated the amount; he bought them "'cause I'd been *waiting* for like so many years." Two Cincinnati interviewees, Jordan Simms and Daniel Moorehouse, likewise lusted after footwear: in this case, Nike tennis shoes. Daniel, now forty, wanted a pair of "hundred-dollar-plus" Nikes because they were "the thing to have."[26] He remembers his parents saying, "That's not happening [*laughs*]. We're not spending a hundred bucks on a pair of tennis shoes that are going to be destroyed in three weeks." He bought the shoes himself, his first independent clothing purchase. Jordan's mother refused to spend more than $50, so he paid the difference out of his savings. These parent-child interactions would perhaps play out differently in wealthier or poorer families. Each young man ignored parental encouragement toward thrift and found ways to buy the shoes they coveted. The rejection of their parents' values and preferences led to momentary claims to autonomy, however limited, and show that socialization is not an uncontested top-down process. There is room for resistance and agency.

Parents taught that caring for clothes was just as important as not blowing a pile of money on them. Travis, who admired his father's style in old photographs, remembered this lesson:

> He had a lot of pride in the things that he had that lasted a long time. So he believed in quality, and then taking extremely good care of the things that you owned. . . . He'd take such pride in saying, "I've had these shoes since I was twenty-five years old and they still look just as good today as they did then." . . . It was important to care for the things that you [had], so showing respect for the things that you owned, essentially.

Al, the third-generation Brooks Brothers suit-wearer, reported receiving a similar message from his dad: "You take care of your clothes." This involved cleaning them, pressing them, and not "throw[ing] 'em on the floor."

Speaking about dress and parents' expectations sometimes triggered emotional recollections. Clark Landon, a salesman from the San Francisco sample, described his parents as "Depression kids." He reminisced about a special hand-me-down cashmere sweater. As Clark told me over coffee in the financial district, "It was my oldest brother's, my middle brother's, and then it was mine." When Clark's mother gave him the sweater, he remembers her saying, "This sweater will last your *entire* life"—here Clark paused, and began to tear up a bit—"if you take care of it." After I responded to this display of emotion with a weak "mm-hmm," Clark said softly, "I still have it." Clothes can encapsulate aspects of our biographies and family connections that we see as meaningful. At the same time, men are socialized not to express emotions such as nostalgia or longing, which is why I was sometimes surprised to encounter such expressions in the interviews.

Hand-me-downs can teach lessons about caring for clothes in less direct ways. Barney inherited "a bunch of [his] grandfather's old clothes" when he passed away. He describes being struck by the fact that his grandfather "had worn stuff for like ten and fifteen years that usually don't last that long, like shirts." He referred to this ability to make clothes last as "a principle that I apply," which "really reflects my values." Barney clearly feels connected to his now-deceased grandfather through their shared commitment to caring for clothing. Like discussions of hand-me-downs, men's stories of learning to wear that most masculine of dress objects, the necktie, were imbued with emotion and significance.

The Ties That Bind?

"A well-tied tie is the first serious step in life," Oscar Wilde supposedly said (or wrote). Leaving aside the predicament this proposition creates for women who want to be taken seriously without wearing drag, I think that many of the men I interviewed would agree. Learning to tie a necktie is a "magnified moment,"[27] an episode that stands out among the everyday, an epiphany involving what will become a mundane action in the white-collar world. Of course, many research participants could not remember learning to tie a tie, and a couple of them admitted that they had never mastered this skill. But eighteen of the interviewees could recall this moment in their dress socialization. Initiations into the mysteries of the tie were not identical and were shaped by men's family situations and specific occasions.

Adam Gerber, a twenty-six-year-old from the Cincinnati sample who worked in finance, echoed those who saw their fathers as paragons of white-collar dress, expressing devotion to his father's method:

> The type of tie that I like to tie—the knot that I like is a full Windsor. And I specifically remember my dad teaching me how to do that. And anytime that I see someone who doesn't have the full Windsor knot, I'm like, "ugh, that's a crappy way to tie a tie. . . . You should learn the *right* way to tie a tie." . . . But what I do remember my dad teaching me was how to tie a tie. And the *right* way to tie a tie.

Jacob echoed Adam:

> I learned how to tie a tie from my father. My dad taught me how to tie a double Windsor knot when I was like seven years old. And to this day I can do it like . . . in ten seconds, in like the darkest room. . . . [*Pantomimes tying*] One, one, and I'm done. . . . He taught me that.

Adam and Jacob were socialized into this specific dress skill and into valuing it as an expression of respectability. Because ties are traditionally only worn by men, by learning to use them properly, young men come to embody masculine ideals, class status, and occupational habitus.[28]

When I asked Graham Houston, who grew up in the United Kingdom, about his father's influence on his dress, his reaction was one of comical amazement. "Oh, God. You just hit the nail on the head. Wow. How many questions in were you? Twelve?" Graham's father was headmaster of a Hogwarts-type English boarding school, where his mother was a teacher. "Talk about bringing your work home with you," he said, describing his parents' strictness with regard to his school uniform of tie and blazer. "The very first time I got my school uniform at the high school," Graham recounted, "there was a whole ceremony about tie tying." In addition to showing Graham how to wear a tie, his father tried to inculcate a sense of appropriate dress. "So for example, right now, he would not be happy about this," Graham said, pointing to his slightly loosened tie as we talked in his colorfully decorated office. Impersonating his father, Graham said bluntly, "If you're wearing a tie, wear a tie. Otherwise, take it off." Graham took a rather formal approach to dressing, which he saw as directly related to his early socialization.

George Wong, a San Francisco participant, remembered transferring to a private high school that required ties: "I tied that tie I think once and just never untied it. I just loosened it and wore it for the whole two years." Other interviewees had also employed this strategy. Luca was one of the only participants to admit his inability to tie a tie, despite being taught. An architect, he rarely wore ties. Now thirty-six, Luca said he asks his dad "every now and then, if I need to [wear a tie]," but since this happens so infrequently, "I forget it almost immediately." This can become a problem: "It happens [sometimes] that I think I still remember it, but . . . I go to work maybe and there's a meeting, and I have to wear a tie. And I try at home." If this fails, Luca said, "I end up asking someone from work to tie it for me." Not everyone becomes, wants to become, or needs to become an expert in the art of the necktie.

Family life in the United States often diverges from the stereotypical middle-class nuclear family in which dad holds a white-collar job. Thus, men's experiences of learning to use a tie reflect the diversity of families. Andy, who described his town as being blue-collar, remembered that his mom tried to teach him, since his father "used to only wear clip-on ties." This didn't work well, and Andy explained, laughing, "Well, I mean, it's not like *she* ever did it [wore a tie]." Dave Baker, a white Cincinnati interviewee who was in finance, told me that he "pretty much grew up with [his] mom and sister"; his parents were divorced and his dad "was hardly around—always had business, always had work." He credits his female-headed household and mother's and sister's influence with his knowledge of fashion and other "random stuff." Dave sounded disappointed when saying about his father, "He didn't even teach me how to tie a tie." He needed to learn this skill urgently as a teenager when his restaurant employer decided to have him work the front of the house: "I had to go across the street to my neighbor, because my mom didn't know." The alternative was, for him, unthinkable: "I didn't want to go into the restaurant and be like, 'Can you tie my tie?'" He uttered this question in a quiet, childlike voice, representing naïveté and helplessness. The neighbor option was less embarrassing.

Men expressed feeling disconnected or alone when the typical line of transmission of masculine skills was broken. Aaron couldn't remember who first taught him the basic four-in-hand necktie knot; his father passed away when he was young. But, Aaron told me, "I learned how to tie every other variation either from YouTube, or I went to the department store and asked a guy how to tie a full Windsor . . . because that was the mid-, early 2000s, so you saw a lot of power ties during that time."[29] In the department store, he had just purchased his first "nice tie" and wanted to make sure he wasn't "looking like a goof." The YouTube option is a new one made possible by the development of the Internet as a source of information and a place that people show off skills and teach others. In offering tying lessons, it fills in for fathers.

Aaron wasn't the only participant to mention department stores. Aiden Curry's father didn't live with the family during his (Aiden's) childhood. His father, who "grew up in the [San Francisco] Bay Area in the sixties and seventies," didn't know how to tie a tie, and this was "a badge of honor for him." Eventually, Aiden needed a tie. Maybe it was for his high school graduation: he couldn't remember exactly. Aiden mentioned to the salesman at J.C. Penney that he didn't know how to tie the tie he had purchased, "and this was in the days before you could go on YouTube." He recalls,

> And this is some random dude working at J.C. Penney with a pencil-thin mustache . . . [and he] taught me how to tie a tie with a brochure. And my dad when he went through, he would always tie a tie like a slipknot and just loosen it and keep it like that and so I was like "Oh great, so I have it tied now, I'm just going to go." You know, just sort of emulating my dad. And the guy was like "No, this is something you need to learn." And he untied it and made me do it again, and then he untied it and gave me the brochure and the tie and sent me on my way. And, I've had that thing for years, and so I knew it by heart.

This anecdote is revealing when compared with the tie stories of other participants and in light of the socialization into white-collar, middle-class norms of dress. Aiden's account of learning to tie a tie is more detailed and sharply remembered than those of some other men. Is this because it was the mustachioed salesman and not his father who taught him? It is clear from Aiden's, Aaron's, and Dave's narratives that if Dad is not available, other men—even strangers—may be called on to impart masculine dress skills (and by extension, dress norms) to younger guys encountering necktie expectations for the first time.

Some participants now find themselves teaching the next generation of white-collar warriors how to armor their necks for battle. Carl, whose advice to his son opened this chapter, described his role as agent of necktie socialization, combining traditional and newer approaches: "I remember teaching my [two] sons, which didn't go all that well. My youngest one got it. My big one I think still struggles with it, although he wears a tie every day now, so he must have gotten it down. But um, I remember going to YouTube and showing them on a YouTube video how to tie their tie. And printing it out and showing them how to do it." Carl's son was just entering the business world and still learning the basics. Carl complained that a couple of mornings he appeared dressed for work with a "bacon collar," a poetic phrase meaning that the collar of his dress shirt had a wavy texture reminiscent of a cooked strip of bacon. "You gotta wear collar stays," Carl remembered admonishing his son.

A couple of participants noted that they were able to tie a tie although their father was not, and others claimed to have taught their fathers or bested their fathers' necktie skills. Lev Asgarov, a New York interviewee, recalled, "I grew up in the Soviet Union. . . . My father was in the military and he hated wearing the uniform." As we chatted on a bench at the edge of the Hudson River over lunch, Lev said, "I remember that I had to teach him how to tie a tie, because the ties they used in the military were clip-ons." Clark, the son of "Depression kids," learned from his father initially. However, Clark later decided he didn't like the type of knot his father used, and he mastered a new knot: "He [Clark's father] would have his tie be kinda slanted like this [*tilts his hand to demonstrate a diagonal line where the knot meets the hanging part of the tie*], where, you know, mine are more horizontal and I think look better, and [are] easier to kind of crimp the tie when you pull it tight." Clark was amused that he had learned something he could teach his father, which is "kinda funny" since as a kid "you look up to your dad." Clark was not alone in saying that he influenced his father's dress.

The Student Becomes the Teacher

Most participants talked about how they felt their fathers shaped their dress ideas and practices, for better or worse; others talked about mothers and siblings as style influences. Yet about half a dozen men turned the tables, describing what we might call *reverse dress socialization*. Here the younger man, the one with less power in the father-son relationship, becomes an expert who can advise his father on how to dress and present himself in the workplace or other settings. The first interviewee to bring up this idea was Ian Geary, a white fifty-seven-year-old who worked in human resources in Cincinnati. Ian's father "wore a suit every day and his suits were all black." Then, "in the sixties, when men's clothing started to get a little color into it," Ian became more interested in style and fashion and began actively changing his father's work style.

> *I* started buying his clothes when I was in junior high. And just started with colored shirts and buying ties and, you know, socks and stuff like that. Well, you know, he would slowly try them. Well, the women at work *loved* what he did. And so he started allowing me to buy his clothes. And I got him to wear the glen plaid suits, or a deep green or something like that. And he always got compliments from the women. So he thought it was great that I could pick his clothes out.

Ian's story is unique in a few respects. In most families, parents or other adults purchase clothing for the household—in many of the families in which the research participants grew up, Mom played this role. While many men recalled their father's style as lacking, most did not report influencing their father as children, though some did as adults. Ian identifies as gay (though he may not have back in junior high). I mention this because his description of the relationship he and his father had through clothing is similar to other male gay-straight relationships that participants discussed. These relationships involved gay men advising straight male friends about style and dress, and men bonding across boundaries of sexual orientation over a common interest in fashion. The fact that these two men were father and son adds another emotional layer to Ian's role as personal stylist. As Ian proudly emphasized, his father "thought it was great" that Ian could shop for him and dress him in styles that attracted attention from women coworkers. This father, in encouraging his son's interests, benefitted from the social prestige that his son's cultural capital won him.

Other participants claimed to influence their fathers' dress as adults. It is not surprising that most of these father-son interactions are taking place in the present or have occurred in the recent past. They have become more commonplace because of heightened social attention in the United States to men's dress and bodies, and newly intensified marketing of clothing and personal care products directly to male consumers.[30] Jon Harper, a twenty-seven-year-old who works in real estate in Manhattan and likes fashion and dressing well, said, "I probably give him [my father] advice. . . . His stuff was kind of old-fashioned, so I try to get him to wear some different stuff." Sometimes actual items of clothing are passed up from son to father rather than passed down from father to son. Bryan, who joked that he learned "some things about what *not* to wear" from his father, told me that now his father "wears a lot of my seconds [hand-me-downs]."

Jeff Michaels's father, a deacon in their church, influenced his style as a young person. Now he is able to return the favor. On a muggy summer morning in New

York's Bryant Park, Jeff, who is in sales, told me his father "likes to look sharp." The problem, Jeff said with a chuckle, is that "he just sometimes doesn't know how to look sharp." Jeff's mother buys clothing for his dad, but so does Jeff. "Every now and then, I'll buy a pair of shoes, and I think he might like 'em," he said, so he will "buy the same for him." Jeff periodically gives his father new watches and ties. Not every father-son relationship lends itself to these interactions, especially if a father is reluctant to talk about style or sees himself as antifashion. Although my husband, Henry, really likes to dress and has educated himself about fashion as an adult, I can't for the life of me imagine him having a conversation with his father about the virtues of flat-front pants or socks with funky designs. Old-school ideas about masculinity may have something to do with the silence around style among most fathers and sons, as shown in Paul's comment that an interest in fashion seems like something his father would not consider "proper." Male bonding within contemporary families may involve sons becoming style experts who advise their fathers, which I see as part of a broader historical trend toward a loosening of patriarchal authority in contemporary families.

Several men said that their moms dressed their dads, period. Frank was one of them. He reported that his mom faced an uphill battle in getting his dad, the attorney, to stop wearing white sport socks with his suits to court. Frank said with a smile, "You know, he's fifty-five or fifty-six . . . [and] he's still getting a 'mom check'" before leaving the house, "like we did when we were going to school." The twentysomething Frank appeared to be following his father in some ways; despite living on his own in another city, he still shopped for clothes with his mother or got her opinion before buying. Michel, the son of a Haitian immigrant father and a Jamaican immigrant mother, recalled that his father dressed in flashy, bright colors until "my mom kind of got him under control." Femi stated simply, "My mom dressed my dad," and he could envision himself in such a relationship: "I'd love to find a woman who, uh, can dress me, 'cause that'd be hot." Femi said having a female partner dress him would "take the pressure off" because "women are a lot more stylish." Since women are stereotypically associated with fashion and assumed to be dress experts, they may fall into—or seize—the role of fashion stylist in their intimate relationships with men (see chapter 5).

Traditionally men would graduate from accepting the dress mandated (and purchased) by their mothers to accepting that mandated by their wives. As one interviewee put it, "I loved shopping as a kid, my mom would take me all the time . . . [and the good thing about] having a girlfriend is you now have an opinion" on clothes and fashion. Caleb saw things changing, though, and explained what he saw as a new interest in dress among his peers who were also in their thirties:

This is just a theory, whatever it is—maybe men went from being dressed by their moms to being dressed by their wives, in the past. I think now, men experience a longer period between college and when they settle down. . . . Maybe in their—as late as their—sometimes in their thirties perhaps, whatever. It creates ten or fifteen years where men have to figure out, how do I shop for myself? What do I buy? How do I dress? How do I wanna look?

This is a powerful argument about how social structure and the life course shape dress and consumption practices. Today a man tends to live on his own longer rather than moving out of his mother's house only to go live with his wife. Men are increasingly seen as, and acting as, autonomous consumers of clothing, whereas in the past clothing was primarily marketed to women.[31] Perhaps I just should have let Caleb write this book.

Connecting through Clothes

We know that class—in the sense of a level of material resources *and* collective identity based on tastes—is reproduced, making social class structures remarkably persistent over time. We know less about the mechanisms, the *how* of social class reproduction. Middle-class and upper-class forms of dress and self-presentation are privileged in our society and people who embody these practices are rewarded. But how do people learn them in the first place? Why, beyond simple economic explanations, is it more likely that a white-collar worker would come from a white-collar family? The studies that have been written about social reproduction do not say much about the process of learning how to dress for the white-collar world. Here I've tackled both the *how* and the *what* of socialization into class-specific norms of appearance, as well as the question of what these norms mean to the people who live by them.

Men's personal narratives show who is being groomed for white-collar work in the private space of the family home (mostly men from middle-class and/ or immigrant families) and elucidate how this happens. Yet there is room for class mobility and adopting new tastes, as illustrated by the men who came from blue-collar homes and tend to look down on their fathers' dress from their new locations in the corporate world. In listening to these men's stories, I was struck by the fact that they were able to learn later what they were not taught at home. They had to seek out other sources of this information (cultural capital), and some of them gave the impression that they were still absorbing the dress standards of their new social group as they moved through their adult lives and careers. To use Bourdieu's vocabulary, you may be able to move from one habitus to another, but it takes some work. And, as my conversations with white-collar men show, your performance of this new habitus is subject to scrutiny and to being evaluated as illegitimate.

Class-based standards of appearance and behavior have a sort of inertia that leads to their replication in subsequent generations. A few men used biological metaphors to describe knowledge of appropriate dress. One research participant described caring about dress and "looking sharp" as something he inherited from his father, saying "Maybe it's part of the DNA." Another, in speaking about his brothers, whom he perceived as more stylish than he, used the same type of language: "I must have missed out on that gene, or something like genes." Realizing that these sensibilities and tastes are not in fact biologically based, he nevertheless saw them as deep-rooted and difficult for him to acquire, making him an outlier in his own family. Others evoked a sense of inevitability to describe their embodiment of white-collar dress norms. For example, one said, "My dad grew up working on Wall Street. . . . He was a very sharp guy." Someone with this background is going to have a head start when it comes to the practical issues of professional dress raised by my interviewees: tie knots, collar stays, sock colors.

The finding that most surprised me while exploring masculine dress socialization was the intense emotion that sometimes accompanied men's stories about their parents and their children. The work-family-dress intersection is imbued with the values that one generation tries to impart to the next but also with the materiality of the bodies of loved ones. People talked movingly about their fathers' aging bodies and morphing styles of self-presentation over time, and about their children's transformation from the busy little bodies of school days to young professionals becoming initiated into the world of paid work. I had expected men's discussions of dress to be purely instrumental and strategic, and was struck by this relational aspect. Some men could step outside themselves and compare their bodies and embodiment to those of their fathers.

One participant had fond memories of a childhood chore. His job on Sunday mornings was to iron his entire family's church clothing. Rather than complaining about this task, he took pride in knowing that he was the reason his family looked good on their way to the pew. His blue-collar family was not the only one that practiced more formal dress (of the type associated with white-collar work) on Sundays. Ironing became a skill that he was able to apply during his move into the white-collar world:

> On a Sunday-to-Sunday basis at least, I was always wearing, you know, suit, tie, things of the sort. I got very used to that as a kid . . . I guess that's where it [my interest in dress] comes from. You know, me having, being

very comfortable in a suit and tie. It was never a problem for me. And even in college . . . going to career fairs and things of the sort, I remember my roommate asking if I can iron his suit for him, 'cause he didn't really know how to iron very well.

Emotion was also embedded in specific items passed from father to son. A man who was eleven when his father died remembers receiving his wristwatch. He said that items "can become yours even if they have somebody else's initials or scuffs on it. You know what I mean? Like, a keychain or a tie bar or a watch can have scratches on it, but it can still be—it's still important because it was something that they carried with them every day." Pieces of clothing or accessories that were often on or next to a loved one's body can heighten a sense of closeness between the person who wears that item and the deceased. Passed-down objects, in this way, make a sort of time travel possible. As one participant put it: "I like timeless items . . . something that can stay within your wardrobe, regardless of what day of the year it is, if it's today, [or] if it's twenty, thirty, forty, fifty years from now. It's something you can pass along to maybe your son, or your grandchild." Interviewees commonly used stories or language that connected three generations of their family's men: their grandfather, father, and themselves, or their father, themselves, and their sons. In addition to material objects, ideas about dress were passed down, including an appreciation for basic skills (e.g., knotting a tie) and a sense of appropriateness. When I asked men to pick a favorite item from their wardrobe, this line of transmission was often invoked. One, in describing his favorite shoes, said, "They're really, really well made. I spent a pretty penny on them, and I'm pretty sure that as long as I take decent care of them, I could hand them down to my son."

Why haven't dress and body been explored as a source of rich insight into men's family relationships before now? What more can we learn if we begin to collect and compare these stories systematically? The men I spoke with described lessons about masculinity, class, work, and professionalism that they received from their fathers (and mothers) through the medium of clothing. They picked up more than just what to wear:

One thing that I learned both from my dad and my grandfather was . . . [how] you present yourself. And we were all tall men, and um, my dad's 6' 4", I'm 6' 3", my granddad was 6' 2". I remember my grandfather saying to me, "Always make sure your neck touches your collar." So when you're walking down the street, you're looking straight up, you're not looking at the ground, your head is not down, you look people in the eye. So there was this way of presenting—The other thing that my father told me that I thought was hilarious: he was in kind of a political job, even though it wasn't supposed to be political, but it was. And he said every time that he had a meeting with someone shorter than him, he always made everybody sit down. And so people would want to talk in the hallway or they would want to, you know, just kind of stand and chat. And because he was such a large person and especially in his time, that was a very tall guy, he would make everybody sit down.

Concepts of acceptable dress and use of the body do not stand alone but are entangled with ideas about self-respect, respect for others, and interacting positively with the world around you. Learning about dress is part of learning to be a man in a particular place and time, and these lessons vary depending on class status and family background. Some of the men in this study were raised to expect to don the white collar, whereas others came to corporate workplaces through different paths of upward mobility and had to learn on the fly.

WATCHES AND SHOES

"It's always the same story. It goes together: usually when you love one, you love the other one. Watches and shoes, watches and shoes." Pierre Molyneux, a French expat with expensive tastes, said these words to me when I interviewed him in New York City. Over the course of my research, men from all three cities mused about everything from khaki pants to tie knots to sports coats, yet a subset of them were fixated on these two items that could be seen as peripheral to a white-collar man's wardrobe.

I met with Aaron Levitt in my campus office on an especially warm June Saturday. If I hadn't been expecting him, I might have mistaken him for a student. He was tall and thin, with close-cropped blond hair and blue eyes. During our conversation, Aaron said, "I think it's important that you invest heavily within . . . I don't wanna call 'em accessories, uh, but that's I guess what they are. Your tie bar, or keychain, or watch." I probed: "Why don't you like the word 'accessories'?" He sighed a little. Being interviewed can be exhausting. Especially when it's a Saturday and the sun is out. "I don't know," he replied. "Being a male . . . I don't have a positive association with the word. I don't think men wear accessories, but . . . I don't think there's a word for, you know, those extra pieces." These were precisely the pieces that some thought made all the difference in a man's image.

In the sedate world of white-collar dress, most men do not wear jewelry beyond wedding bands and the occasional pair of cufflinks (which, in some offices, are seen as too attention-grabbing)—and wristwatches. Some participants described themselves as "watch guys." One bought himself a watch as a reward upon getting a promotion at work. Now when he looks at it, it reminds him of a goal that he set and met. Another received an IWC brand watch as a gift. Online, IWC watches start at a few thousand dollars and top out at the price of a boat or a nice house in most midrange U.S. markets. He called it "obnoxiously expensive," something he couldn't afford in a million years, and it was one of his favorite items. A third man talked about inheriting his grandfather's watch and what that meant to him. It wasn't worth much money, he said, but "it's from the sixties, and it's got a cool look to it."

George Wong, who worked in sales support, was always looking at watches and planning his next purchase. He liked saving up and then splurging on a piece of wrist candy. "I only have two right now, but hopefully I will grow the collection," he chuckled. "Not to like flaunt or show off," George qualified. "It's just so I can

say, hey, I did something and I can afford this, and it's something that not everyone can afford." He thought of watches as a thank you gift to himself for his hard
work. George bought his first pricey watch at a turning point in his life. He had
just quit a job he had been "busting his ass" at, and he had just become a father.
The watch was a symbolic way of celebrating the inauguration of a new phase in
his life and a way of demonstrating to himself and others the confidence that he
would find another, better job. George also thought about how watches factored
into the sales encounter. "A couple of times, customers have noticed the watches
. . . [or] I noticed they have a nice watch and I say, 'Hey, nice watch,' and they say,
'Hey, you too, I noticed yours.'"

Then there are the shoe guys. Some shoe guys are also watch guys, as Pierre
claimed. Pierre's father was a shoemaker, so he had been raised to appreciate
quality craftsmanship and to buy shoes that would last. Others come to shoes via
hip-hop culture, collecting sneakers and allowing the passion for shoes to bleed
over into their everyday office dress. Even more than watches, shoes were thought
to communicate something about who a man was and how much effort he put
into his self-presentation.

Keith Rogers, an African American former marine, said he could shop for shoes
all day. "I think shoes say a lot about a person." Why do shoes have this symbolic
property? "I think 'cause it takes a lot of effort to keep them clean. . . . It's just like,
if you wash your car and your tires are dirty, the car looks a mess." (Cars, are, of
course, another manly stand-in for status.) There is a tactile element to keeping
shoes clean: "You touch them, you have to polish them." And women—"especially
women"—notice shoes. Keith said that there was a myth out there that "if a man
doesn't take care of his shoes, he won't take care of his kids."

While Keith talked about polishing and caring for his own shoes, other interviewees mentioned the pleasures of getting shoes shined. Some who could afford
it preferred leather-soled shoes, which could be resoled instead of thrown away
when they wore out.

When he wanted to feel confident, say, on the day of a big meeting, Clark
Landon told me, "I'll put on a nice-lookin' pair of shoes, and I'll shine 'em."
There's something about wearing well-made, cared-for shoes that "makes me feel
that I'm on my game, and makes me feel dressed up." His sensory experience
mattered, too: "When I walk, especially in leather shoes, you can hear them goin'
click-click-click, and I feel differently." The external affects the internal. Wearing
these shoes—shoes that announce his presence in the hallways before anyone can
see him—makes him stand and walk in a new way.

Nice shoes and nice watches don't come cheap. People in the know can ascer-
tain by looking at these accessories what was spent on them. What level you're at.
What you can afford. How seriously to take you. How much to charge you.

After interviewing seventy-plus white-collar men, I began to reflect on the
watches and the shoes. They represent not only status but also middle-class

orientations toward quality or elite tastes for luxury. Two images came into sharp focus:

> *The gold watch: traditionally given to the U.S. white-collar "organization man" upon retirement. Like the watches that some research participants talked about buying for themselves, it marked a milestone, concretized his hard work. Maybe he also needed it, since his newly lowered income might not allow him to buy another watch in his lifetime.*

> *The suited businessman getting a shoe shine: on an elevated, throne-like, cushioned chair, in a public place, served by other men (often men of color), who literally labor at his feet. The shoe shine embodies the luxury of removing the grime associated with urban perambulations, putting image on the list of priorities, caring about the details of appearance. It is a masculine activity (how often do we see women getting shoe shines in airports or train stations?) linking class and body, and a visible marker of cerebral rather than manual employment.*

PUTTING ON THE UNIFORM
Choice, Obligation, and Collective Identity

Dress norms, which we begin learning from an early age, are shaped by a need to balance conformity with individualism. Questions of individual expression versus conformity, self versus society, and personal versus collective identity have fascinated social thinkers for centuries. Many men encounter dress codes and uniforms early in life; and like adults, children have a range of reactions to being obligated to dress like everyone else. Before considering the question of whether white-collar work dress constitutes a uniform and analyzing adult interviewees' views on uniforms, it makes sense to begin with men's childhood experiences with required clothing. The aim of uniforms is to train the body to represent certain roles and statuses, and uniforms also raise the possibility of concrete consequences for violations.[1]

School Days

Uniforms prepare young people's bodies to accept conformity and value looking like one of the group. Sean Albertson, a white thirty-eight-year-old in the San Francisco area, reminisced about his Boy Scout uniform: "I loved wearing it and . . . my dad loved it. He was always the one, you know, [saying] 'Make sure you keep your uniform clean,' and 'You did a lot of work for this.'" Through this specialized group attire, the concepts of work, achievement, uniform dress, and presenting an acceptable appearance were impressed upon Sean. For many middle-class men in this study, as chapter 2 demonstrates, early dress socialization pointed toward future employment in white-collar work. More than Boy Scout uniforms, which few men mentioned and which are worn relatively infrequently, school uniforms emerged as a tool for training young men in white-collar embodiment.[2]

Some men loved school uniforms, others despised them, and some simply accepted them. One of three men who complained about school uniforms justified this dislike by saying "I believe in individuality. . . . There's no personal identification there." Another said that having to wear khaki pants every day in high school led to his "disdain for khakis" to this day. Yet most interviewees offered positive or neutral evaluations of school uniforms. For example, one interviewee mentioned the "sense of entitlement and privilege" he got from wearing a private school uniform as a New York City schoolchild. Daniel Moorehouse, a white forty-year-old interviewed in Cincinnati, spelled out the connection between his school uniform and current work dress:

> I went through thirteen years of Catholic school where we never dressed down. I mean, we were never—I never in all the years that I went there . . . was allowed to wear jeans to school. You know, you were required to wear a collared shirt, you were required to keep your—a guy had to keep his hair off his collar. So having that type of structure, you just did it. I think being in that sort of mode all those years, to me it wasn't really that big of a change [to dress for white-collar work].

Jon Harper, a white man in the New York sample who had transitioned from college to the workforce just a few years earlier, did his primary and secondary education at private schools that required uniforms (one of which currently charges about $40,000 per year in tuition). He described college as the one time in his life when he had complete choice about what to wear each day, and he saw this as unusual. Aside from that period, "I had to wear suits and my [school] uniform my entire life." It's easy to see how the body can be trained through the routine of wearing school uniforms, which in Jon's case consisted of a coat and tie, very similar to what he wears to work now.

The regime of school uniforms, like the office dress codes described in chapter 1, puts the onus on students to stay within the bounds of acceptable dress. Graham Houston, who grew up in the United Kingdom, recounted wearing uniforms to school and claimed that, rather than being reprimanded by teachers for dress code infractions, "kids end[ed] up policing themselves." In some cases, school uniforms even prepared students for social class tensions that they might encounter as adults. Recalling his education in a "Harry Potter-style boarding school," Nigel Peters, another British man, said he was "preconditioned" to not question the uniform. However, when he and his schoolmates would leave the school grounds for the surrounding town (as Harry Potter and his friends finally did in *The Prisoner of Azkaban* film), Nigel said, "We stuck out like sore thumbs. So, the other kids who lived nearby, you know, they would try and ambush us, because there was no concealing you. We were the rich kids at boarding school, and they weren't, so . . . [*trails off*]" The social inequalities between his classmates and children from the town were visually represented by their dress, leading Nigel to become a target. There was a trade-off involved in conforming: he sacrificed individual expression through dress but gained social and economic privilege, learning to meet the embodied expectations of his social class. Most men in this study make a similar exchange.

Research participants' reflections on school uniforms highlight the purpose of these uniforms in social and economic context and lead to the main question of this chapter: Is contemporary white-collar work dress a kind of uniform? Men have their own answers to this question, as we'll see. Yet we can't stop there, as the discussion of uniforms raises the larger issue of conformity. Conformity (and its opposite, resistance or deviance) has been a major concern of sociologists since the birth of the discipline. Some of the most significant works on U.S. corporate life in the twentieth century identified conformity as a defining feature of this social world, usually painting it as negative. Likewise, theories of fashion and dress are preoccupied with the conformist as well as individualizing functions of clothing. The men in this study, experts on their own work lives and the constraints of the corporate workplace, talked a lot about conformity. This chapter explores their opinions and experiences of conforming to white-collar dress norms. I conclude with the accounts of men (six in the core group of interviewees and three others) who have served in the military, pushing the investigation a step further by asking whether the ways men talk about military uniforms resemble the ways they talk about white-collar work dress. Conformity is part of these military narratives too, with departure from dress norms incurring harsher penalties for service members than for civilian workers. White-collar men and military men (and those who have been both) emphasize the positive aspects of wearing clothing that immediately communicates their status and occupation, their privilege and respectability.

Is Men's White-Collar Dress a Uniform?

From the beginning of my research on white-collar men's work dress and identities, I wondered whether today's looser dress codes count as a uniform. It seemed reasonable to consider the gray flannel suits of 1950s America a uniform, but what about today's businessmen?[3] Were they, for all intents and purposes, wearing uniforms to work? I asked a couple of straightforward questions about uniforms in each interview (e.g., "Have you ever had to wear a uniform?"), but men often brought up the idea of uniforms before I got to this question, or in answers to what I initially saw as largely unrelated questions. So the uniform appears to be a meaningful symbol.

Many interviewees employed the word "uniform" to describe typical work dress in the corporate world or to illustrate how men in the same company or office dressed alike. For example, two employees from the same large Cincinnati corporation, interviewed separately, both told me that they and their colleagues jokingly referred to the "[Company A] uniform," consisting of a button-down shirt (often light blue) with dark dress slacks or khakis. This description could fit probably three quarters of the men working in Cincinnati's mostly business casual white-collar sector, yet these men saw it as the uniform identifiably associated with their company.[4] It was common in Cincinnati, a smaller city with a handful of really massive white-collar employers, for research participants to stereotype employees of these companies by their dress.

The idea of workplace-specific uniforms was not limited to Cincinnati. One New York City interviewee described his recruiting firm as having a uniform, remarking with a chuckle that "everybody has matching shirts, 'cause they all buy them from the same place." When I asked him to clarify whether people had identical shirts or just similar shirts, he said: "I call it the [Company B] shirt . . . basically a blue checkered shirt. I think at *least* eight people, including me, own it, have that shirt." When I wondered aloud whether people sometimes came to the office wearing the exact same shirt, he said, "It happens all the time," and that his coworker Ray was actually wearing it that day. Rolling his eyes up to the ceiling and mentally scanning the office, he asked himself, "Who else has it on?" This shirt, the interviewee said, "is worn at least three, four times a week, by different people. There's days where two, three people are wearing the same shirt. Same tie. Everything. It happens." While matching shirts might not be common in other workplaces (and no one else described this degree of uniformity, so Company B is likely a bit of an outlier), many men used the word "uniform" to describe dress at their company and others.[5] One of these men was Domingo Sala, a thirty-eight-year-old Filipino navy veteran in the San Francisco sample, who described his workplace dress this way: "I mean, when you look at the guys [I work with], it's kind of like, almost uniform, because everyone's wearing a button shirt, but they just might have a different print on it. . . . Every day it's going to be just like a uniform . . . button shirt, long-sleeved."

When I asked research participants to describe the most stylish man in their office, some said they couldn't because "everybody dresses the same." Nicholas Georgiou, a white thirty-nine-year-old I spoke to in Cincinnati, seemed perplexed by what he referred to as the "uniform" worn by some of his coworkers.[6] "They don't have to wear khakis and a golf shirt every day, but they choose to do that, and I don't know why." Nicholas reported observing white-collar men in Dockers and loose-fitting dress shirts, with their cellular phones clipped to their belts:[7]

> I see them in my building all the time. They work at [ABC Bank] or something. . . . They wear that at work. They wear it in the evening. They wear it on the weekend. That's just sort of like their uniform. . . . It

doesn't look particularly flattering, and I just wonder, what drives that? Is it that they don't care? Is it that they're depressed?

Here Nicholas identifies uniforms in the corporate world as something worn by other people. Compare this with the account of Jack Harrison, a white thirty-two-year-old also working in Cincinnati:

> I feel like it's just so much like a uniform. You know what I mean? Like, [it's] easy for me to get dressed in the morning.... I've got some options as far as color, but outside of that, you know, it really is a uniform. . . . It's almost mindless.

These examples show that the uniform is inherently value-neutral. Nicholas detests what he sees as a uniform, actively choosing more creative dress for himself, whereas Jack enjoys the simplicity of his daily uniform. For some research participants, "uniform" is not a dirty word.[8]

A few men espoused a more expansive concept of the uniform, beyond particular companies or occupational niches. "Men wear uniforms every day," said one. Travis Jones, a thirty-nine-year-old of Afro-Caribbean descent who lives and works in New York, agreed:

> There's a uniform for every role, there is a uniform for every profession. . . . There's some limitations relative to being a professional in my industry [advertising]. So as cool as I might think this skateboarder kid looks, I can't adopt that for me, yeah, and I'm not sure if that's who I am anyway. But I can appreciate that, [and say] "Wow . . . he knows exactly who he is," and he's wearing—there's the uniform. Whether he has a pair of Vans on,[9] pair of skinny jeans, and a, like a super low-cut V-neck T-shirt, like, he's looking exactly the way he should look for what he's doing. So he's got his uniform on.

Travis expresses the idea that all people have uniforms that fit their work—and out-of-work—personas and roles. He can't trade uniforms with the skateboarder he sees on the street because of the constraints of his occupation. But his work dress is distinct from the uniform of his clients in the finance industry, for example: "You go down to Wall Street, and it's like, blue suits, black suits, blue shirts, white shirts."[10] Travis is fortunate to have a uniform that he feels more comfortable in than the clothing associated with the Wall Streeters or skateboarders he comes into contact with in his daily life in the city. Patrick Flowers, a forty-two-year-old self-identified "white dude" working in Manhattan, expressed a similar logic:

> A lot of jobs require pretty specific kinds of clothing, and . . . I think there're some people that we just see as the same. Like, if you're working

in a burger place, you know, you wear the apron and the hat. And if you work on a fishing boat, you wear so-and-so. And if you worked in the sort of finance [area], you wear the—the freaking Thomas Pink shirts[11] with the graph paper designs and the French cuffs [*laughing*].

A few interviewees pointed out that white-collar uniforms had a level of flexibility built in. Men could add "a little twist"—for example, by expressing their personality through ties or cufflinks, even if they were required to wear conservative suits every day. Several men argued that today's business dress may be a uniform but definitely not in the way that it was in previous eras.[12]

Conformity and the Corporate Look

Some interviewees voiced concerns about the uniformity of dress in the white-collar world, whether or not they used the term "uniform." John Wentz, who worked in a tech firm in the San Francisco area, said, "If everyone is dressing in suits, you're not that special, you know what I mean? It's just another form of homogeneity." When I asked Andre Leung, another San Francisco interviewee, about uniforms, he said he didn't like them "because my idea is, it limits your individuality, your uniqueness." Phil Blum, a retired native New Yorker whom I interviewed in San Francisco, expressed disdain for the type of gray suit "that you would see on anybody . . . like that's the uniform." Phil asked me, "The mayor of New York [City], you see how he dresses?" Then, shaking his head sadly: "Pure corporate." I replied, "Yeah, that's his world, that's where he came from." Phil was disappointed in then-mayor Michael Bloomberg because his dress had "no flair." Echoing these concerns was Patrick:

> I think people are also just kind of scared. And you know, your workplace is where your food is coming from . . . and there's just, like, conformism in a lot of . . . business cultures. . . . Just yesterday somebody [I work with] was kind of talking about . . . being unified and [*energetically*] "like the military!" And I said, [*scared voice*] "Like the military?" And she saw this as like, yeah, we should be more together like . . . [under] one flag. Like, what flag? [She said it would show] we're all together, like the military. And I said, that's not what I want to do. If I wanted to be in the military, I would be in the military, you know?

Nearly all my interviewees discussed conformity, and their views tended to contrast with the ones I've just presented. Most saw the tendency toward sameness in dress and self-presentation as either an unequivocally good thing or a necessary evil in the white-collar world. But uniformity in dress, work practices, and collective identity raised concerns for some men. For at least a century, sociologists have voiced similar worries about excessive conformism and its links to power and obedience.

Social Scientists' Takes on Conformity

As I tell undergraduate students, sociology is the study of people in groups. For the most part, people conform to at least some of the basic norms of the social groups to which they belong, though there is usually room for some resistance or individual expression. Bureaucratic organizations, including the companies most white-collar men work for, would cease to exist without reasonably predictable behavior on the part of the organization's members. Many U.S. and European social scientists, especially after the genocidal horrors of World War II, were suspicious of conformity and social pressures that could result in blind obedience by group members. Fascinated by the question of what would make ordinary people engage in the violence perpetrated by the Nazi regime, social psychologists including Stanley Milgram (famous for his 1961 experiment in which research subjects were willing to administer potentially lethal electric shocks to total strangers) and Phillip Zimbardo (whose faux-prison experiment in the early 1970s produced similarly disturbing results) pointed out our dangerous propensity to conform and accept prescribed roles unquestioningly. The sociologist Robert Merton, while recognizing the need for some conformity in organizations, also saw the perils of overemphasizing rules and rule following, arguing that excessive conformity could become a paralyzing straitjacket of red tape.[13] Herbert Marcuse critiqued "the system," a name he gave to the predominant forms of social relations structured by institutions such as work and school. Marcuse expressed alarm over the lack of organized opposition to capitalism, the apathy of citizens living in supposed democracies, and the general "suppression of individuality" in modern society.[14] More recently, scandals such as the implosion of the energy company Enron due to its duping of investors have shined a spotlight on the threats posed by conformity and unthinking obedience in the corporate world.[15]

Intellectuals have related the conformity versus individualism dynamic to people's dress. Georg Simmel, considered one of the founders of sociology, wrote more than a century ago about the role of fashion in dictating dress norms and behaviors. By fashion, he did not mean the avant-garde or the trend-setting but the practice of keeping current by wearing what most people in one's social circle were wearing: "a standard set by a general body." Accepting this standard, being in fashion, ensured that a person would not call attention to himself: following the (implicit or explicit) rules for what to wear is "a positive adoption of a given norm [that] signifies nothing." Stepping outside these norms creates "conspicuousness or notoriety," so most people follow along.[16] In this way, fashion and dress resemble other aspects of social life, as "the whole history of society is reflected in the striking conflicts, the compromises . . . between socialistic adaptation to society and individual departure from its demands."[17] Fashion, in the opinion of Edward Sapir, a scholar best known for his linguistic theories, is an area in which "a measure of compulsion on the part of the group" constrains "individual choice from among a number of possibilities."[18] Far from being a frivolous or private matter, dress concretizes the relationship between self and society, a relationship characterized by both friction and cohesion.

Sociologist Herbert Blumer, writing in 1969, critiqued Simmel for saying that class determines dress, while admitting that "people thrown into areas of common interaction and having similar runs of experience develop common tastes."[19] It's as if Blumer had been hanging out in the offices of my research participants! He does not explicitly define "fashion" but writes that it

> introduces a conspicuous measure of unanimity and uniformity in what would otherwise be a markedly fragmented arrangement. If all competing models enjoyed similar acceptance the situation would be one of disorder and disarray. . . . If people were to freely adopt the hundreds of styles [of dress] proposed professionally each year . . . there would be a veritable "Tower of Babel" consequence. *Fashion introduces order in a potentially anarchic and moving present.*[20]

Though Blumer notes that which styles "carry the stamp of propriety" can change, dress norms help hold a modern "moving society" together.

The most famous books about work life in U.S. corporations also highlight conformity. In *White Collar*, C. Wright Mills makes the bold claim that "the twentieth-century white-collar man has never been independent," going on to explain that "he is always somebody's man, the corporation's, the government's, the army's."[21] Mills did not find much individuality or originality in this social setting, arguing that "white-collar people are the interchangeable parts of the big chains of authority that bind the society together."[22] In *The Organization Man*, journalist and former corporate employee William H. Whyte bemoaned the degree of homogeneity he encountered in office and suburban life in the post–World War II era. The organization man was an ultracommitted white-collar worker "who most urgently wants to belong."[23] Whyte found that younger, fresher employees were most likely to favor blending in over expressing individualism. In his words, these men (and he refers only to *men*) are "well aware that organization work demands a measure of conformity—as a matter of fact, half their energies are devoted to finding out the right pattern to conform to."[24] But as they moved up the corporate ladder, Whyte's interviewees said, it "gets worse," and standing out becomes even more of a risk.

Fictional depictions from the 1950s express similar critiques of conformity in U.S. companies. In Sloan Wilson's best-selling novel *The Man in the Gray Flannel Suit*, the protagonist Tom Rath comes to a revelation after traversing a rocky stretch at the beginning of his white-collar career, telling his long-suffering wife:

> I really don't know what I was looking for when I got back from the war [World War II], but it seemed as though all I could see was a lot of bright young men in gray flannel suits rushing around New York in a frantic parade to nowhere. They seemed to me to be pursuing neither ideals nor happiness—they were pursuing a routine. For a long while I thought I was on the side lines watching that parade, and it was quite a shock to glance down and see that I too was wearing a gray flannel suit.[25]

Here the suit, a style of dress commonly used to identify the man of business, the masculine white-collar worker, is described almost as a permanent brand on the body. For the fictional Tom Rath, the gray flannel suit symbolizes conformity and being just like everyone else. It is relevant for my discussion in this chapter that, at the beginning of the novel, Tom has recently left military service, an experience that forever changed his way of seeing and being in the world. The book's author, Wilson, was also a veteran of World War II, as was William H. Whyte. Along with Mills, these writers directly compare military and corporate bureaucracies. The ideas of uniformity, conformity, and anonymity in the white-collar workplace seem to lend themselves to military metaphors. Drawing on conversations with veterans of more recent vintage, I explore the military-corporate link toward the end of this chapter.

In her now-classic *Men and Women of the Corporation*, published in 1977, sociologist Rosabeth Moss Kanter describes the managers at the company she researched:

> They were not exactly cut out of the same mold like paper dolls, but the similarities in appearance were striking. Even this relatively trivial matter revealed the extent of conformity pressures on managers. Not that there were formal dress rules . . . like the legendary IBM uniforms, but there was an informal understanding all the same. The norms were unmistakable, after a visitor saw enough managers, invariably white and male, with a certain shiny, clean-cut look.[26]

Kanter argued, as have more recent scholars, that business organizations' orientation toward conformity inhibits diversity because hiring managers tend to look for people who are like them.[27]

These foundational writings on dress and corporate conformity raise important questions, such as where uniforms and other required dress fit into theories of social life and group cohesion and how contemporary U.S. society differs from earlier time periods. Issues of dress are directly related to ongoing dialogues among scholars about the nature of the relationship between social structure and individual agency.[28]

This tension between conforming and standing out, between the group and the individual, appears throughout the accounts of the men I interviewed. As seen above, they tended to consider their mandated work wear a type of uniform, though some disagreed, pointing to greater freedom in professional dress than in previous eras. I did not uncover any studies of the colloquial usage of the term "uniform," but academic research distinguishes between uniforms and non-uniforms. One study posits that dressing similarly is not the same as wearing a uniform, which signals membership in a specific organization.[29] Another argues that "uniforms are all about control" and that "most people have had experiences of uniforms and these encounters are memorable."[30] I did not find this to be true for my interviewees: more than half of the men said that they had never worn a uniform for work or school, and some of those who had worn uniforms found the experience unremarkable (in contrast to a few of the men quoted at the beginning of this chapter).[31] In general, research on uniforms highlights the ways they train the body, as in my analysis of school uniforms.[32] Most scholars do not consider business dress—even that worn by the gray-flannel-suit types of the 1950s—a uniform. However, the men I spoke to often thoughtfully discussed the issues of conformity raised by dress codes, called "the most unstructured form of occupational clothing," as well as by uniforms.[33]

The Strategic Embrace of Conformity

Most participants in this study described the corporate environment as encouraging or even demanding conformity. This description did not surprise me, as it showed continuity with the findings of Mills, Whyte, Kanter, and others who had written about the white-collar world in the twentieth century. Conformity is promoted not only by intangible social pressures but also by enforcement of dress codes and norms and by informal social control (for example, through office gossip). Many interviewees consider fitting in and blending in the goals of work dress. Luiz Rodrigues, born and raised in Brazil, depicted Brazilian dress culture as more overtly sensual and flashier; both men and women tried to make a splash with their clothing. In contrast, he described the white-collar masses of midtown Manhattan: "I . . . never see anybody in the subway in the morning that make[s] anybody turn their heads to see because [they're] dressed too differently or too extravagant." The goal in dressing for work, according to Luiz, was to "try to fit without creating much of a big shock, big wave, when you enter." Many interviewees characterized corporate dress regimes as based on sameness, even monotony. One called the clothing he and his coworkers wore "the kind of look that you would see in 90 percent of the professional companies, corporations in America."

Discussions of fashionable work dress also touched on the topic of conformity. San Francisco interviewee Brad Jennings equated conformity with fashion à la Simmel, saying, "I watch everyone else just a little bit; so if I see a style trend going in a specific direction and everyone starts doing it, like a lemming I start doing it too, because I guess you kind of want to be in unison." Bob Liu, a fifty-three-year-old in Cincinnati, said he was "conscious enough of fashion . . . for my dress to sort of follow that." Then he added, "Not in any sort of cutting edge way, just very [pause] conventional." Bob's main concern when it comes to fashion was not looking horribly out-of-date. Yet given the noticeable pause before the word "conventional" in the recorded interview, I'd guess it may have been difficult for him to admit the conformist motivations for this fashion consciousness. Bob's comments recall Simmel's claim that fashion simultaneously "satisfies the demand for a social adaptation . . . [and] the need of differentiation" among individuals.[34] While Bob prefers to think of himself as a unique individual—which of course is true to an extent—he is also conforming to what he sees as current dress standards. Luiz, Brad, and Bob all point to the mandate to not stand out, which I'll discuss more in a moment.

What surprised me about the research participants' claims that conformity was rampant in their office settings was that, in general, these men were pretty much okay with this scenario. The complacency toward conformity shouldn't be read as an expression of men's individual desires. In many cases, men didn't particularly enjoy this aspect of their job, but they saw conforming through dress and other behaviors as necessary for getting ahead. When I asked Joseph Davis, an African American man working in Cincinnati, how he felt about the dress code at his office, he employed this reasoning: "Whatever a company says the policy is, if you want to work there, you just do it. . . . It's pretty much a black and white situation." Other interviewees agreed with Joseph, making such comments as "It behooves most people to stick with the mainstream"; "[Try] fitting within that norm, not putting your own spin on it, not getting too crazy"; "You have to modify to some degree your own personal expression to make sure that what you're wearing isn't distracting." These men, one of whom called the narrow dress expectations in his healthcare company "unfortunate," didn't seem to spend a lot of time worrying about the reasons behind their workplace's dress norms; for them, the strategic response was to simply follow them.

The key to successfully dressing for work, according to these white-collar men, was to aim for "fitting in." Their narratives supported Simmel's claim that men try to dress in ways that do not call attention to themselves. Ed Hatcher, a white executive who had spent nearly forty years working for the same corporate conglomerate, was one of the more vehement defenders of workplace conformity:

> If I came strolling in here with like a suit on with a yellow bowtie and I made sure everything [*mimes checking his outfit to ensure everything is in place*], people would look at me like, "What's wrong with that guy?" . . . I think if you go extreme on anything, [and] this philosophy extends way past dress, you know, zealots of any form are potential trouble.[35]

Later in our conversation, Ed reiterated: "I want people to say, 'Look at that guy, he looks like he didn't just fall out of a tree; he looks professional.' I don't want somebody to be, 'What's that guy doing? Trying to make people look at him?'" It was not only older workers like Ed who espoused the virtue of conformity in white-collar work. Thirty-six-year-old Vince Lo told me that when it came to his work dress style, "I don't want to rock the boat." Vince, who worked in finance in San Francisco, partly attributed this decision to his company culture and his peers' behavior: "I'm not a person who does rock the boat, and neither are the people that I work with." Frank Miller, a twenty-four-year-old working in Cincinnati, placed value on "looking like you belong," a major concern among other interviewees who had recently graduated from college. A few men described dressing to fit in as "playing the part." There is an element of performance, of convincingly executing the role of white-collar businessman, in men's narratives.

What happens when men don't conform to expectations? When they don't pull off these performances? Gossip can be an effective tool for social control and promoting compliance with group norms.[36] In the men's accounts of dressing the part in their work lives, gossip was something to be avoided. Ryan Carter, a white twenty-five-year-old in Cincinnati who favored flashier dress than he felt comfortable using in the workplace, told me, "I do see people who are in my function who wear kind of colorful-type shirts and it looks like you're going to a nightclub. And people talk about that behind their back, like, 'Hey, did you see so-and-so, the shirt he was wearing today?' And so I'm cognizant of that." Aaron Levitt, who at age twenty-four was just starting his career in healthcare administration in the Cincinnati area, had been thinking about how to put his best foot forward at his new office:

> I wanna step in a little bit under the radar. I don't want people to notice me for what I am or am not wearing. . . . You know, like I don't want

that to be the discussion piece of, "So what do you think of our new employee Aaron?" I want it to be, you know, he's qualified, he's intelligent, he helps out, he's exciting, you know, he's enthusiastic. Something of that nature. I don't want them to say, "He dresses really well."

For Aaron, a younger, thinner guy influenced by the contemporary fashion of slim-fit suits, the balance he sought was to wear clothes that fit his body, but to do this in a way that "nobody's gonna look at you and say, 'Wow, did you see what he was wearing today?'"

Most men in the study agreed that it was important to avoid commentary about their clothing, a desire that fits with traditional stereotypes of masculinity in the United States (i.e., real men don't care about clothes or dress in attention-getting ways). These stereotypes position men as active subjects rather than objects to be looked at.[37] Trevor Robins, a white architect in Cincinnati, typified these concerns, performing the following analysis of what he called his "psychology": "I never thought of it this way before, but that would almost be a failure [*laughing lightly*] of mine for being noticed because of my dress. I mean that—that—that's crazy, but I . . . kind of like stay under the radar that way. I mean or, just—just do my work." It seems from this interview excerpt that even thinking about being called out on his dress gets Trevor a little flustered. Many interviewees expressed similar distaste for being noticed or talked about because of their appearance. In the words of New Yorker Timothy Stein, "I tend to dress not to be noticed. So you know, what's the goal of dressing? . . . The goal of dressing is more to not stick out, it's to look professional and look important."[38] This opinion was shared across occupations and age groups; however, there were some geographical differences in my findings.

Consider these three quotes, by men from each of the cities in the study.

> We also live in a very conservative area here in Cincinnati where people don't wanna be flashy and show off or anything, or [be] seen as, you know, rocking the boat and trying to stand out, as opposed to just putting your head down and being a good worker bee. (Nicholas Georgiou, Cincinnati)

> Ultimately, I like to stand out a bit—but not in an obnoxious way. . . . But I do like something that defines [my style] in the sense of being simple, sophisticated, but also unique in a tasteful way. (R. J. Logan, New York)

> I'm dressin' for my work environment. And—I'm dressin' to be good enough, I mean, that would be a pretty accurate comment, I'm dressin' to be good enough. (Clark Landon, San Francisco)

These three views on what Timothy called "the goal of dressing" for work represent the patterns I found in each urban site and fit the depictions of local dress cultures woven throughout the research participants' accounts.[39] It makes sense that in "conservative" Cincinnati, white-collar workers want to make noncontroversial clothing choices and be good worker bees. The New York interviewees found it harder to ignore fashion, working as they did in a global epicenter of style innovation. Many, like R. J., were interested in fashion and maybe pushed the envelope a bit in their work dress, but they were required to balance their fashionable leanings with the need to not stand out "in an obnoxious way." Clark's aim to dress "good enough" is reasonable in San Francisco, with the most casual dress regime of the three cities and residents' reputation for being relaxed about matters of dress and appearance.

The men most likely to seek out a space for fashion and/or individuality within the required dress were those in New York and San Francisco. Almost no Cincinnati men articulated concerns about maintaining their individuality in workplace self-presentation. Luke Gottlieb, a white thirtysomething in business services in New York—who appeared at our interview wearing a thick-striped button-down shirt and bold polka-dot tie, both in a toothpasty aqua-and-white color scheme—told me with a smile, "I definitely have, I would say, a fun style. . . . Always professional. But, you know, perhaps maybe a little more color and a little more enthusiasm than some of the other people here. But I'm not the loudest dresser. [*Quieter*] I'm probably up there." Luke highlighted his need to express himself through his work wear. He claimed to do this not to elicit a "Whoa!" reaction (as he put it) from his coworkers but because he "genuinely like[d]" the things he wore.[40] He surmised that "women really like to wear clothes 'cause it's fun," and argued that such creativity and joy in clothing didn't have to be the sole province of women: "There is a degree of that for men as well with what they wear." Luke was not alone in playing up the individualistic aspects of generally conformist corporate dress. One New York interviewee said he wanted to dress appropriately for work but worried about becoming a "corporate stooge"; another saw wearing cufflinks as a way for even the most buttoned-up, conservative bankers to show their personalities.

When I asked Carlos Calle, interviewed in a suburb of San Francisco, to name his favorite item of clothing, he answered without hesitation: "My socks." After he showed me his socks for the day, some relatively sedate black-and-gray argyles, I asked whether he thought wearing what he called "funny" socks communicated something about him to others. His answer focused on expressing his individuality but also on the desirability of changing people's perceptions about HR professionals like him. The message, according to Carlos, was that "I can be fun too. HR can be fun." Pete Costa was one of a few San Francisco participants who mentioned tattoos as aspects of white-collar embodiment that were becoming more acceptable in the local business milieu. As we chatted over lunch in the city's financial district, Pete told me, "I have a sleeve tattooed on my arm, and I don't feel bad about having that [at work]." He added that being visibly tattooed in the workplace "doesn't seem like a [big] thing at all. . . . A lot of other people have them [tattoos] too." A contrarian reader would point out, of course, that this comment is also conformist, as what makes tattoos acceptable is that others in the office have them. However, this acceptance of individualized embodied expressions such as tattoos stands out when compared with the more formal dress culture of New York or the more uniformly business casual environment of white-collar Cincinnati. Thus, location matters for men's strategies of conforming and for how much individuality they feel able to inject into their work appearance.

What about *Real* Uniforms?

It's all well and good to show that some white-collar men in this study used the word "uniform" to denote their professional dress and to demonstrate (strategic) commitment to conformity in their workplace self-presentation. But I want to go a step further in exploring the question of whether workers' dress in corporate America counts as a uniform. The best way to do this is to compare the accounts of men who have actually worn uniforms—as a requirement of their military service—to the accounts of those who have not.

The incorporation of military veterans into the white-collar workforce is one major difference between the gray flannel world of the 1950s and today. In fictional and nonfictional works on corporate life from the midtwentieth century, veterans were perceived as integral participants in the business world. For-profit bureaucratic structures and chains of command were seen as being inspired by military models of organization. However, with the transition of the United States to an all-volunteer military after the Vietnam War, the percentage of veterans in the corporate workforce has decreased. According to data from the Census Bureau and the Bureau of Labor Statistics, 11.8 million veterans are part of the U.S. labor force today, making up about 7.7 percent of the working population.[41] The first census conducted after World War II (1950) identified 13.8 million veterans in the civilian workforce, or a bit more than 33 percent of the employed population at the time.[42] In my core interview sample of seventy-one white-collar men, only six (about 8.5 percent) had served in the military. Three of these men had served in their home countries before moving to the United States, and only one was currently a member of the reserves. I asked these veterans about the experience of wearing their military uniforms, and I also reached outside my main group of interviewees to speak to three other former servicemen.[43] One worked in corporate customer service (in a far-flung suburb of New York City), one worked as a technology consultant in the entertainment field (and lived in Manhattan), and one worked in education (in Cincinnati). So I interviewed a total of nine men who had served in uniform in the United States or abroad. For the U.S. men, all branches of the armed forces were represented— army, air force, navy, and marines. In devising questions on military uniforms, I also drew on my nine years as the spouse of an active-duty U.S. marine (*Semper Fi!*). I benefited from this secondhand experience of service members' dress and from being able to consult with my husband, now in the corporate work world himself.

As we might expect, interviewees who had served in uniform described conformity as more of a demand in the military than in their civilian jobs. They linked the conformist elements of dress in the armed forces directly to their work activities. Wilson Turner, who said he came from a long line of British military men, described the uniform as "functional." He evoked both conformism and anonymity by saying, "It's there so you disappear," a view other veterans also expressed. For Wilson, the uniform is useful because "it breathes" and has pockets to carry things that you need. But he also recognized and appreciated the symbolic aspects of dress uniforms (called "mess kits" in the United Kingdom), which he said the ladies love: "One side of it [the uniform] saves your life, and the other side is pomp and circumstance." Hans Schroeder had served in the German army and liked the way that military uniforms, like school uniforms, built esprit de corps. He said, "You don't stand out. It's one team, one organization. . . . Uniforms are not bad." These ideas of not standing out and of being on the same team, as seen earlier, were also relevant for white-collar men without military backgrounds.

Keith Rogers had served in the U.S. Marine Corps. When I asked why the military, and especially the corps, was so picky about uniforms, Keith's answer went right to the practical aspects of warfare:

> You have to be squared away[44] at all points, because if you're out in the field [in a real or practice battle situation] and they say be at twenty meters, and you're at nineteen . . . that bomb would have been—at 20, you'da been clear of it, but if you want to do something that's not precise as you're told, it sets everything off. Everything has to be in order. You can't have the uniform out of sync and then say, "Well, hey, this operation flows effortlessly." It's not going to happen.[45]

So while someone like me, who has never served in the military, might bristle at "precise" instructions about how many inches from the edge of my sleeve my chevron patch should be, Keith saw such specificity as useful because in a war scenario being just a bit off could get you killed. In our conversation, Keith also stressed the value of uniformity in creating collective rather than individual identity and claimed that the dress rules for marines were unaffected by geographic location. He explained, "I mean, you just can't just come down a street like, 'Oh, okay. He has a nice uniform. . . . But he don't look like the rest of us.' No. So, yeah, you got to have uniformity. You go to Camp Pendleton, they're the same. You go to LeJeune, Quantico: everybody has to be the same."[46] In this aspect, military clothing norms are different from those of the white-collar world, which, as we've seen, are affected by geographic location and local dress cultures.

Keith's description reminded me of a phrase I found while perusing the U.S. Marine Corps uniform regulations:

> Eccentric and faddish individual appearances detract from uniformity and team identity.[47]

The idea that individualism may be detrimental to the team also cropped up in white-collar men's discussions, which addressed the tension between looking "nice" or expressing oneself and looking like "the rest of us." One implication is that looking different will cause people to talk about a man's dress, something to be avoided both on military installations and in the corporate office. The marines I spoke with mentioned that as they went up in pay grade, they were able to buy higher-quality uniform items rather than the "paper shirts" that they were initially issued; however, they bought these items because they would allow them to better meet dress rules or to make clothes last longer, not to stand out or be original.

The consequences for violating required dress rules are different in the armed services than in the corporate world. Several veterans mentioned the routine enforcement of dress regulations, which sometimes involved embarrassing or punishing the offending soldier, sailor, marine, or airman. Wilson used the term "sack of shit" for a serviceman in a sloppy uniform, a synonym for what the marines call a "shitbag."[48] Since I had become familiar with this term as a marine spouse, I asked ex-military interviewees about it. When I uttered "shitbag" during my conversation with Keith in his office, he laughed loud and hard for a full four seconds, then said he hadn't heard the word in years, since he left the corps. According to him, it means "just looking like a slob. . . . You really don't take care of yourself, you're probably out of shape. . . . You're just [wearing] wrinkled [clothing] . . . looking like Otis from [the] *Andy Griffith* [show]."

Alan Salazar, another former marine who now worked in corporate America, saw a shitbag as someone who didn't take pride or care in his appearance. He identified possible psychological roots of this slack self-presentation: "He maybe has some insecurities about himself; therefore it projects onto the way he wears his uniform. . . . [He doesn't really] want to be there." Like many other white-collar interviewees, Alan saw lack of attention to dress as potentially signaling some internal lack of confidence or self-esteem; interestingly, failure to conform is interpreted here not as an overvaluing of the individual self but as its devaluation. This idea appears in the official uniform regulations as well, which state that "wearing the uniform should be a matter of personal pride to all Marines." The marine who deviates from the strict dress standards draws negative attention to himself.

The veterans I interviewed had many positive things to say about their military clothing, even the one who told me that he burned his uniforms when he separated from the air force (more on this in a moment). The sharpness and "classiness" of the uniformed look—and its supposed effect on women—was one reason some men said they joined the military. Daniel, who had served in the U.S. Army, told me he liked the simplicity of wearing the uniform. His explanation was reminiscent of the white-collar men who like suits because they narrow dress choices: "There's less decision making when you get up."[49] Wearing a uniform, said Daniel, is so regimented that "it's a no-brainer, anyone could put it together." It causes less stress than nonuniform dress because "it's so straightforward." Thus, although some men who hadn't been in the military were horrified by the idea of wearing a uniform, for most who had served in the armed forces, the lack of choice and the predictability of uniforms were seen as advantages.

Keith mentioned the confidence and change in body language that came with wearing a uniform: "I think your posture sort of straightens out. . . . You already walk straight, but it's more of a sense of pride." Several veterans highlighted the positive social interactions that resulted from wearing their uniforms in public (e.g., strangers thanking them for their service).

> Dress blues, which I didn't wear often, but when I did, I would stop traffic. . . . I remember going through [the] St. Louis [airport] and I was surprising my parents, and I had on dress blues, and I was walking down the gate area, and it was just like parting the seas, just [people] looking at me. (Keith Rogers)

> One time I went to the public library and I had on my full uniform and by people just coming up to shake my hand (they didn't know me), my gloves were dirty like I just mopped the floor with gloves. . . . People honking horns, things like that. In the airport people would just stop and look just like, as if I was famous. . . . *Now* I couldn't pay anybody to look at me. (Keith)

> I felt good about it [wearing my uniform in public]. I felt respected.
> (Claude Whitfield)

> We did the whole Portland Rose Festival thing. . . . Everyone was waiting
> for the navy guys to come and like walk around town. And they were
> like, "Hey, can we take a picture?" And I was like, "Wow." They kind of
> gave us a little status and it was kind of fun. (Domingo Sala)

> I feel like I get a lot more looks, always positive. . . . But I definitely get a
> lot more questions like, "Oh, why are you wearing it? What branch are
> you in? How long have you been in it?" And those sort of things; like I'm
> stopped a lot more on the street, when I wear my uniform. . . . I don't
> mind it. . . . I take it as a compliment. (Sam Wahl)

Although these seem to be experiences specific to wearing military uniforms in
public, there are similarities between these quotes and others from nonveteran
interviewees about how it feels when your dress garners respect in public settings.
Al Elkin, who likes to wear suits even though his Manhattan office is business
casual, sounded a lot like Keith and Domingo when he talked about wearing his
suit around town:

> When I wear a suit, the recognition I get and the way I'm treated when
> I'm in a suit versus casual is entirely different. People get out of the way
> of you on the subway. People move out of the way and give you respect
> on the streets and subway when you're in a suit.

Al's suit seemed to do for him what Keith's dress blues uniform did for him in
the St. Louis airport; the visual image they employ of people deferentially making space for someone who is dressed importantly is almost identical. Of course,
dressing up or dressing differently in public can also lead to danger or negative
consequences. In a scene quite different from the one he described in Portland,
Domingo recounted a time that he and his uniformed friends were verbally ha-
rassed by passing motorists and pedestrians as they walked around Chicago. As
the men I interviewed communicated clearly, dressing in a way that draws attention is, if not something to be avoided, an action that carries with it some element of risk. The very clothing that makes military and business men stand out
in public—marking them as respectable and traditionally masculine—is what
makes them blend in at work.

For the veterans I interviewed, with the exception of the reservist, wearing
military uniforms was part of their past. I asked the men two questions about
the aftermath of military service: (1) What did they do with their uniforms when

they got out of the military? and (2) Did any of the dress habits they developed in the military carry over into their civilian lives? Their answers drove home the ways that clothes become imbued with emotion and memory, as tangible reminders of embodied personal histories. Clothing is tied to our sense of self. A couple of the ex-military men didn't know where their old uniforms were and didn't seem overly concerned by that fact. Keith said he had gotten rid of everything except his dress blues (the most formal and iconic of marine uniforms), which he called his "museum piece." Alan told me that he had kept pretty much all of his uniforms neatly arranged in the garage, where—as his wife complained vociferously during our interview—they took up way too much space. Alan's son was about to ship out to boot camp, carrying on his family's military tradition; perhaps this was one reason Alan had held on to his uniforms. When I asked Claude what he did with his air force uniforms after his time was up, I jokingly added, "Did you burn 'em?" I was still chuckling when he replied earnestly, "Actually, I did. I burned 'em." He had a couple friends over, threw the uniforms in a garbage can, and lit them ablaze. What did this gesture symbolize for him? "It was just freedom. I had my life back. No one could tell me what to do."

After finding out what had happened to his uniforms after he left the air force, I was surprised to hear from Claude that many of the clothing-related routines he had developed in the military stayed with him. When he first enlisted (for economic reasons), Claude was a "complete rabble-rouser." He claimed that he detested the way that uniforms had to be hung a certain way, with "the jacket line facing the left, [and] one inch in between each hanger." He found this organized system incomprehensible at the time, yet confided, "I find myself now using it in my everyday life." Claude wasn't the only veteran who saw continuities between his military and his civilian life.[50] Domingo still emulates the "nice and crisp" style he needed to have while in uniform. He said he wouldn't mind wearing a suit to work rather than his current business casual dress: "When I'm in a suit, it's like, 'Wow, I'm confident.' . . . In my uniform, I would go out around town [and it was] like, 'I'm in my uniform,' you know, 'I'm representing the country,' not just the company." Sam Wahl, the navy reservist, told me that when he returned to his regular life after basic training, "my day was much more regimented. . . . I would wake up at six o'clock every day, shave a lot more frequently . . . get my hair cut more often." Indeed, none of the veterans I interviewed had facial hair; though to be fair, neither did most of my interviewees. Sam shows that expectations for military embodiment go beyond uniform dress to personal grooming and other aspects of appearance that bleed into civilian life.

On the other hand, a few former military men I spoke with didn't see their experience in uniform as changing their dress habits. Keith, for example, said that he was already a fastidious dresser when he joined the marines; so not only was the adjustment to military dress easy, but the transition back to civilian life didn't involve changes to the way he thought about clothing and self-presentation. Here's how he described the fit between his personal penchant for dressing stylishly and the Marine Corps's uniform: "I just like to look neat. So before I even thought about the military, I said, well this is the sharpest group. . . . If I have to wear what everybody wears, let [me wear] what I perceived is the nicest-looking military outfit out there, hands down."

Keith's statement echoed those of white-collar interviewees who said that the emphasis on presenting an acceptable or professional appearance suited their personalities and preference for dressing in a certain way.[51] They described dress codes as fitting the way they already liked to look.

Uniforms and Nonuniforms

This chapter asked a question to which there is no simple answer: Is white-collar men's contemporary work dress accurately described as a uniform? In short, it depends on whom you ask, though I am inclined to say yes. Many of the men in this study used the word "uniform" to label their dress and/or the dress of other men they encountered in the business world. Others thought that perhaps several decades ago, white-collar dress was a sort of uniform, but that this was no longer true. I investigated men's accounts of school uniforms and military uniforms, "real" uniforms that socialize people into dressing and carrying their bodies in particular, regimented ways. I see school uniforms, especially the prep-school versions with coats and ties, as preparing men for work in corporate offices. This socialization may be part of the inculcation of middle-class dress norms discussed in chapter 2. The narratives of nine veterans of the armed forces, seven of whom now work in corporate America, show many similarities to the narratives of the larger group of white-collar men in this study. Themes such as confidence, the positive effects of dress on social interactions outside of work, and the benefits of not standing out appear in both sets of stories. Men receive positive reactions to wearing both suits and military uniforms in public, partly because of the associations between these types of clothing and traditional masculinity. Since it is believed that "real men" wear these things, they generally experience privilege as a result of this masculine embodiment. Yet the very same dress, when worn in their work settings, makes them blend in to the point of invisibility. Anonymity and exceptionalism are two sides of the same coin.

The issue of uniforms and nonuniforms brings up a potent social dynamic: the tension between conformity and individualism. This is a constant area of inquiry and theorizing in social science: What holds people together in society?

I was not surprised that most men saw conformist tendencies in their offices and work lives, but I was surprised that only a handful complained about this homogeneity. Rather than clamoring for more ways to express their individuality through dress (or other practices), most research participants demonstrated what I call a *strategic embrace of conformity* when it came to dress.[52] The main goal for most of these white-collar men in dressing their bodies for work was to not "call attention," as Simmel phrased it in his essay on fashion. This effort to not stand out relates to traditional views of masculinity in the United States, in which men do the looking and women are to be looked at; it seems improper to some men to be gazed on by workmates because of clothing choices. Microlevel incentives to conform to dress expectations include receiving praise and avoiding punishment or gossip.

The acceptance of conformity in dress raises the possibility of conformity in behavior. The anonymity associated with dressing and behaving like others in a social group can potentially lead to acceptance of wrongdoing and fear of challenging the status quo. If conformity is valued highly by a company (or an economic sector), this may inhibit efforts to increase the diversity of the workforce. In such a system, we can guess that those in power will tend to remain in power, and we begin to envision a possible future in which social controls are not resisted or challenged—as in Aldous Huxley's dystopian novel *Brave New World*.

Mills's and Whyte's critiques of social conformity in the 1950s may seem a bit hyperbolic and certainly convey a judgmental tone, yet they were rooted in real-world fears of the dangerous consequences that blind obedience within organizations can have. These concerns have been underscored in recent scandals such as the U.S. military's Abu Ghraib prison abuses and the Enron debacle. Of course, my interviewees were not involved in these ethical breaches, and I have no reason to believe that they are not upstanding citizens. I see their strategic embrace of conformity as just that—a strategy for increasing their chances of upward mobility and financial success. I get what the sociologists and novelists are worried about when they critique extreme conformity, though some degree of conformity with social norms seems necessary for smooth everyday interactions and functioning organizations.

TAILOR TALES

If you buy something off the rack and it doesn't fit, you feel like you're wearing your dad's suit.

Right now, you're seeing a lot of twenty- and thirty-year-olds who are really excited about dressing up again.

There's two guys: you get the guy that's the obsessive clothing guy, who's really into it, and the other guy is showing up because he trusts you and needs to look good . . . two different types of clients.

—Quotes from interviews with three men in the custom clothing business

The tailor shop occupies a smallish white building with a navy blue awning across the front. On my first visit, the display window next to the front door displays an outfit composed of a light blue button-down shirt, gray-striped seersucker shorts, and a yellow bowtie—it is obviously springtime. Directly to the right as you walk in, there is a counter; opposite it is a round table smothered in a swirl of folded ties. The walls bear caricature-type prints of men in Victorian-era formalwear. Richard, the owner, emerges with a yellow tape measure festooning his neck, and I follow him to the back. We pass through a showroom with clothing and accessories, then a narrow hall with fitting rooms, arriving at a somewhat worn leather loveseat in a stately kelly green. A side table holds miniature water bottles and a stack of napkins. The antique trunk serving as coffee table holds recent issues of *Sports Illustrated*, a travel magazine called *Departures* (with a feature "Where Men Shop in New York"), *Cigar Aficionado*, and *Men's Health*. A large shelf divides the sitting area from another part of the room, each of its compartments holding small leather-bound books of fabric swatches. Atop the shelf sit an antique radio and some other dignified masculine bric-a-brac, and next to it stands a folding screen covered entirely with vintage business cards. Behind me on the wall are some framed vintage *Esquire* magazine covers. To my right are a matching green leather chair, a tall podium-type table, and a glass cabinet full of catalogs, in front of which are stacked some vintage suitcases in a purposefully messy fashion. Directly across the trunk-table from where I'm sitting is a bright, airy room in which I can see two sewing machines, quiet at the moment.

Richard and a female sales assistant are helping a woman who is getting some clothes made for her husband and some alterations done for herself in preparation for the Kentucky Derby in two weeks. She is chatting about a business associate of her husband's, who is worth 250 million dollars but is "so down-to-earth." She mentions the buying of a company as casually as I would discuss a trip to Target.

When I speak to Debbie, who works in the sewing room, she comments that the men who come here are very interested in clothes. She says they come and sit and look through the fabrics in the leather binders and ask what all the other guys are doing. When I ask if it's because they want to be different, she says no. They don't want to stand out; they want what others are wearing. This is more important to them than being in fashion. Every person who walks through the door, and every staff member I see, is white. In this wealthy part of town, the cars in the parking lot include a Porsche, an Infiniti, and a Mercedes. Golf and skiing are discussed by staff and customers (one says to Richard, "You ski?" and the response comes: "Not as much as I used to.").

Driving to the tailor shop several weeks later, I ask Henry (my husband, and research assistant for the day) about his expectations. He's had things tailored, remembers being fitted for his uniforms back when he was in the marines, and he got some custom suits made on a trip to Ecuador a few years back, so he doesn't think that getting a custom sport coat and shirts will be that different. "I hope they don't expect me to know everything," he said. "They should know enough to guide me in picking things out. Also, if I'm going to spend a lot of money, I want a lot of options." I ask him whether having men touch him will be uncomfortable, and he says no, he thinks of it as a doctor visit.

In their consultation, Richard asks where he would wear the sport coat, and Henry responds that he would wear it to work and outside work. Richard asks what other similar coats he has, and Henry lists a gray, a brown houndstooth, and a black velvet with pinstripes. He says he doesn't love the way these jackets fit: a bit loose. Richard remarks that the under-forty crowd is asking for more fitted clothing, and this has completely "changed my business in the last six months."

Richard's advice: stick to dark colors because they will go with more things, don't go for big or bold patterns (when Henry points to one pattern, Richard shakes his head and says "too bold"), and avoid too heavy a fabric because it gets hot when worn indoors. "This is going to be your favorite coat," Richard tells Henry. "You want to be able to wear it with everything and not have people say, 'He always wears that.'"

When Henry selects a dark blue fabric with a faint red windowpane check, Richard comments, "This has been a great coat for us." This reminds me of the seamstress's observation—that clients often want to know what other guys are wearing. Perhaps Henry is not interested in getting what everyone else was getting, so Richard clarifies: "But when I say this is a popular coat, you don't have to worry about seeing yourself coming and going. I've sold maybe twelve coats from the whole [fabric] book."

A tall, dark-haired man (who I'd guess is approaching fifty) comes into the sitting area and apologizes for interrupting. The man gestures to Henry, who has now moved on to perusing fabrics for the jacket lining, and says, "This is so much fun, innit?" "Yeah, it is," replies Henry, as I picture the shrinking credit limit on our next Visa statement.

A sales associate, James, comes back to help Henry get measured. He approves of Henry's final choice, saying, "I'm sure you have some gray pants." Henry nods and says that yes, he's got a couple. James says with authority, "The gray pant is the number-one pant in your wardrobe." By now Henry has chosen a lining, gold satin with tiny darker dots. We turn our attention to shirt fabrics.

"Here comes the hard part," says James. "Let's get you measured." Henry stands and James removes a sheet of paper from the wooden pulpit-like stand at the edge of the room. Before he begins to fill in this form, James asks Henry whether he wants French-cuff or button-cuff shirts. Button-cuff. He asks about the collar spread, touching his own collar to say, "I use a medium spread, because I can wear it with a tie or without." That's fine. James asks, already anticipating the answer, "No pocket?" Henry says no, he's worked with too many Brits to wear a pocket on his shirt. Henry faces the back of the shop as James approaches with his measuring tape, joking, "Okay, turn your head and cough." (Interesting, in light of Henry's earlier reference to a doctor's visit.) He proceeds to measure the chest in a few places, the belly, waist, neck, biceps circumference, and arm length, standing mostly behind his customer and noting each measurement on the form. Henry will tell me later that he felt comfortable being measured and touched by the salesman until a female employee walked past, and then he felt awkward, also becoming more consciously aware of my presence then. I smile to myself when I recognize the song playing on the radio during this moment of physical closeness between the two men: John Mayer is indeed crooning, "Your body is a wonderland." "Do you always wear a big watch?" asks James. Henry says yes, looking down at the black-and-silver Movado on his left wrist (he's a bit of a watch guy). I ask James if that was a question relevant to the fit of the shirt and he says that yes, he will have the shirt cuff made slightly bigger to account for this.

James leaves for a minute, returning with a gray blazer from one of the racks in the showroom. Henry slips it on, mumbling something about being a forty-four long. James measures across the top of his back and takes some measures of his shoulders as well. He asks, referring to the coat style, two button? Yes. Side vent (the "house style")? Yes, this is fine with Henry. James pulls out a wooden, L-shaped gadget, which features a tiny glass tube filled with amber liquid in which a round air bubble floats, reminiscent of a carpenter's level. When I ask about it, he explains it is a Perkins device—named after its inventor—that measures the roundness or slope of the shoulders and upper back. The resulting number is two and three-quarters inches. James produces another device shaped like a generous wedge of pie featuring the same liquid and bubble. This he sets on the top of Henry's shoulder, near his neck. A difference emerges between the right and left shoulder measurements. James calls Richard over for a second opinion, asking if he should round down, diminishing the difference, or up. Richard, hurrying back to the busy front of the store, calls over his shoulder, "It's a half inch or it's nothing; don't do a quarter of an inch." James seems ready to protest, and his boss says energetically, "Yeah, but look at his thumbs!" He means the way that one hangs lower than the other when Henry's hands are down at his sides. In nearly two decades of marriage, I've never noticed this before. I imagine how horrified a woman would be by this two-person examination and discussion of her body's asymmetries, but it isn't bothering Henry. I ask if this unevenness is typical, and James says yes, adding that the more "in shape" a guy is, the more even the slope will be. So bodies are naturally asymmetrical, but men can make them more even by pursuing the body-as-project.

"Ten years ago I would have thought, 'Why would you wear that to work? That seems so unprofessional.'"

"You don't order alcohol unless they do first. You don't touch your food until they touch theirs. You kind of mirror their movements, because you're assuming . . . that's what's gonna make them the most comfortable. So, same thing with your attire . . . follow the leader."

"When I wear a suit, the recognition I get and the way I'm treated when I'm in a suit versus casual is entirely different. . . . People move out of the way and give you respect on the streets."

"We need to have the appearance of not only being a creative person but someone who's stylish and knows . . . what's going on in society."

If you talk to a woman about wearing something dressy, that's a *huge* open window… and men's clothing for the most part isn't body-revealing."

"The head of the company is . . . very conservative, but very well-dressed. . . . He'll always wear dark shoes, solid ties, probably a white shirt . . . very simple yet very powerful. And you can tell he's wearing very nice stuff. Very well fitted, so it's probably all custom. I certainly noticed that."

"I enjoy clothes, I really do. I like looking at different types of patterns, different colors, not your standard stuff. I experiment a little bit here and there."

"They really don't expect it, so I figure with me being a black male in corporate America, to walk into a conference room suited up, they're like, 'Wow, what's going on? Who is that?'"

"*I don't mind* wearing suits.
I actually think they are comfortable."

"I think a number of people
believe that by buying more
spacious clothes, they will look
slimmer, which is obviously
a misconception."

THE METROSEXUAL IS DEAD, LONG LIVE THE METROSEXUAL!

In 1904, social theorist Georg Simmel, in an essay on fashion, described a character he called "the dude."[1] He wrote that "in the dude the social demands of fashion appear exaggerated to such a degree that they completely assume an individualistic and peculiar character." The dude "leads the way" when it comes to fashion and dress. He is characterized by "the mingling of the sensation of rulership with submission . . . the mixing of a masculine and a feminine principle." Was Simmel the first sociologist to identify the metrosexual, about a century before the term was coined?

Silly or Serious? Metrosexual(ity) as a Social Category

Try engaging in a conversation about the meaning of the term "metrosexual" without smiling. It's impossible. For many Americans, the word and the concept it represents just seem silly. In my interviews with corporate men, mentions of metrosexuality nearly always involved laughter and joking. Yet I would argue that the hubbub around the figure of the metrosexual is rooted in something very real, something that we should take seriously. Men's bodies, grooming, and dress are subject to greater scrutiny than in past decades,[2] and some men's reaction to this heightened surveillance of their looks has been to take greater care in their appearance-related decisions and behavior.[3] My focus on white-collar men's work lives—and the stories they tell about themselves as men and workers—is a useful way to ground a discussion of the meanings of metrosexual. The corporate workplace is an everyday, but high-stakes, setting for self-presentation, making it a place where metrosexuality is discussed, observed, and critiqued. Most of the scant scholarly research on metrosexuality relies on media or celebrity examples, whereas I prioritize men's definitions and experiences. Men refer to popular culture in their explanations of what it means to be metrosexual (or not), which places my investigation in conversation with these previous studies. As with other potentially stigmatizing categories, the imaginary lines separating metrosexuals from non-metrosexuals can be alternately blurred and reinforced. Typically, an interviewee identified the metrosexual as the man who went just one or two steps further than he did in the care and display of his body.[4]

Here I explore what the word "metrosexual" means to white-collar men, whether in their opinion the term corresponds to some reality of men's bodily presentation, and how this social category intersects with others that are used to label men's style and sexual orientation. This chapter is based on thirty interviews with a diverse subgroup of men in San Francisco, New York City, and Cincinnati in which the word "metrosexual" was explicitly used and discussed. These were drawn from the larger sample of seventy-one interviews and the three supplemental interviews with military veterans. In some cases, I was the one who injected the term into the conversation, but more often the interviewee used it first. Of these thirty participants, 37 percent were from the New York City sample, 30 percent from Cincinnati, and 33 percent from San Francisco. Most (twenty-three out of thirty) identified as white, with some using more specific or colloquial terms, such as "white Jewish," "WASP," or "white dude." Of the non-white respondents, three identified as black or African American, one as Indian, one as Afro-Caribbean, and one as Filipino. One participant who would probably be classified as white in daily life identified as Jewish and by the national origin of his immigrant parents. Seven of the thirty interviewees (23%) identified as gay, and gay men from each city were represented in this group. The men worked in areas such as sales and marketing, healthcare administration, finance, recruitment, IT, and architecture/design. A few of the men thought about the metrosexual image as part of their jobs in creative or marketing occupations, and this colored the ways they spoke about the label. The youngest participant in this subgroup was twenty-four, and the oldest, a retired salesman, was seventy-one; the average age was thirty-nine. These men were pretty typical of the larger group of interviewees in that the proportion from each city was roughly equal, most of the men were white, and they represented a range of occupations and ages.[5]

Making Sense of Masculinity

Before we can examine how metrosexuality fits into contemporary (corporate) U.S. masculinity, let's take stock of what social scientists have written about masculinity and the relationship between gender and sexual orientation in recent years. The oft-cited pioneer of this field of study is Raewyn (née R. W.) Connell, whose 1995 book simply titled *Masculinities* introduced the concept of "hegemonic masculinity" as well as the semantic tradition of pluralizing "masculinity" to indicate that there are different ways of embodying male gender in modern society.[6] The book defined hegemonic masculinity as the dominant form of masculinity in a given society at a particular point in history and as the linchpin of gender inequality between men and women. Connell later refined the concept in order to prevent misunderstandings of hegemonic masculinity. Rather than being monolithic or totally determinative of men's gender experiences, hegemonic masculinity coexists with "multiple masculinities," even in the practices of one man or group of men.[7] Connell and Messerschmidt also highlighted the need to understand the "regional and local constructions of hegemonic masculinity."[8] Yet research on men's lives has seldom used a comparative focus that would allow for place-based differences to surface.

In the United States and Europe, Connell stated, "gay men are subordinated to straight men by an array of quite material practices."[9] Gay masculinity was perceived, according to Connell, as the opposite of heterosexual masculinity; the dividing line was clear, and straight men enjoyed higher status at the expense of gay men. Peter Nardi's 2000 collection *Gay Masculinities* showed that thinking about masculinities (plural) could help scholars understand how men performed gender. Nardi's book also beefed up the empirical research available on gay men and gay identities.

Just as Nardi's book expanded on Connell's concepts, Demetrakis Z. Demetriou (possibly the coolest-named gender theorist ever) argued that hegemonic masculinity didn't only work as a top-down social phenomenon. Demetriou claimed that hegemonic masculinity was not only influenced by, but also co-opted, certain aspects (e.g., practices) of marginalized masculinities, which are associated with less privileged men—racial and ethnic minorities and gays, for example.[10] This selective hoovering up of alternative masculinities would lead, Demetriou theorized, to the emergence of "hybrid masculinities" that would actually serve to reinforce hegemonic versions of masculinity by making them "dynamic and flexible."[11] Hegemonic masculinity bends rather than breaks, thus extending its reign. It incorporates just enough of marginalized masculinities that men who don't share in all the benefits of hegemonic masculinity still accept it and even believe in it.[12]

So gay and straight masculinities are not completely opposed; they are in contact with each other and sometimes in cahoots. What does this mean for friendships or collegial relationships between gay and straight men in the white-collar world? Dwight Fee's chapter in *Gay Masculinities* explores friendships between gay and straight men, stating that "the two groups share more experiences than is commonly thought."[13] This is perhaps especially true of gay and straight men in the corporate world, who share similar social class status and work in similarly structured organizations. Basing his analysis on interviews with gay and straight men whose friendships cross boundaries of self-identified sexual orientation, Fee shows how both sets of men benefit from these relationships. He claims, somewhat hyperbolically, that these friendships blur the borders separating straight and gay men as collectives, "scrambling or redirecting the gendered systems or signifiers that have historically positioned sexuality (or sexual orientation) as the determinant of gender."[14] Building on Demetriou's idea of hybrid masculinities, sociologist Tristan Bridges's research with an eclectic group of men shows how straight men borrow elements of gay culture and even (jokingly) describe themselves as "gay."[15] Bridges finds this phenomenon mostly among white men, and refers to the styles straight men borrow from gay men as "sexual aesthetics" (a concept that includes but is not limited to dress and other bodily practices). He claims that such borrowing leads to a reinforcing rather than a smudging or erasing of the gay-straight border. The chapter you are reading answers Bridges's call for research that explores "the diverse ways in which gay aesthetics are understood and utilized by straight men."[16] My analysis in this chapter supports some of the theories and analyses I've summarized here and challenges others.

Academic versus Popular Definitions

As two of my interviewees reminded me, the word "metrosexual" became famous through the Bravo network makeover program *Queer Eye for the Straight Guy*, which premiered in 2003 and featured gay men turning straight men on to "metrosexual" tastes in grooming, fashion, and home decor. A *New York Times* article published around the same time investigated marketing focus groups targeting "metrosexuals,"[17] and news outlets were already documenting a backlash to the "metrosexual movement" by the following year. Scholarly interest in both *Queer Eye* and the metrosexual label seemed to peak around 2005.[18]

There is some agreement that around the turn of the century—the century we're in, that is—Mark Simpson, a British journalist, coined the term "metrosexual," defining it as "a single young man with a high disposable income, living or working in the city" who had a narcissistic, consumerist approach to crafting his physical appearance.[19] Scholars claim that "a short and concise definition would be inevitably partial" and that the concept of metrosexuality has "extensive and multilayered" meanings.[20]

There is some debate over whether the *metrosexual* category is exclusive to *heterosexual* men (as implied by the way the two words almost rhyme).[21] While lay descriptions depict metrosexual men as being more "in touch with their feminine side," some scholars do not accept this reductionist definition, perhaps because of the overly general idea of femininity that it suggests. It seems that two underlying aspects of the metrosexual are connected and sometimes confused: the "aesthetic" and the "erotic."[22] Aesthetic metrosexuality involves a heightened attention to "appearance, fashion, and grooming with an element of conspicuous consumption," whereas erotic metrosexuality "refers to the overt eroticization of the (male) body as a visual pleasure in mainstream media . . . and a certain open-mindedness regarding same sex desire."[23] Some writings on metrosexuality emphasize the extent to which this social category has been used by marketing professionals to identify new markets and products to sell to them.[24] Many participants in this study refrained from attributing the metrosexual stereotype solely to marketing schemes, arguing that it was probably exploited rather than created by Madison Avenue. Yet even if a label is invented by marketers, it can come to take on new meanings and uses and even be adopted as an acceptable identity by those whom it classifies. (Think of tweens or soccer moms, for example.)

So the ivory-tower set has put forward some ideas for thinking about the category of metrosexual, its propagation, and its identification with media and advertising. But how does the average white-collar guy define this term, and how often does he hear it in his daily life in and outside of work? More important, how does metrosexuality relate to conformity, privilege, and the successful embodiment of masculinity in this setting?

Interviewee Wilson Turner, a Brit working in a staffing firm in San Francisco, told me, "If you say metrosexual, you know exactly what we are talking about." In fact, I encountered quite a range of opinions on what metrosexual means and whether it is a positive, affirming label or an insult. Sometimes individual men held conflicting opinions on whether metrosexuality was a good or a bad thing. In general, they highlighted dimensions of the stereotype that align with "aesthetic metrosexuality." According to Dave Baker, a white twenty-four-year-old finance professional in Cincinnati, a metrosexual was "always a hundred percent concerned with [his] appearance all the time." While the original definition of metrosexuality in Mark Simpson's writings entailed being young and single, the participants in my study never mentioned age or marital status as being part of the metrosexual category. Simpson's metrosexual had a "high disposable income," yet socioeconomic differences were not a focus of men's discussions of metrosexuality. Of the thirty interviews in which the word was mentioned explicitly, six men said that they had been called a metrosexual (with a variety of reactions to being so labeled), and three told me that they had called other men metrosexual. As twenty-seven-year-old Rohan Mehta said, "I have two friends, you know, who dress very nicely and . . . I've called them, you know, hey, yo, you're metro." Rohan's slangy, jocular delivery shortens "metrosexual" to "metro," a move that foregrounds the aesthetic aspect while downplaying the erotic.

It seems that, for these white-collar men, there are at least three possible reactions to being called metrosexual. They could embrace the label, reject it, or accept the label after verifying its exact or intended meaning. Those who reacted negatively to being called metrosexual complained about the exaggerated concern with appearance that it connotes. Louis Katz, a fifty-eight-year-old "white Jewish" man from New York City, complained about the way the word is used to demean certain styles of masculinity. "There's a lot of guys," he told me as he ate lunch in his office, "where, if you seem like you care about your appearance at all, they're like [*in a pinched, analytical voice*] 'Ohhh, you must be a metrosexual,' you know, and it's kind of looked down on. It's a derog—you know—among *guys*, it's derogatory." Graham Houston, originally from the United Kingdom and now working in Cincinnati, described liking to dress nicely for work, but stated adamantly, "I'm not a metrosexual in any way or anything like that." Negative definitions of the metrosexual included someone who "spends far too much time in front of the mirror," who takes two hours "putting down [his] hair every morning," or the gym-tanning-laundry proponents of the MTV reality show *Jersey Shore*.[25] Luke Gottlieb, a white man in his thirties who works in Manhattan, described the negative image memorably: for him, being a metrosexual implied "an obsessive concern with appearance . . . to the point where it was almost like annoying. It's like, come on. Be a man." Part of this resistance to the aesthetic rigors of metrosexuality seems to be rooted in what scholars call hegemonic masculinity. These negative reactions imply that part of the privilege of being a man in U.S. society lies in not being judged on appearance in the way that women are. Voluntarily giving up that privilege can cause a man to be looked down on by other men. As Dave put it, "I think you could be ostracized if you were on [the] extreme of always so well manicured." These lay definitions of metrosexuality are markedly more negative than those proposed by scholars and cultural critics.

Yet some of the men who recognized and articulated negative definitions of metrosexuality also saw a bright side. Graham was clear about not identifying himself as a metrosexual, yet he told me that the metrosexual concept showed "how men were changing" in a positive way, "that jeans and T-shirts were no longer good enough, and to celebrate a sense of style is a good thing." Rohan, who migrated to the United States from India as a teenager, said he wouldn't mind being called metrosexual:

> I think it's a compliment [*laughs*]. You know, I mean, you would say it to a person who dresses very nicely, who *does* care about their appearance. I mean, I don't see anything wrong with that. . . . They're doing it for themselves or whatnot. And I don't think it should be taken in a bad way. . . . If some people do call that to me, I wouldn't take it in a bad way. I would be like, "sure." It doesn't matter to me.

Echoing Rohan, Sean Albertson (a thirty-eight-year-old white man working in marketing in the Bay Area) valued the prototypical metrosexual's ease in stepping outside the traditional masculine box. Being called a metrosexual, he said, "just means you're in tune with style. . . . It's okay for you to wear a pink shirt and not feel uncomfortable about it." For Sean, metrosexual meant embodying confidence and style through "wearing trends [and] fashion."

As I chatted with Claude Whitfield, a black forty-year-old with a military background, in a café in gentrified Harlem, he embraced the label of metrosexual, though it had taken some time for him to arrive at this position. He told me between bites of salad, "It [being called a metrosexual] don't bother me now. At first I used to be really offended, [but now] I even refer to myself sometimes, you know, as a metrosexual, because I do probably take care of myself more so than probably the average guy." He didn't seem completely comfortable proclaiming this, as he then said, "Um . . . ," paused for a good two seconds, and then qualified his statement: "At times, I guess." Unlike Claude, other men I spoke with did not see metrosexual as a label taken on by an individual but as a label that was imposed. Pete Costa, a thirtysomething working in corporate retail in San Francisco, claimed that the word was used less than in the past: "A couple of years ago that was the term that was kind of around." And it was always a label that came from outside the individual: "No one really ever claimed it for themselves but there was—you would label other people, right?" In this way, one of my colleagues argued convincingly when I gave a talk on this chapter, the cultural figure of the metrosexual is similar to the infamous "hipster."[26] You know it when you see it, and it's almost always embodied by someone who is not you.

Domingo Sala, a Filipino interviewee from the San Francisco sample, expressed respect for the avant-garde fashion choices of the men he called metrosexuals. For them, he said, stylish dressing just "comes naturally . . . and you can see they're just so confident" in the clothes they wear. He seemed impressed by men who could keep up such a personal style all the time and stated that some men just "dress like that now and then, and for those days they feel confident and they are just walking around like 'I'm that dude.'" Domingo was one of the few interviewees who indicated that metrosexuality was something men could dabble in rather than being a 24/7 lifestyle. He perceived potential negative ramifications of embodying metrosexual-identified style, though, stating that when confronted with fashion-forward men, some men would show "their negative side" and criticize them. In the face of such negativity, Domingo seemed intrigued by "people who carry that natural metrosexual attitude." Interviewees' invoking of both positive and negative connotations of the metrosexual social type indicates that this figure raises questions about the proper way to perform masculinity.

The deep divisions in men's views on metrosexuality support scholars' claim that masculinity in the contemporary United States is undergoing shifts and transformations. Before enumerating the pros and cons of being stereotyped as a metrosexual, we should ask whether or not this is a term that white-collar men are hearing and using on a regular basis.

Is the Metrosexual Dead? Did He Ever Exist?

Several men noted that the term "metrosexual" was heard much less nowadays than when it first became popular. Here are quotes from some of them, implying that this term is not fresh, although ideas and images associated with it may still be circulating.

> I feel like that fizzled a little bit. . . . I feel like it's died down. (Adam, Cincinnati)

> I think that was an invented term. (Graham, Cincinnati)

> I think it's dying out. (Nicholas, Cincinnati)

> The term died a quick death. (Brett, New York)

> It ran its course. (Travis, New York)

> I think metrosexual is nothing but a rebranding of the term "pretty boy." . . . The term's just a little bit maybe passé, [but] I'm sure there'll be another one. My thing is: pretty boy. And it'll come back around I think in some other shape or form. (Luke, New York)

> Whatever happened to that guy? [*Laughs*] I don't know. (Pete, San Francisco)

In the list above, only one San Francisco interviewee states that "metrosexual" is disappearing.[27] Indeed, the fading of the term was noted by most of the men who mentioned it, except in San Francisco, where it seems more prevalent. Five of the eight San Francisco men who used "metrosexual" in our interview claimed to still hear the term on a regular basis in and outside their workplaces. I'll return to this geographical distinction later when discussing the issue of sexuality, as San Francisco differs from the other two cities in important ways, offering some plausible explanations for the word's greater popularity there.

Intrigued by the way that a word purporting to represent a large group of U.S. men could increase in popularity, then flame out, I asked participants when they thought the term began to be used less. Most of them said that the word was bandied about more frequently five to ten years before (roughly 2000–2007).[28]

But the word being used less often in daily conversations does not mean that the idea of the metrosexual is dead. Interviewees claimed that the changes among the professional men they knew over the last half-decade or so had rendered the term redundant. That is, we are all metrosexuals now (if "we" represents middle-class men in corporate workplaces).

Several men said the bite had been taken out of calling someone metrosexual, making comments such as "I don't think it's a bad term anymore" and "It's just a label for normal." The New York City participants were the most certain that the metrosexual phenomenon had become mundane by the second decade of the 2000s. Nigel Peters, who is originally from the United Kingdom and goes back often for business and to visit family, told me, "I think now a lot more men are metrosexual and you know, have manicures, pedicures, those sorts of things, and probably wouldn't have twenty years ago, so. . . . It's sort of definitely like more cool, more sort of hip, more normal." Jeff Michaels, a black forty-year-old working in sales in Manhattan, said that the shift in men's dress, especially outside of work, was making the word "metrosexual" obsolete: "Now that (I personally feel like) a lot [of men] are dressing more appropriately or more professionally . . . it's a word that's kind of fading away." Jacob Burstein, a young gay New Yorker in marketing, asserted that "you can no longer look at someone, and because their belt matches their shoes, assume that that person is gay." He went on to say, "I think we've evolved very rapidly in the last couple of years. . . . People are realizing that it's a socially *acceptable*—and it's really a[n] *expected*—thing to dress well." In this scenario, the word "metrosexual" becomes less meaningful as more men (straight men, Jacob implied) approximate the metrosexual stereotype by "dressing well" and putting effort into their appearance. R. J. Logan, a straight newlywed in New York, who told me he's often mistaken for a gay man by both gay and heterosexual people, took Jacob's argument a bit further, remarking that the emergence of the term "metrosexual" made it possible "that a straight guy can be interested in what he wears more. . . . I think it [the word] has lost its power, in the sense that, people are, like—it sort of evolved into a whole demographic in a way." While the term may still be stigmatizing, then, some of the practices it evokes are not stigmatized any more. As R. J. understands it—and he was not alone in this view—the word loses its power because the things that metrosexuals supposedly do become seen as normal.

This reference to a metrosexual "demographic" by R. J., who happens to work in marketing, is not an arbitrary word choice. The few scholars who have investigated what's been called the metrosexual movement point to the role of advertising and media in helping foment the acceptance of new ideals of masculine appearance and the new metrosexual norms my interviewees described. Whether or not they, like R. J., worked in marketing, research participants recognized the invisible hand of the capitalist marketplace in the propagation of metrosexual images. Daniel Moorehouse, a white forty-year-old in corporate retail, identified the metrosexual category as a way that advertisers (perhaps even his own company) get more guys to try "trendy stuff." Two men mentioned the television program *Queer Eye for the Straight Guy*, which featured a team of gay "lifestyle experts" performing makeovers on heterosexual men that involved changes to dress, grooming, eating, and interior design. As with other makeover shows, one objective of the program was selling the products that the "queer" savants pushed on their straight pupils.

David Coad discounts the explanation that metrosexuality is about men incorporating more supposedly feminine practices and orientations.[29] Yet Graham, who works in marketing and is interested in new strategies targeting male consumers, defined the metrosexual as "somebody who was well put together, that was in touch with their feminine side, I think was the mark—. . . was the way the advertising tried to sell it." While Graham began to refer to metrosexuals as a preexisting market for products, he then reworded his explanation to convey that advertisers were trying to create this market by invoking a nascent metrosexual prototype (a strategy that he thought reductionist yet somewhat effective). Similar marketing messages have been used to target gay male consumers for years.[30] Luca Constantino, a Manhattan architect originally from Italy, thought the metrosexual image portrayed by advertisers gave men permission to prioritize—and spend time and money on—their looks: "The whole metrosexual thing . . . was the perfect way to market it, right? So now guys think, oh I'm a metrosexual; I can care about my hair." Of course, as the negative connotations listed by the men make clear, men's "caring" about appearance contains an element of risk because it defies some traditional ideals of masculinity as encompassing brain and brawn but not beauty.[31] Practices such as buying beauty products or following men's fashion, which "smacks of insinuations of femininity and/or homosexuality,"[32] are embraced by the prototypical metrosexual (as well as by many men who reject the label).

Location, Location, Location

The word "metrosexual" obviously invokes sexual orientation or sexuality. The first part of the word, *metro-*, in Simpson's original definition of the term, denotes an urban location where this image or identity is cultivated, thrives, and is recognized. Cities are also important to the development of white-collar identity, as Mills wrote:

> White-collar workers are city people; in the smaller cities, they live on
> the right side of the tracks and work "uptown"; in the larger cities they
> often live in the suburbs and work "downtown." The city is their milieu
> and they are shaped by its mass ways.[33]

Three geographic comparisons emerged in discussions with participants: urban
versus nonurban, different U.S. cities, and United States versus Europe.

Pete, who worked for a retail company in San Francisco, described his everyday life as taking place in a "metropolitan bubble": within that bubble, fashion
and dress mattered more than elsewhere. Espousing a similar urban exceptionalism, Brett Mason, who grew up on the West Coast and now lived in "the suburbs
in New Jersey," highlighted the metropolitan definition of the concept as a way of
defending its usefulness. "I think there is validity to it," he told me as we chatted
in the slightly claustrophobic break room of his Manhattan office. "I definitely
think that people in metro areas do pay more attention to style and fashion than
people in non-metro areas." Based on his experience, he remarked, "There's definitely a cultural divide as soon as you go over the Hackensack River [into New
Jersey], [or] you get five miles outside of—off of both coasts, there is definitely a
shift in fashion" and the level of attention to dress. Other men who had moved to
the New York City area from elsewhere, or who left New York to live and work in
other parts of the United States, declared the uniqueness not only of large cities
but of New York itself. Jonah Weil, who moved to San Francisco from New York,
went as far as equating New York-ness with metrosexuality: "I'm sure people
have called me a metro. . . . I mean I'm a typical New York person, so it wouldn't
surprise me." In these thirty interviews and many others, men from all three cities referenced the role of New York as a fashion capital and a place of heightened
awareness of dress.[34] In general, research participants thought that living in a
city—rather than suburbs or rural areas—makes it more likely that a man will
engage in behaviors associated with metrosexuality.

How does location within the United States matter for the usage or usefulness of the metrosexual label and for men's beliefs and practices? In comparing
my three urban research locations, I found definite differences in men's work
dress. Interviewees with knowledge of different U.S. cities pointed to the diversity of style norms, and the reported prevalence of the term "metrosexual" varied
by region. For example, Nicholas Georgiou, a design professional in Cincinnati
who often traveled to New York and Europe, mused that "in the Midwest things
move slower, so I think people [in Cincinnati] would probably think that [the
metrosexual] is still a fairly new concept, whereas in the coast it's not at all." This
brought to mind the famous and probably apocryphal quote attributed to Mark
Twain: "When the end of the world comes, I want to be in Cincinnati, because

it's always twenty years behind the times." Location constrains and shapes work dress decisions, in combination with occupational sector, organizational dress codes, and men's place in office hierarchies. R. J., who was interested in fashion and had moved to New York City from the small midwestern town where he grew up, found his new social milieu liberating: "I think it's more forgiving in New York, because everyone is sort of like a little bit fashion-y. . . . If I were to wear something like what I'm wearing right now, with like pink shoes [*gestures toward his pink espadrilles*], in the Midwest, I would be a little more on guard for some sort of comment." This statement points to the differing degrees of normalization that metrosexuality has undergone in different locales and to the greater visibility of what Connell calls "marginalized masculinities" in some global cities. R. J. claimed to be accustomed to negative comments on his clothing, but he still dressed slightly more conservatively when he went back home to visit. From the perspective of many interviewees, it seems that although more men in big cities might embody the metrosexual stereotype, because of the normalization of practices associated with this stereotype in these cities, they might escape being classified as metrosexuals. A dress decision that might cause a man to be labeled metrosexual—or homosexual—in a small town in so-called middle America might fall in the "normal" range in a place like Manhattan, passing as unremarkable.

Those who had lived and worked in other urban places referred to these experiences in order to compare cities' distinctive styles (what I call local dress cultures). Several Cincinnati interviewees used the word "conservative" to describe not just their city but the entire Midwest geographic and cultural region of the United States. Daniel, who had spent time in Europe during his military career, put it this way:

> I just think you're looking at a midwestern town that's going to be conservative by nature. You go to New York, you go to L.A., San Francisco, it's going to be different. You know, 'cause they're much more trendy, and we're just a little bit more conservative here.

Daniel's statement not only compares Cincinnati with the other cities in my study but also demotes this metropolitan area of about two million people to just a "town" in relation to larger, more globally oriented metropolises.

When I asked men to tell me about their most stylish male coworkers, some pointed to European men in their offices as having superior taste. (It is thus unsurprising that some European men I interviewed named themselves as the office style leaders.) Domingo, who worked in healthcare administration, referred to a European coworker who is "always up to date." He pantomimed his coworker checking out someone's work clothing and saying, "Oh, that's last year's?" Domingo described this man's clothing choices:

> He's like totally always got this paisley shirt . . . and he's wearing these white pants and it's like, oh man, this guy is ready to go! Where's he going? The club or what? But um, yeah, he looks so professional, right? . . . It still flows, right? So I'm like, alright [*nodding in approval*].

Participants who were raised in Europe or had spent time there were struck by the differences in appearance and dress between Europe (specifically the United Kingdom, France, Germany, Greece, and Italy) and the United States. Daniel, the former globe-trotting serviceman, claimed that the attention and effort involved in European men's dress and self-presentation would be seen as "comedic" in the United States. Graham, who had lived in New York, Cincinnati, and the United Kingdom, critiqued the limited options for U.S. men:

> It seems so antiquated here (in America) . . . there seems to be three or four buckets and that's it. You know the sports jock, the preppy, you know, and . . . versus Europe, where there are far more nuances and where men in fashion are celebrated just as much as women. You know, I probably have just as many shoes as my wife. And my American friends have maybe three or four pairs of shoes, that's it.

Rather than blaming American men for their supposed lack of style (as most of the European interviewees—and many of the U.S. ones—did), Graham pointed to the different cultural settings and the limited models of masculine self-presentation. As he was not from the United States, Graham seemed not to mind being different from his "antiquated" American friends. Several research participants who were from or traveled to Europe purposely did much of their clothes-shopping there. When they could not visit the continent, they would order items online or pop into stateside stores of European brands or designers. It seemed that many of the behaviors and preferences that were labeled metrosexual in the United States would not be seen as remarkable or unusual in the European hometowns of some of my participants. Moreover, some men who performed practices that could be stereotyped as metrosexual enjoyed their association with European styles, which they saw as superior. The consumption of European clothing and accessories conferred a certain cosmopolitanism on a man's dress, a theme appearing throughout the interviews. Cosmopolitan style sensibilities and behaviors that signal cosmopolitan leanings (e.g., shopping for clothes in Europe) were seen as desirable by men interested in dress and fashion. Their ideal version of masculinity involved the consumption of luxury, sophisticated, or hip goods—often purchased in other countries or in shops that were seen as outside mainstream knowledge or tastes. At the other extreme, some men bought clothes—including work dress—at their local Costco stores and did not emulate this cosmopolitan style, even if they did travel transnationally.[35]

Even men who were critical of the metrosexual label (for example, saying that there was nothing new to this social type or that it was all a marketing ploy) saw some truth in the "metro" prefix. As Georg Simmel and subsequent theorists have argued, despite differences among cities, there is something about urban life that ups the stakes of self-presentation through dress. My interviewees—lay theorists of their own social realities—agreed. For example, men who worked in downtown Cincinnati—where major corporations, large law firms, and big banks tend to have their headquarters—felt that they were held to higher standards for dress and self-presentation than many of their suburban counterparts.[36] The interviewees' discussion of the importance of urban location implies that the dispositions and practices associated with metrosexuality are more easily found in larger cities. However, because of the collective progression toward metrosexuality as a new norm, these urban white-collar men might be less likely than their suburban or rural counterparts to actually be called metrosexuals.

Putting the Sex in Metrosexuality

While the workplace is often seen as an asexual space, for men, "sexuality is often a question mark, an unspoken disturbing presence, in everyday organizational reality."[37] Gender, sex, and sexuality are often entwined and yet undiscussed in men's relationships with men. In this context, "metrosexuality becomes a queering practice that diminishes the divide between homo- and heterosexuality."[38] Ian Geary, a gay man in his fifties who worked in corporate retail, claimed that the term "metrosexual" had its origins in the gay community:

> Metrosexual started off as a derogatory term for straight men who were really gay. So, everybody knew that they were gay. They probably had a boyfriend. They probably, you know, edged into the gay community somehow or other, but when you saw them on the street, they had a wife and kids. They had a very strong, uh, gay sensibility. They had a fashion sense. They had all the classic gay marks and yet they were living this straight lifestyle. And so that term was really used in a derogatory way [by gay men] for men who were too timid to be themselves.

In view of his etymology of "metrosexual," Ian thought it humorous that the word had come to be used so widely and was embraced by some straight men.

He remembered three men with whom he had previously worked who glee-fully called themselves metrosexuals. He also took to calling them metrosexu-als, but with the original meaning he attributed to the term. Breaking out into knee-slapping laughter, Ian recalled his interactions with these men he suspected of being gay, despite their claims of heterosexuality. It was funny, he said, because "their meaning was 'I'm fashionable' and all this . . . [and] my meaning is just, 'you haven't come out yet.'" With another peal of laughter, he pretended to ad-dress these men: "You're just a midlife crisis waiting to happen." The assumption (by scholars and laypeople) that only heterosexual men can be metrosexual is rooted in the idea that a gay metrosexual is redundant.[39] However, Ian was not the only person who saw the category of metrosexual as connected to or connoting ideas about (homo)sexuality. Some who discussed these connotations tried to rhetorically untangle "metrosexual" from sexuality, giving us a window into how men, both gay and straight, think and talk about sexual identity.[40]

Although I had not anticipated it, talking about metrosexuality was an effec-tive way of getting participants to speak about sexual orientation in some detail.[41] The topic of metrosexuality often came up when I asked about the stereotype that gay men are more fashionable or better dressers, a stereotype that was cri-tiqued or accepted by men in both sexual orientation categories.[42] Jim Shaw, a middle-aged gay man, laughed when I asked him about this, saying people "cer-tainly wouldn't think that of me . . . because I don't dress the part." Brett, who is straight, claimed that "people"—by which I presume he meant heterosexual men like himself—"don't want to look gay." He went on to say that if you are "too fashionable," others might assume that you are gay. He saw some truth in the stereotype that gay men dress well, although he also thought that some gay men were "rather terrible dressers." Brett perceived fashion as a potentially risky area, and not just because of the danger of being mistaken for a gay man: "I don't even know if it's mostly [about people] thinking that you're gay. It's just like you're trying to put on airs . . . trying to be too stylish." This idea of "airs" seems to in-voke American middle-class ideals and anti-elitist sentiments, such as the dress ideologies many interviewees were socialized into (chapter 2). In white-collar occupations that involve interacting with a variety of people, as many of the men's jobs do, looking approachable is more important than looking "too styl-ish," which could convey aloofness or a sense of superiority. Trying too hard to produce a particular level or style of dress runs counter to ideals of hegemonic masculinity, in which "real" men eschew appearance-related concerns and novel fashions. Brett's contradictory views on whether dress and style can communi-cate gay identity were typical of other interviewees. Luca, who came out as an adult, felt freed of this concern once he began living openly as a gay man. He told me, "I sort of thought to myself, huh! I can wear anything I want now."

Barney Nicks, a straight white financial consultant in his late thirties from San Francisco, mentioned the conflation of gayness with metrosexuality in people's perceptions of him. As we chatted in his glass-walled office overlooking San Francisco Bay, I asked Barney what he thought people meant when they used the word "metrosexual." At first, he fumbled for words, then took a deep breath and exhaled powerfully into the microphone clipped to his lapel, before defining metrosexual as "a heterosexual guy who's really into being polished and dolled up," noting the "effete, effeminate suggestions that would come with" the label. Barney said that men used the term "metrosexual" to poke fun at each other or themselves for being too concerned with appearance. Yet not only men wield "metrosexual" as a tool for drawing social distinctions; so do women. Barney told me that women he had dated had "teased [him] a little bit" about his attention to fashion and style. He recalled one ex-girlfriend saying, "You are the gayest-dressing straight guy that I know." While he insisted that this was a compliment and that he didn't mind, he momentarily put himself in the shoes of other men who identified more with traditional masculine ideals: "Some people might have . . ." He began but did not finish this sentence, implying that some people (read: some heterosexual men) would be less nonchalant about being called metrosexual, with the connotations of gayness that such a label carried.

Some men felt that the category of metrosexual opened up a sort of third way, a space for straight men who were interested in fashion and did not want to be stereotyped as gay. As Daniel put it, "When the word 'metrosexual' came out . . . people [men] could get away with being more trendy and fashion without people looking at them *that way*" (like many of the interviewees, Daniel used "people" to mean only male-sexed humans). Domingo echoed this sentiment, saying, "That's where that whole metrosexual thing came [from], right? Try to eliminate that . . . 'If you dress good, you're gay.' No, you're just a metrosexual." The difference from more traditional forms of masculinity in the United States is still noted, but the man being labeled is not placed in the category of gay or homosexual. He is not completely excluded from the privileges of hegemonic masculinity. "I don't think," said Rohan thoughtfully, "*that* [metrosexual] is taken as bad as somebody who would call you gay." Though not one of the thirty men who used the term "metrosexual," interviewee Tom Marino referred to "a certain personality type, but that doesn't necessarily have anything to do with being a homosexual. It just has to do with being somebody that's . . . ultraconscious of their image, I guess, and likes that . . . kind of like fashion-y look." Before metrosexuality, was "excessive" attention to bodily self-presentation or fashion among middle-class men assumed to be a marker of gayness? Some of the interviewees' statements seem to support such an argument, although most agreed that such assumptions could not be made in today's dress climate.[43]

The word "metrosexual," according to some of the men with whom I discussed the term, can be used without the intention of classifying someone as gay and yet still be interpreted in this way by the target of the labeling. Consider this excerpt from my conversation with Joseph Davis, a married, thirty-two-year-old African American who identified as straight.

> *Joseph*: Being someone who has always pretty much been an [*slight pause*] outgoing dresser, or being called a metrosexual by tons of women, and . . . [*laughs*]
>
> *Erynn*: You have been called that?
>
> *Joseph*: Oh, yeah. Yeah, yeah. . . . So being someone like that, I think, um, it [paying attention to dress and style] was never really looked upon as a negative thing. . . . I think like twice, two or three times I was called that. First time was probably like ten years ago. And [*slight pause*] when the individual said it, I had never even heard the word before. I got offended 'cause I'm like, you know . . . [*laughs*]
>
> *Erynn*: "What does that mean?"
>
> *Joseph*: "What you trying to say?" you know. But then, you know, when they explained it, I was like, "Ohhh. . . ." I was like, "Well, I don't know. Maybe that's me? I don't know." So, um, I don't . . . when I've heard it I don't think it was considered a negative thing. I think they were trying to define a man who, uh, takes his appearance and does the . . . I don't know, he may [*slight pause*] get his fingernails done, or he may . . . which I don't do that, but I'm just saying, he may do that, he may [*slight pause*] whatever, he just stay up on himself in that manner, so I think they were just trying to use it as a [*slight pause*] defining word versus insulting me. I didn't take it as an insult.

This exchange is illuminating for several reasons. First, Joseph tolerates the label "metrosexual" but after initially being upset by it because he thought it meant that he was being called gay. He "didn't take it as insult" only after he figured out exactly what his interlocutor intended. This is one of three common responses to being called metrosexual, along with outright acceptance or utter rejection. Second, even though Joseph accepts the metrosexual designation (as long as it doesn't connote gayness), he still dissociates himself from certain grooming activities that he seems to see as potentially feminine, such as getting manicures. I have maintained in the transcription here the pauses and laughter in Joseph's speech, which show that he may be somewhat uncomfortable or reluctant to fully accept the metrosexual identification, seemingly because of lingering associations with homosexuality. We can see why being labeled metrosexual (especially by another man) might lead Joseph to become defensive: "What you trying to say?"

Other interviewees saw the use of the term—especially by men to describe men—as simply a more polite or socially acceptable way of calling someone gay. Gay men were most likely to claim that "metrosexual" was used to mean "gay" in certain situations—particularly in the workplace. This was relevant to participants Adam Gerber in Cincinnati and Jacob Burstein in New York: white gay men in their twenties who were not "out" in their workplaces.[44] "My boss calls me one [a metrosexual]," chuckled Jacob as he sipped coffee in the living room of his Manhattan apartment. He went on: "And that's funny because he doesn't know that I'm gay. So I kind of like laugh in my head whenever he calls me that. It's like, you know, if you could put two and two together, you would probably figure it out." Jacob's boss, who is older than he is and presumably straight, seems to know this rule of contemporary corporate America: it is okay to call someone a metrosexual, but not okay to call him gay. Perhaps the lesser sting of the metrosexual label in recent years has to do with the (at least rhetorical) distinctions that have been made between metrosexuality and homosexuality. That is, as some gender scholars have suggested, hegemonic masculinity is flexible enough to include metrosexuality but still marginalizes activities and identities marked unequivocally as homosexual. This separation between metrosexual and gay makes using the word in and outside the workplace acceptable; thus it can be used to hint at gayness while allowing the speaker an out if he is challenged on his use of the word. Perhaps this declawing of the word "metrosexual" is related to the increased acceptance of gay identities in U.S. society. Since I did not ask the men whether and to what degree they found being called gay insulting, I can only speculate about this point and can't directly compare their opinions on being labeled metrosexual versus being labeled homosexual.

Some men relied on a detailed distinction between metrosexuality and homosexuality to emphasize the aesthetic rather than erotic dimensions of the metrosexual category or to reject the category all together. Over lunch in a small café in Cincinnati, Nicholas (a white thirty-nine-year-old who works in a creative design firm) complained, "I don't like the word 'cause I don't think it has anything to do with somebody's sexuality. So I don't even know why that's thrown in there." Louis, a New York interviewee, was ready with an anecdote when the topic came up:

> This morning, this guy sitting over there [*motions to another part of his office*] referred to me as a metrosexual. I was like, [*scolding voice*] "Don't

call me that." That's—First of all, nobody uses that term anymore. . . . And it's like, it has nothing to do with sex anyway, so I don't understand that whole—that whole thing.

These men, who identified in other parts of our conversation with some stereotypically metrosexual interests such as fashion design and clothing construction, strongly rejected the sexual connotations of "metrosexual."

When I asked Frank Miller, a Cincinnati interviewee in his twenties, if the stereotype that a well-dressed man must be gay was still around, he answered, "Not among educated people." He said being concerned with your appearance and clothing "isn't about being gay, it's about being professional and looking like you belong" in the white-collar workplace. Frank told me about a friend in his social circle who dressed in "very fashionable clothes," sometimes accessorized with cowboy hats or cowboy boots (which may be the norm in other parts of the United States but are somewhat exotic in this part of the Midwest). "We give him a hard time about that," Frank told me with a chuckle, "but not because we think he's gay." The man in this anecdote and men like him who are the most fashion-forward in their group of male friends sometimes step outside the bounds of traditional masculinity into more daring fashions.[45] But this behavior doesn't necessary lead those around him—or at least those who consider him a friend—to label him as gay. His friends might call him a metrosexual or make fun of his style, but this does not automatically throw his presumed heterosexuality into doubt. As San Francisco-based Jonah put it, "I mean it's a very, very fine line between how a well-dressed gay guy dresses and how well-dressed nongay guy dresses."

As I see it, there are at least three possible levels of analysis when it comes to the metrosexual label and individual men. First, there is the question of whether or not a man accepts or rejects the label for himself: does he identify as a metrosexual, or "metro"? Second, do his accounts of his own body-related and consumption practices fit his own or others' definitions of metrosexual behavior? Third, what does he actually do in his everyday life? This third area for analysis is a black box, as I did not systematically observe research participants and in most cases did not have occasion to see them socially. The link between levels one and two (label and self-described practice) is variable. That is, some men rejected the metrosexual label for themselves yet claimed to engage in practices—or visibly embodied characteristics—that are associated with metrosexuality in many people's minds, including mine. These practices or looks may include, for example, wearing slimmer-cut clothing that reveals the shape of the body or using products to sculpt or spike their hair. Other men self-identified as metrosexual but did not describe or appear to be involved in many stereotypically metrosexual body or dress practices. These contradictions illustrate what makes social research on gender identity simultaneously challenging and fascinating.

I was struck in our conversations by the way that some men, despite their sexual orientation or self-rated stylishness, described an interest in dressing well as a possible way of bridging gaps between (some) gay men and (some) straight men, or as something that existed outside of traditional classifications of sexual identity. Claude, a straight man who grew up in a black neighborhood in Chicago, had gotten used to talking fashion with the gay men he encountered in his new hometown of New York City: "It's more, more straight men [that call men metrosexual]. . . . I think a gay man would just be like 'Oh, well you dress nice' or they'll even go as far as naming, like, what I have on, whereas a straight man would probably be like, you know, 'You're a metrosexual,' or you're so this or so that." Claude liked the chance to interact with gay men around their common interest in clothing. He felt that they appreciated his style choices, whereas straight men judged him harshly, distancing themselves from those choices, which might be perceived as gay. Barney (the "gay-dressing straight guy") also told me he liked getting complimented by gay men.[46] R. J., a straight man from the New York sample, recounted being hit on frequently by gay men before getting married, attributing the lower levels of interest afterward to his shiny new wedding ring. He thought his fashionable dress was the reason for this earlier attention. The historical moment and location are significant for gay men's potential forwardness with men in mixed (gay and straight) settings.[47] Some interviewees also evinced a characteristic associated with "erotic metrosexuality," as conceived by masculinity scholar Jan Wickman—a willingness to be a potential sex object and tolerance or even openness toward same-sex desire.

Jacob also saw dress as allowing men to reach across boundaries of sexuality. He told me, "I think more guys are becoming learned about how to dress well." In the southeastern U.S. city where his boyfriend resided, he told me (invoking stereotypes I heard from other participants about southern men's more formal style), "everyone is dressed well . . . everyone is dressed well, and they're not [all] gay." Nigel, who did not self-identify as a metrosexual, referred to a new sort of détente between gay and straight men when it came to style. He told me matter-of-factly, "I'd say from my experience: Yeah, the more gay people I get to know, the more fashion advice I take from them and [*laughing*], you know, appreciate it." One of the gay men in his life was his girlfriend's best friend. Nigel said this friend would sometimes call him up if he was shopping and ran across an item of clothing that he thought would look good on Nigel. Jacob recounted that friends had asked him to go shopping with them in the past, saying that they wanted his opinion; he implied that some of these friends were straight men. I interviewed two men who worked in the same office, one straight and one gay, who both claimed to shop together outside of work. Interestingly, many straight men described their relationships with their wives or girlfriends, mothers, and sisters as involving shopping together and accepting advice on clothing choices (see chapter 5). The role of fashion maven, then, seems to cast the gay friend in a typically feminine social role.[48]

So if some gay and straight men are connecting with each other through fashion and clothing, how do these practices relate to metrosexuality as a social category? It is possible that straight men may adopt metrosexual practices and affinities while still rejecting the metrosexual label. Alternatively, if some men are able to reject the negative definitions of metrosexuality or identify positive aspects of this new label, they may be able to embrace it as a potentially positive self-identification. There seems to be evidence of this acceptance of the label, however tentative, by straight men in my study. Perhaps this nascent self-identified metrosexuality reflects lower levels of homophobia among heterosexual men, and just maybe some stereotypically metrosexual interests could act as a sort of bridge between fashion- and style-conscious gay and straight men. This bridge could lead to new types of sociability between members of these groups, especially in the white-collar workplace, where appearance matters more than in some other types of work and where being an out gay man is increasingly accepted.

In the views of the men I spoke with, gay men and straight men are only recently dressing more similarly than they did in the past.[49] Yet several men (both gay and straight) affirmed stereotypes of gay men dressing differently, so this bridge seems to be a relatively new—and still probably somewhat tenuous—development. Research suggests that gay men in Italy enjoy the "semiotic ambiguity" of current men's styles and that wider acceptance of gay aesthetics could increase gay men's standing in society.[50] Yet my findings echo those of other scholars in that friendly relations between gay and straight men, or straights' adoption of gay tastes, do not equalize their social status or erase stereotypes based on sexuality.[51]

Moving beyond Metrosexuality?

There's the right, the appropriate balance of, of being sort of like, the manly man and equally concerned about their appearance. (Travis Jones, New York)

Our customers probably don't see themselves as metrosexuals—they are shopping for clothes, but they are having scotch, and doing something that's very manly. (Owner of custom tailor shop, New York)

> I think in general it [metrosexuality] just elevated the standards of what guys are supposed to care [about], anyway, so I think even like a straight guy, girls still want dudes to look like . . . a dude, right? They don't want them to look like fluffy and all put together. (Sam Wahl, San Francisco)

Examining metrosexuality, a label that could be hastily dismissed as trivial, nonsensical, or a marketing gimmick, sheds light on how men think about and "do" masculinity and lets us see how they view a new social category-in-creation (or in decline, depending whom you ask). I would not argue that the metrosexuals, men who are increasingly consuming appearance-related products, are somehow duped by Madison Avenue or have warped priorities. In speaking with white-collar men—some of whom identify as metrosexual—I did not see evidence of what some sociologists might call "false consciousness," that is, a misunderstanding of their social and economic position and an adoption of ideas that somehow oppress or limit them. In fact, I saw just the opposite. As metrosexuality influences mainstream men's ideals and practices, the norms related to appearance change, including within white-collar workplaces. Men earning their livelihood in these workplaces are strategic actors who choose to (selectively, partially, or completely) adapt to new conditions of employment, including expectations around what interviewees called a professional image.

As Travis indicates, many white-collar men engage in balancing acts as they aim to be seen as masculine yet also present an image that their coworkers, bosses, and clients see as appropriate—well dressed yet not extravagant, well groomed yet not excessively "manicured," neither out-of-date nor overly trendy. They must conform to what these other people in their work world expect, at least to some degree. The thirty interviewees who spoke about the metrosexual gave contradictory definitions and disagreed about which types of men fit these inherently unstable definitions. This lack of consensus demonstrates that the rules for embodying masculinity in socially acceptable ways are in flux and that hybrid masculinities are indeed emerging. Most of the men in Cincinnati and New York saw the term "metrosexual"—and the need to point out or label metrosexual men—as passé. According to some participants, the metrosexual is not extinct but has become the new norm that middle-class men in urban centers aspire to or embody in their dress and grooming practices. This normalization is made possible in part by men's insistence that there is a difference "between *having* gay tastes and *being* gay."[52]

The term "metrosexual" held more relevance for the men in the San Francisco group, with a majority of San Franciscans who used the word in our interview saying they still heard it often. Why would this be? If any city were to be seen as lagging behind cultural trends, it would be (by the assessment of many of the research participants, and Mark Twain) Cincinnati, not a West Coast, global city such as San Francisco.

A plausible explanation for this puzzle combines: (1) the participants' descriptions of metrosexuality as set of common interests that linked some straight and gay men and (2) the particular demographic realities of San Francisco, to which we now turn. In general, scholars of masculinity argue that gay men hold less social power than straight men, who are more closely associated with the dominant, hegemonic, form of masculinity.[53] However, San Francisco is perceived as a gay mecca and has a larger gay population than many other U.S. cities, with 15 percent of residents identifying as nonheterosexual, compared with the estimated national average of 3.5 percent.[54] In such a setting, it is possible that economic and social inequality between straight and nonstraight men may be more muted. White-collar straight men in San Francisco would likely have more contact with gay men in the workplace than would their counterparts in Cincinnati, or possibly even those in New York City. There are certainly many gay men in the city who occupy positions of economic, social, and political power. If we focus on corporate San Francisco, gay men are well represented, even at the highest levels of management.[55]

Let's think about the higher representation of gay men in San Francisco's population and possible implications for the workplace. Heterosexual men in San Francisco, as strategic actors in corporate settings, may find it advantageous for their careers to befriend or at least have positive working relationships with gay white-collar men.[56] Gay men, who are stigmatized in the wider society regardless of their level of social acceptance in a particular city, may also see the benefits of forming social bonds with straight men in the work world. The lingering use of the term "metrosexual" in this urban locale, then, might be due to the greater need and opportunity for men who have some common interests to connect across the divide of sexual orientation.

The term "metrosexual" does connote gayness and/or effeminacy, at least for some of the men I spoke with. However, according to my research participants, the effeminate connotations are stronger with the social category of gay; this is generally true even if participants admit knowing (or being!) gay men who do not fit the effeminate stereotype. It's possible that, more than their counterparts in the other two cities, straight men in San Francisco use the label metrosexual to protect themselves—or other men—from being labeled gay. Straight men may be more likely to be mistaken as gay in an area with a large gay population. Another theory, related again to the particular characteristics of the Bay Area, is that if metrosexual connotes homosexual, in a space with large numbers of gay men, being called gay is just not a big deal.[57] Thus, men in this setting do not resist the metro moniker.

Strategic alliances between some gay and straight men, based on metrosexual-identified behaviors and shared knowledge and interests (cultural capital) could turn into broader social networks that increase individuals' status and social power (social capital).[58] This does not mean, of course, that gay and straight men can't form cross-group friendships for reasons other than these strategic motivations, or that they might not find other ways of bonding aside from metrosexuality. But in an urban location in which nearly every man's heterosexuality is questioned at some point and middle-class gay men have achieved some visibility and social acceptance (an accurate description of San Francisco, according to some men I interviewed there), straight men's hold on hegemonic masculinity seems to be less crucial to their social standing.

So over time, as gay identities become less sanctioned socially and appearance-related behaviors previously associated with stereotypes of gayness become normalized, being classified as gay just might not matter as much to straight men. Although gay masculinities are certainly still stigmatized (as my findings confirm), the privileges associated with traditional masculinity may be less apparent to straight men, leading to their nonchalance about metrosexual labels and practices. My interview data don't allow me to speculate on the relationship between the rising social acceptance of gay identities and of metrosexuality, but I see these two trends as related and as indicating shifts in understandings of masculinity. There is evidence in the men's accounts of the selective incorporation of gay aesthetics and tastes into hegemonic masculinity that Demetriou theorized and Bridges documented.[59]

Straight men's willingness to entertain or embody the metrosexual image could be seen as a way of symbolically sharing some of the privileges of hegemonic masculinity with gay men, of letting them into the club (or at least into the waiting room of the club). Straight men may even see their gay counterparts as superior in certain aspects of self-presentation: remember Nigel's comment about taking fashion advice from gay men? Of course, this perception overlooks gay men's experiences of homophobia and the constant critiques of their performance of masculinity, reifies stereotypes about gayness, and inherently defines gay masculinity as more superficial, but there are other consequences. In everyday life, sharing or bonding over fashion and other concerns could take the form of positive, friendly work relationships, fostering the preferences and opportunity offers that make the corporate world go round.

If metrosexuality, especially in San Francisco, but also in other cities, can act as a new means of linking gay and straight men across boundaries of sexual orientation, what are the possible outcomes of this phenomenon? As I mentioned, one critique of the theory of hegemonic masculinity argues that rather than obliterating or completely subjugating "marginalized" masculinities,[60] hegemonic masculinity shores itself up by incorporating select aspects of these "other" mas-culinities.[61] By doing this in a symbolic way, rather than fully granting equal social power to marginalized men, members of the dominant group—in this case, white, middle-class, heterosexual men—actually strengthen their own he-gemony over other men. Simultaneously, they maintain gender inequality, de-fined here as the power of men as a class over women as a class.[62] In the words of sociologist Tristan Bridges, straight men's "reliance upon gay aesthetics expands 'acceptable' performances of straight masculinity, but does so without challeng-ing the systems of inequality from which they emerge."[63]

It is probably not a coincidence that, among my interviewees, men of color were more likely to embrace a metrosexual identity than were participants who identified as white. These black and brown men are already associated with marginalized masculinities and thus have less to lose by claiming alternative or less traditional masculine identities. They also may be more comfortable with being called or calling themselves metrosexual, as this fits with stereotypes about black and Latino men as skilled or flashy dressers who are able to pull off feminized styles without diminishing their masculinity in the eyes of others.[64] Whereas white men's conformity to narrow ideals of masculine self-presentation is a means of preserving their privilege, these minority men are less privileged to begin with, and different kinds of dress and expression are valued in their communities.[65]

While I see the positive side of gay and straight men's bonding over metro-sexuality, I can also see two dangers. First, if at least some gay men are able to draw on their links to men who embody hegemonic masculinity, they may use the ensuing privileges and power to advance members of their own sex at the expense of women (just as heterosexual men have typically done). Perhaps gay men in the corporate world have already been doing this. But tighter connections to straight men, and the new status they might achieve through those alliances, may provide them with more power to enforce these preferences.[66] Second, I'm reminded of a quote by cultural critic Susan Bordo: "I never dreamed that 'equal-ity' would move in the direction of men worrying *more* about their looks rather than women worrying less."[67] The question is, What are the short- and long-term consequences of the fetishizing of the male body that metrosexuality involves? On the micro level, men who participate in normalized metrosexuality stand to gain socially and materially—for example, by attracting romantic partners who appreciate the metrosexual look or by being seen as more promotable at work. On the other hand, men may engage in activities that make their masculinity and sexuality suspect to proponents of more traditional gender performances. These activities may make a sizable dent in their wallet, especially for young men on the lowest rungs of the white-collar hierarchy. On the macro level, men's increased spending on appearance-related products adds up, fueling a men's-marketing behemoth that feeds on the new insecurities and aspirations that it creates and promotes in men. In the end, metrosexuality is another set of pressures on white-collar men to conform to particular norms of self-presentation. They react to these pressures by either adapting to the new norms (which can carry social risks *and* benefits) or rejecting them in favor of embodying hegemonic masculine privilege.

ZUCK'S HOODIE

Within a day of beginning research for this book in San Francisco in May 2012, I had been told the exact same story by two different interviewees. Here is a snippet of that first conversation, with Wilson Turner, a corporate recruiter:

> *Wilson*: I think you should find some tech-y people and talk to them.
> *Erynn*: Some tacky people?
> *Wilson*: Some *tech*-y people. Go find your Zuckerbergs and that sort of lot, because—I mean, they're multibillionaires. Although that was funny, because Zuckerberg got into trouble with the City for not dressing up.
> *Erynn*: Really? I didn't hear that story.
> *Wilson*: Well, it was a whole thing. I didn't hear all the details of it, but he had analysts and the portfolio managers with the older firms [who] were saying they felt that Zuckerberg was rude and was actually showing up in flip-flops and jeans and was actually being disrespectful to the City, who were actually helping fund him, raising capital . . .

Aside from my apparent denseness, a couple of things in this interview excerpt are worth highlighting. First, Wilson is British; ergo he says "the City" instead of "Wall Street." (The equivalent of New York City's Wall Street district on the other side of the Atlantic is the City of London, where banks and financial firms are concentrated.) Second, Wilson was recounting the media coverage of an event that had happened a couple weeks before. Mark Zuckerberg, the young CEO of Facebook, had visited financial organizations in New York and other East Coast cities to drum up support for the company's initial public offering (IPO). He wore jeans, though Wilson was mistaken about the flip-flops. Yet the item most discussed (and blogged and tweeted about) was Zuckerberg's hooded sweatshirt, or "hoodie."

On day two in San Francisco, I interviewed Aiden Curry, who had worked in public relations for several Bay Area high-tech companies. When I asked Aiden whether tech businesses had their own slant on workplace self-presentation, he told me the same story: "About two weeks ago, prior to the Facebook IPO, Mark Zuckerberg and the rest of their organization went on a road show"—the term for visits to investors by executives whose companies are going public—"and Mark

Zuckerberg met with a roomful of Wall Street investors wearing a hoodie, and I don't know if you saw the hubbub around it . . . ?" I nodded. By this time, I had looked up the story online. Aiden continued, "This one particular investment banker . . . said it was really disrespectful. So that's . . . a very corporate—like, it was some Morgan Stanley guy [or something]—that's a very corporate place." For Aiden, as for Wilson, this encounter was meaningful because it illustrated the technology sector's "more laid-back approach to style."

The men I interviewed in the San Francisco area were still alluding to this Zuckerberg-meets-investors tableau a few weeks later. Sean Albertson, who worked in sales for a tech company, said,

> The whole hoodie thing, the Facebook thing, I think that was a joke, you know? I think that was—you know, it's great for being on Facebook's campus. Absolutely, you know, it's your company, do what you will at your company. And in fact everyone's got this Facebook mission statement where they have the hoodie,[1] so I respect that, that's part of the company; but when he's out in front of investors trying to raise money . . . It's key in New York, these banks, and now he's trying to get his company public and he responds to shareholders, not himself. . . . I respect the individualism, absolutely, and I think there is also a time [to] I wouldn't say conform, but just acknowledge and respect what you're doing. . . . I would take the hoodie off. It caused so much controversy.[2] I would listen to it, I was reading it, and I was like, "This is a joke." And my dad was furious, like, "I have never!" Oh my God, I couldn't believe it. He's asking for billions of dollars.

The word that all three of these men used to describe the debate over Zuckerberg's apparel choice was "respect."

The media coverage of "Zuck," as he's nicknamed, and his hoodie emphasized the critique from the finance industry—that such dress signaled immaturity or flippancy—and the response from his supporters, who stressed the Facebook mystique of being young and cool.[3] Even before the Wall Street tour, the hoodie had been Zuckerberg's trademark: he was referred to in the press as "hoodie-wearing boy genius," "the social network's hoodie-wearing head honcho,"[4] and "hoodied techno-guru."[5] Humorous headlines detailed "Hoodie Gate" and jokingly proclaimed "Zuckerberg Wears Hoodie, World Ends."[6]

Why was this an important story for interviewees to tell a researcher who was investigating the meanings of white-collar work dress? I believe this anecdote, the related media circus, and the men's need to retell the story crystallize two concerns of and about men in the corporate workplace.

A clash of cultures, or at least business models. Tech companies are seen as departing from old-school business models, and this divergence is embodied in informal dress codes. In this sense, the hoodie is "the opposite of a Hermès tie, the favored accoutrement of Wall Street."[7] Interviewees who worked in or around the high-tech sector often talked about the new easygoing corporate cultures ushered in by CEOs like Zuckerberg. What could be more delicious and newsworthy than "the inevitable culture clash that occurs when a 27-year-old titan of California's freewheeling startup culture meets the buttoned-down world of Wall Street"?[8] Media reports often compared Zuckerberg to Apple's Steve Jobs, also seen as a genius who blazed a new sartorial path with his uniform of black turtleneck and jeans. Men in my study were often moving between these two business worlds and strategically adjusting their dress (or their reactions to others' dress) for each setting.

Man as company. Let's not forget that the sweatshirt is, after all, a "piece of Facebook merchandise."[9] This is branding at its finest.[10] The idea that the man, through thoughtful use of dress, can embody the collective resulted in some unlikely journalistic comparisons. In these analogies, Zuck becomes Bill Belichick (the New England Patriots coach who wears his team on his body in the form of a hoodie; in fact, his nickname is "Hoodie"); he becomes Nelson Mandela (the South African revolutionary-turned-president who eschewed suits in favor of more traditional silk garb); he morphs into Fidel Castro (the Cuban leader who dressed like he was still fighting in the Sierra Maestra even after becoming the establishment).[11] The common thread connecting these fanciful comparison figures is their hypermasculinity, a quality not often associated with pale, thin tech geeks like Zuckerberg. The idea of representing one's company is not relevant only for owners and CEOs, however. As seen in my interviews, the average rank-and-file worker may also be called upon to embody the company.

Mark Zuckerberg is not the only representative of the tech world whose encounter with investors has drawn scrutiny, furthering the "clash of cultures" narrative. In the fall of 2013, Twitter executives visited Wall Street in the run-up to their IPO. Dick Costolo, then Twitter CEO, was critiqued for not wearing a tie, though he did opt for a blazer rather than a hoodie. The discussion over techie tie wearing took place, not surprisingly, on Twitter, with Costolo tweeting good-humoredly, "You know, I try to spend a few extra minutes each morning asking myself which shirt you'll like best and YOU DON'T EVEN CARE!"[12]

Future tech CEOs visiting Wall Street now have another option. Just days after Zuck's hoodie raised a ruckus about appropriate business wear, the San Francisco-based clothing company Beta Brands released the Pinstripe Executive Hoodie, a hoodie-blazer mash-up made of fine suit-quality wool.[13]

WHAT ABOUT WOMEN?

Gender and Dress at Work and Home

> Those guys that really care, you know, they're comparing suits. [*deepens voice, imitates American accent*]. "Hey, yeah, where'd you get your suit from? Oh, how much did you pay for your suit?" . . . It's definitely more macho with the men. And then with the females . . . [They] all look well presented and professional. But then I think there's sometimes . . . when someone pushes the line a little bit too much, you tend to get more backlash from the females than the men. . . . There was that one case where someone looked like they were going to the beach, and it was actually female employees that complained.
>
> —Nigel Peters, thirty-eight, straight, engaged, New York, sales

> I'm a heterosexual male. If you ask me if I dress for women, absolutely. Do men dress for other men? Absolutely. They certainly do. I dress thinking there's ego involved: ab-so-lutely. And anybody that says they're not, they're lying to ya. 'Cause you like the compliments. It feels good. You look good. You feel good. All that stuff. . . . I also dress because I want to be recognized. I want to be distinctive. . . . Would I prefer to be recognized by women? Absolutely. Will I reject that compliment from a guy? No. But it feels [*light laugh*] better when it comes from a woman.
>
> —Al Elkin, forty-five, straight, married, New York, human resources

> Guys figure out—more or less figure out—what they want to wear in their twenties, and then they stick with that pretty much . . . until their wives make them change, like maybe in their fifties.
>
> —Aiden Curry, thirty-two, straight, engaged, San Francisco, public relations

Despite the current attention to men's dress on television (*Mad Men*), in print (*Esquire, GQ*), and online (men's fashion blogs such as *A Continuous Lean, The Sartorialist, Real Men Real Style*), it is still assumed that women are more interested in—and more knowledgeable about—clothing and fashion.[1] This stereotype means that the fashion industry still sees women as its primary market. And in everyday interaction, women are expected to pay more attention than men to the image they present through dress. There are at least two possible explanations for this. The first is an essentialist argument: women are somehow naturally predisposed to care more about dress. The second is an argument about social environment: women are subject to greater pressures to look and dress in certain ways. Men in this study employed both types of discourses. As a sociologist, I reject the first argument, that women are hard-wired to worry more and know more about dress and appearance. Research tells us that males and females are socialized differently from early infancy. I think the second explanation is more accurate, as it is rooted in an understanding of gender inequality in contemporary society.

The disproportionate demands on women to pursue more perfect bodies and to dress impeccably or at least respectably are well documented.[2] In this chapter I highlight research participants' takes on the stereotype that women are more "into" clothes, and I show how they use explanations that invoke nature (as feminine essence) and social environment. As seen in the quotes above, interviewees differentiated between men's and women's dress-related behaviors in the workplace, claimed that women coworkers were more likely than men coworkers to be censured because of their dress. They discussed dressing to attract or impress women in the office and beyond. Heterosexual men reflected on how their wives or girlfriends influenced their style of dress day to day and over time. Talking with men about women yielded insights on the links between gender, dress, and appearance in middle-class America. These narratives demonstrate the relationship between men's dress conformity, their views of women as "other," and their gender privilege.

How Many Women Is Enough?

Before delving into participants' perspectives on women and dress, I want to present some of their opinions on workplace gender inequality. I didn't bring up the issue of gender inequality or sexism as I didn't want to alienate male interviewees or put them on the defensive. I asked men about the breakdown of male to female employees in their offices in order to get a picture of whom they were interacting with at work. I was surprised to find that eight interviewees from various employment sectors responded to this factual question with commentary on gender imbalance and gender inequality. Marc Hoffman, a white man in his early fifties who ran a Cincinnati architecture firm, told me, "It's getting a lot better," although "it's still a lot of men." He estimated that 40 percent of the employees in his office were women and 60 percent men. However, when it came to partners who held a share of the business, he said, only one-eighth were women. This is typical of the greater representation of women in the lower ranks of many U.S. companies. Maybe Marc was just telling me what he thought I wanted to hear. Or his comments may reflect a personal desire for greater gender parity in hiring and promotion.

R. J. Logan expressed a similar opinion about his field of marketing, saying "There [are] still a lot more men than women in the industry, which is somewhat unfortunate." He asked me if I had watched the television show *Mad Men*, which portrays a Madison Avenue ad agency in the 1950s and 1960s. In the program, men tend to be the bosses, and women act as assistants and secretaries (though this changes somewhat as two female characters achieve upward mobility). R. J. commented, "I think that dichotomy still exists, in the way that like, advertising is a very sexist environment. . . . It's very hard for a woman to become a creative director and be involved with the idea and concepting [phase]." He went on to remark that "most of the women I know in advertising are in production . . . outside of the idea process." He thought that women in his business felt more pressure to "be presentable" and always have "a smile on their face."[3] R. J. concluded by saying that "there is a degree of racism and sexism within advertising that sort of puts certain expectations on some people . . . but not on others." I may have been nodding vigorously at this young white man as he expounded, sounding a lot like a sociologist, "If you're a white male, you're more likely to have a lot more privileges and a lot more freedom in terms of what you can and can't do. . . . This is all, of course, unspoken." In his analysis of gender inequality, R. J. directly connected the unequal status of men and women in advertising to the demands placed on women's appearance and demeanor. He saw both women and people of color as disadvantaged by stereotypes of the ideal ad man as white, as seen in *Mad Men* and other pop culture products. Participants working in advertising supported R. J.'s claim that their field was male-dominated, but most did not explicitly critique it as he did.

Men in finance also commented on gender imbalance and inequality. Sergio Rivera, who worked at a New York City bank, gestured beyond the glass walls of the conference room where we chatted, explaining the spatial and function-specific separation of men and women employees.

> Well, this side [*pointing to one end of the long, narrow, open office space*] for example, is all operational. . . . The desk secretary works over here. So I'd say like 90 percent of this side is female. And then on that side

[*pointing to the opposite end*] is the trading.... There's plenty of females, but they all do kinda like support work—at least in my space. And so [*pause*] in my little world, they're all men.

Like many interviewees, it seemed that Sergio might not have spent much time thinking about the concentration of women in lower-paid roles in his workplace. The pause we see in the interview excerpt may suggest that he was deciding whether he wanted to admit that his team was "all men."

Another participant from the world of finance, Timothy Stein, seemed less concerned about the absence of women in his type of position than about my perception of this gender imbalance. A white man in his late twenties, Timothy worked in analysis and investment at a hedge fund. "We haven't had many interviews with women for jobs," he said, then clarified that he couldn't remember interviewing "a single woman for any positions other than [administrative] assistant, sad to say." Timothy said that more than anything, this was "a commentary on the job pool," with few applications from women candidates ("I can't even think of a female résumé").[4] Even within finance, which he characterized as "male-dominated," his type of job was "particularly male-heavy." "To be fair," he went on, "I wouldn't blame the other people around me for it; it just is what it is." As he apparently racked his brain to think of recent hires who were women, Timothy remembered a female intern who was identified through a "general casting call" at a prestigious local university. Applying a gender-blind logic of meritocracy, he said, "She was the best one, [so] she got the job." Half-joking, he added, "So there, we do hire women."

Notice how Timothy's description of gender inequality in his workplace and field differs from R. J.'s. Yet both men come up blank as far as how to solve the problem. These men see gender parity as a goal, or at least pay it lip service, but don't seem to have the motivation, the tools, or the standing to push their organizations toward this goal. Nevertheless, these men and a handful of others did acknowledge in our conversations that women are underrepresented or disadvantaged in the white-collar workplace. The interviewees' evaluations of women's work dress take place in the context of limited advancement opportunities, lower salaries, and subordinate status of women in most of corporate America, all of which privilege men.[5]

Women and Dress at Work

Women Just Know More/Care More

In describing their female coworkers, men draw on the stereotype that women are more knowledgeable about fashion (defined as currently popular styles of dress) and more interested in crafting a particular physical appearance. Many expressed the opinion that their women colleagues dressed "better" than the men in the office or dressed up more.[6] They attributed women's supposedly superior or more formal dress to greater interest, knowledge, or motivation rather than to different rules for men's and women's dress.[7] John Wentz, an engineer in the San Francisco area, summed up the essentialist view in techspeak: "Women are more *front-loaded* to care about how they look." Rohan Mehta, from the Cincinnati sample, agreed, saying, "Women are a lot more fashionable. . . . They know how to pick clothes . . . [they] will remember what shoes [a] colleague was wearing." Ethan Mueller, a Cincinnati interviewee who professed ignorance about both men's and women's fashion and said that most employees in his marketing department were men, saw a difference in his male and female colleagues' dress:

> The guys that I interact with the most . . . not that they don't care how they look, but they're just—it's not top of mind for them. It's not a concern. . . . I think for most of them anyway, it's not a conscious decision of "I want to look really nice today" or "I got a nice new outfit that I want to wear," but the women that I know . . . now, I think it's not top of mind for them either, but it's closer to the top of mind than for the guys.

Taking an almost clinical stance, Ethan compares how two sets of coworkers prioritize dress, employing a marketing phrase ("top of mind") used to describe brand recognition.

Several men who saw women as more concerned with their dress or more in the know about fashion trends pointed to this as an undesirable preoccupation. When I asked New York interviewee Femi Banjo whether he thought that the men he worked with at his tech firm cared about their appearance or dress, he offered the tongue-in-cheek reply: "Nah, 'cause then we'd be women," followed with a quick "Sorry." Ron Varick, whose human resources department was made up primarily of women, said that whereas men like him thought carefully about the image they presented in their work lives, they differed from women in their goals. "It's not to *please*," he explained, "whereas I think women enjoy the compliment. I mean everybody enjoys compliments. But [with women] I think there may be a searching for that in some ways. [*More quietly*] I don't think men do that so much." Although the words Ron chose were neutral rather than judgmental, there is a weakness implied in the idea that women dress to please or to solicit compliments. They are portrayed as valuing the opinions of others, perhaps as much as or more than their own. Brett Mason, whose advertising office employed more men than women, agreed that men had more of an "inward focus" when making decisions about what to wear. Basing his assessment on market research scenarios that he encountered in his job, as well as observations of his colleagues, he said,

> I think that women are much more outward-focused. Whereas I think men are much more internal, internally driven. Women are communicators, and they connect with other people, whereas men are much more of the lone wolf. . . . When we've got focus groups in here, women talk [*loud inhale*] about *any*-thing, they're just so much more communicative. And then you have a group of guys, you ask them their opinion on anything, you get one-word answers.[8] It's just, that is just such the dichotomy of men and women.

Brett's description employs stereotypes about gendered differences in behavior and orientation toward the social world. Brett claimed that, as social "communicators," women may be trying to "connect" with others—to start a conversation of sorts— through dress. These gender distinctions don't portray women positively. Brett implies that women talk too much—although he directly benefits from their talking during market research—and that the "lone wolf" is kind of cool, if less valuable as a focus group participant.

In contrast, Clark Landon, whom I interviewed in San Francisco, described what he saw as women's greater preoccupation with dress and angling for compliments as a rational and even strategic behavior. He began by saying that women's prioritization of appearance had "less to do with the work environment" and was more "'cause they're just *gals*" (the classic essentialist argument), but then added,

> The guys, I'd say [are] not so much [concerned with dress], because we're all wearin' more or less the same thing, and it just functionally doesn't make a lot of difference. If you dress really nice, no one would probably notice, you dress terrible nobody will notice, whereas if the gals dress up, people give them compliments, if they don't dress up, they don't, so . . . there's some reward, there's some return on investment there for the gals.

Here, Clark uses business language ("return on investment") to say that women have greater incentive to put thought and effort into their work dress. Clark doesn't imply that women are weaker or inferior but that they make strategic choices based on what will pay social dividends in the workplace. These rewards for embodying femininity are part of an unequal gender system that begins with socialization in childhood.

Although in general men depicted their women coworkers as both more interested in and more knowledgeable about dress, a few contradicted this stereotype by asserting their own knowledge in interactions with women. Dave Baker was a single, young, straight man who sometimes went clothes shopping with women friends. He recalled saying to a friend on such an excursion, "'You're going to think that I'm—that this is the most homosexual comment I can possibly make, but . . . that dress has a *really high* bust line.'"[9] He recounted that his friend expressed surprise, "not expecting that I would know that." Dave attributed his knowledge of clothes to "growing up with girls" as the only boy in his single-mother household. His story places the (heterosexual) man on equal footing with his woman friend when it comes to fashion know-how.

Although their office culture was an outlier in this sense, two interviewees who worked together in a New York business services firm agreed that their male coworkers were actually more concerned with their dress than were the women, "much more than is healthy, probably," in the words of one. These men recognized that they and their coworkers defied the "societal sort of aspect that fashion is much more a women's thing in general." I think that since their office was a sales environment characterized by high-pressure competition, dress became just one more aspect of work life that the male employees turned into a contest. In any case, some men challenged the idea that women are more schooled or interested in dress and fashion.

Clothes Talk(ers)

Men backed up their assertion that women care more about dress with the observation that they were more likely than men to talk about clothes in the office. Daniel Moorehouse, who worked in corporate retail, gave an example: "I do have a coworker who sits close, a female who's very trendy, and I'll hear her talk a lot about the newest shoes she's bought . . . to other female coworkers." Jordan Simms, who also worked in retail and was the only male member of his work team, described feeling somewhat left out of women's dress discussions:

> We joke about the fact that we come together in staff meetings and they're all complimenting one another's shoes and jewelry, and I'm usually kind of laughing about that because [*slight pause*] I don't relate, and they know I don't relate, and rather than making it an awkward [situation], which it really isn't, we laugh about it. They all know that fashion is not something that is high on my priority list.[10]

Ted Demetriou marveled that some of the women who worked in his Cincinnati marketing firm had "shoe calendars up on the walls." When I asked Ted what a shoe calendar was, he described calendars that had photographs of "all the different shoes, 'cause they love their shoes so much." According to Fabricio Silva, employed in public relations in New York, "it's like more natural for women" to comment on their coworkers' dress or talk about clothes in the workplace than it is for men.

So what happens when men cross stereotypical gender boundaries and talk about clothes in the office? Apparently much of this talk happens with women rather than other men. Nicholas Georgiou, a fashion-conscious heterosexual man from the Cincinnati sample, said, "my female coworkers ask me for advice [about dress], and I'll seek their advice as well, 'cause . . . most guys aren't that into fashion. I just don't know why." Jacob Burstein, a New York interviewee who identified as gay and professed an interest in clothes and style, thought that he was more likely than his straight male coworkers to talk to women coworkers about dress:

> You know if I'm a guy—If I'm a straight guy, and I see a woman, you know, I just think "boobs!" But . . . as a gay guy, I'm able to say, "Wow! I like her shoes. I like the way she did her hair, those earrings, it sort of matches. It's really great . . ." So . . . I think it's different for me.

When straight men spoke about this topic with each other, it often took on an element of competition (as in the New York workplace described above) or was seen as strange or laughable, somehow unmanly, as Brett commented: "My desk-mate is fairly fashionable, and we discuss fashion a bit. Sometimes I do feel like we're a couple of girls talking about where to get the latest shirts and pocket squares and tie clips. But I think that that is . . . important to the creative directors in our office." Talking about fashion at work can make straight men like Brett feel like "girls." He justifies it as being worthwhile for men in his creative field, especially the higher-ups. Even when men are going against the grain and talking about clothes, the language of what is normal for men and women is still used. To focus on the body and dress rather than downplaying these things is to sacrifice an element of masculine privilege and to associate oneself with femininity, a subordinated identity in male-dominated work settings.

Given the ubiquitous stereotypes about men's and women's dress knowledge, it is not surprising that interviewees often expressed feelings of discomfort or found themselves at a loss for words when discussing their women coworkers' clothing. Most participants easily answered my question of what men in their company wore to work. But many appeared flummoxed when I asked what the equivalent of that male work dress was for women, when I inquired as to what women wore to the office, or when they were trying to explain women's dress.

"I don't know how to describe it," was a typical response. Ethan put it this way: "I am by no means a women's fashion expert, so I'm sure there's a lot of things they're wearing that I don't even pick up on." Here again, men claim to be less attuned to dress distinctions. Domingo Sala remarked that he had seen women wear capri-style (cropped) trousers to the office, but then he immediately second-guessed himself, asking, "Capris are the short pants things, right?" When talk turned to what women in his field wore to work, Timothy hedged, "I'm dangerous as an observer of women's fashion, I know so little." Jonah Weil, whom I interviewed in San Francisco, echoed these denials, saying, "I don't know much about girls' fashion."

Jonah's use of the term "girls" was consistent with the way most interviewees talked about their female coworkers. Although men sometimes used "women" to refer to their colleagues, "girls" was the more common label.[11] At first blush, "girls" may seem the logical counterpart to "guys," a label that participants often used to refer to themselves, male coworkers, and men in general. Yet "girls" connotes youthfulness, inexperience, and lower social status. Some men used it as the feminine equivalent of "men," which made the distinction even starker.

Two aspects of gender difference emerged in my conversations with men about women's dress. First, women's and men's work wear are seen not as equivalent, but rather as completely different modes of dress. There is no real female version of the business suit, concretely or symbolically (apologies to Hillary Clinton's pantsuits, but it's just not the same, in these men's view). Participants also described women's and men's business casual dress as not comparable. For example, while interviewees had definite ideas of what business casual dress was for them and other "guys," it seemed more difficult for them to articulate what articles of clothing a woman might select to meet this dress code. Marc exemplified this disconnect between women's and men's clothing when speaking about appropriate dress in his relatively casual workplace: "A man could get away with a real nice pair of jeans, a black T-shirt, and put a jacket on. . . . I don't know what the equivalent is for a woman in that type of attire." I noticed that when talking about what clothes women wear to work, men tended to use the word "fashion" even when I didn't use it in my questions. Using "fashion" to categorize women's but not men's clothing reinforces the idea that dress is a distinctly gendered practice. It also paints fashion as a feminine area and work as a masculine area, portraying women as out of place in the work world.

Second, the potential for sexual desire to enter into cross-gender work interactions partly accounts for men's reluctance to comment—even to a researcher in a private, confidential interview—about female coworkers' clothing.[12] One of the victories of the women's movement in the United States has been the institutionalization of sexual harassment training by employers. Although I did not ask specifically, I would guess that most of these men have been given some guidelines by their companies about avoiding sexual harassment or have attended meetings or trainings on this subject. Perhaps they have heard about or witnessed legal battles related to harassment in their companies. Some men favored a cautious approach with women colleagues, and a few spoke directly about fears of harassment accusations. For Carlos Calle, a gay man who would thus perhaps be an unlikely target of harassment complaints from women, conversations with women employees about dress code violations were still uncomfortable. He said that although no HR person wants to have those conversations, "I can do it. . . . It's especially tough when I have to talk to a female about that, but it's part of the job."

Barney Nicks, who ran a financial firm in San Francisco, was adamant about his reluctance to speak with women about their work wear, saying that it is "rougher, as a guy, telling women how to dress . . . because you are vaguely creepy about it if you go too far." He avoided confrontations over dress issues, even when some of his women employees complained about a new coworker who wore "tiny dresses" to work. Fed up with what they saw as her inappropriate dress, they told Barney, as he recalls, "Well, we're going to talk to her if you won't." He reported responding: "Okay, you do that." Dress codes take on a whole new meaning when you are the owner of a smaller business, as Barney explained:

> [In] a bigger company, you can be sort of really Taylorist about it and write these detailed codes, [but] in a smaller company, it's more complex, because *I* am writing the code. . . . It's like, "What am I going to say?" . . .[13] I'm really concerned about allegations of sexual harassment. I'm very, very concerned about that . . . and there's always a weird dynamic because I'm at an age where, you know, it's not inconceivable that I could have a romantic relationship with one of them [the women employees]. . . . I'm just terrified of allegations of sexual harassment because stuff like that affects your reputation.

It's not only business owners who think about sexual harassment when deciding whether to talk about women's dress. Nigel, who said clothing was a big topic of conversation in his office, referenced sexual harassment issues, saying, "You'll be careful and make sure you can say . . . in an office environment, 'Oh your dress looks nice.'" One interviewee, who had migrated to the United States for work as an adult, said that despite being into fashion and clothes, he refrained from making comments at work about what women were wearing. If you are going to compliment a woman's outfit, he said, "You have to know her very well." But he could comment on a man's clothing, as sexual harassment is still perceived as a cross-gender offense: "You can do a comment if they're the same sex as you." His advice was "don't say anything, because you never know in this country."

The narrow definition of sexual harassment as something that men do to women in the workplace, and something that might involve comments about dress and appearance, continues. Possible women-on-men harassment is dismissed as a joke. Carlos, for example, recounted a time that he wore some tighter khaki pants to work on a Friday. One of his women coworkers, who knew that he tended not to wear jeans in the office, remarked on his pants. According to Carlos, their dialogue went something like this.

> *Female co-worker—let's call her Bettina*: Uh, those are almost jeans.
> *Carlos*: Why do you say that?
> *Bettina*: Uh, they look different.
> *Carlos*: What does that mean? What does that mean? Tell me more. Actually, no, I don't want to know.
> *Bettina*: No, they look nice, they just look nice.
> *Carlos*: You're looking at my butt, that's what you're—[*laughing*] Look up, stay professional, please.

Apparently it is so unusual for women to blatantly check out and comment on men's dressed bodies at work that it becomes a source of comedy rather than a sexual harassment issue. There is, of course, the added factor here that Carlos is gay and out, at least to this coworker. Perhaps Bettina thought she could ogle him with impunity, since it wasn't going to lead anywhere or give him the wrong idea.

Women's Dress as a Problem

I wondered whether participants knew of someone in the office getting into trouble for what they were wearing. Many said yes, telling stories about women employees who had been spoken to (or spoken about) because of what was seen as inappropriate dress. Vijay Singh, who worked in sales in New York, said: "It's usually the girls. It's like toooooo summery, like too much like a summery, going-out dress, or something like that—Like, why would you sit in front of a client [wearing that]?" Other interviewees sketched a similar image of women wearing cocktail dresses to the office. For example, Carl Adelman, who ran a business services office in Manhattan, said it would be a problem if "a woman came in [to work] with a fancy-looking dress that wasn't business-accepted." Carl's neologism "business-accepted" referred to clothing seen as suitable for the office environment.

There were two potential problems with women's work dress, according to the interviewees: it was too fashionable or, more commonly, too sexy. Women usually got disciplined only if their dress was seen as too sexy; if it was too trendy, they might get talked about behind their backs, but bureaucratic consequences were unlikely. Ed Hatcher, who worked in corporate retail and categorized himself as a conservative dresser, informed me, "We got some people that really go a little overboard in trying to be fashionable and they kind of look stupid." When I asked him to clarify whether he was describing men or women or both, he said, "women trying to be a little too current." Ed's comments are reminiscent of negative stereotypes in the wider society of women as easily influenced by fads and trends while losing sight of common sense.

The women described as shaking up staid office settings with their dress wore clothes that were deemed too body-hugging or too revealing.[14] Ted, who worked in advertising in Cincinnati, told me that the attire of "some of the women designers . . . can get interesting, especially in the summertime." When I asked what he meant by "interesting," there was a slightly awkward pause as he silently pondered his choice of words, then said, "A little bit more risqué." Louis Katz pointed to similar issues among his female coworkers in Manhattan, describing a colleague who "dresses much too young and wears really tight, short skirts, and she's in her fifties, and it doesn't look right." Sergio said that in the bank he worked at, short skirts and "really low-cut blouse[s]" would be frowned upon, but that there weren't really any consequences for women who chose such clothing, and a few did.

Ian Geary told a story that took place at a midwestern company he had previously worked for:

> [The CEO] was coming through this big huge hallway lobby thing with a contingent of Asian officials. You know, it's like all the guys in the black suits and the cameras kind of clustering. . . . And it was a Friday. And there were three young women walking in front of him with their jeans too low and their T-shirts too high. There was an edict that [following] Monday that jean Friday was gone. . . . He said, we can*not*. If people cannot figure out how to do this, we are not doing it. . . . And we're like, what?!?! And part of it was, they were really moving into the world, expanding out in a reach they had not had before. And [*deep breath*] it's like [*lowers voice almost to a whisper*] do you know what a sacrilege [it was] for these Asian men to see, you know, women's skin? [*Laughs*]

In this encounter, men who are high-status corporate officials briefly share space with presumably lower-status white-collar women workers. Ian was shocked that a seemingly minor faux pas on the part of a few women—a gap between tops and waistbands—resulted in all employees losing their privilege to wear jeans on Fridays. His account presents a snapshot of how bodies matter in global business capitalism at the micro level, reminding us that transnational business is driven by people like these men. Ian prefers more lax dress rules over what he (or the CEO) seems to imagine Asian customs might be. He critiques the employer's prioritizing the Asian business partners' supposed sensibilities over employees' comfort and satisfaction. One linguistic detail in the men's accounts is worth mentioning here. When interviewees used the word "people" in their discussions of work dress, I could usually infer that they meant only men. Yet when they spoke of dress infractions in the workplace and used the word "people," it became apparent they often meant only women, as in the CEO's message to his workers (*people* cannot figure out how to do this) and Ed's complaint about fashion-conscious coworkers (*people* who go overboard trying to be fashionable). These habitual ways of speaking about white-collar work entrench the conception of men as the default, normal workers and women as potentially trouble-making interlopers.

Even for women in positions of authority in the corporate hierarchy, sex and sexuality can be read into dress decisions. Caleb Green, interviewed in San Francisco, had put some thought into this conundrum:

> A powerful woman executive or businessperson who's attractive, she has a super advantage over a powerful male executive who's a male among males.[15] She has that added edge that people may be attracted to her, and that kinda encouragement can go a long way, or that kinda mojo can go a long way. I think that's a double-edged sword. It can be tough for women.

Caleb suggested that women in male-dominated environments, like the white-collar workplace, could wield their attractiveness (and their ability to be a sex object for straight men) as a strategy for success. However, the flip side of that coin, he points out, is that this status as a sex object—especially when highlighted by particular forms of dress—could also disadvantage women or weaken their position in the organization.

Many interviewees cited examples of women's being disciplined for dressing in a way that was deemed inappropriate for the work setting, but they also brought up more indirect means of social control, such as gossip.[16] Rohan said that in his department, if "someone" (he did not specify man or woman) was perceived as being dressed inappropriately, he observed his coworkers "pass[ing] a comment here and there." Typically, it was women who were talked about negatively in the office, by both men and women. Luke Gottlieb remarked that men in his office made fun of women's dress—sometimes explicitly, as in a teasing e-mail featuring a picture of Benjamin Franklin that was sent around to lampoon the ruffled collar of a female coworker, also a recipient of the message. Louis's women colleagues, whom he saw as dressing too young, "elicit[ed] a lot of comments on a daily basis." And while white-collar women were likely to be gossiped about in their offices for showing too much skin or taking fashion risks, there might be other consequences. Carl, who worked in recruiting, recalled that occasionally after sending a woman job candidate to interview with a corporate client, he got negative feedback, such as "a call from a client that says . . . I can't believe what she was wearing." Although the candidate is not an employee of Carl's organization, her dress is a reflection on its ability to select prospective employees who will "fit in" with clients' companies.[17] If her self-presentation were seen as unprofessional, the client may let Carl or his staff know.

From what I could tell by talking with men about women's work dress, gossip was a more common reaction than direct confrontation or discipline. The negative consequences if such gossip gets back to the commented-on employee are obvious. But what could this mean for women if the talk went on only behind their backs? On the one hand, if the gossip doesn't get back to the woman employee, she may be spared an embarrassing situation. On the other, if she doesn't hear the gossip, she could miss an opportunity to be socialized into what is seen as appropriate clothing for her office, occupational sector, or local white-collar dress culture, affecting her career opportunities.[18] Men's fears of addressing perceived clothing infractions head-on because of the potentially sexually charged nature of cross-gender office interactions may also keep women from learning about (and from) their missteps.

While most participants claimed that the more frequent cause of controversy (albeit muffled or backstage) was women's work wear rather than men's, some sympathized with the women's plight. A couple of men specifically blamed the fuzzy boundaries of women's work dress for their being criticized for adopting specific styles. Vijay said he thought it was harder for women to decide what to wear to work, remarking, "I guess there's no formalized dress" for women comparable to a men's suit. This makes it harder for women to blend in at work in a white-collar world that values conformity, as we've seen.[19] Ian noted that women could get into more trouble with their work dress "because the boundaries are less clear." He said, "If you talk to a woman about wearing something dressy, that's a *huge* open window . . . and men's clothing for the most part isn't body-revealing." Here we see women's sexuality and sexualized bodies (especially when wearing "revealing" clothes) as threatening the order of the corporate workplace. The absence of definitive demarcations of acceptability for women's attire, according to these men, was the reason their dress decisions might be seen as problematic. Whatever the reason, women are seen as bodies out of place.

Several interviewees agreed that men had it easier when it came to dressing for work. Dave, for example, thought that the bar for white-collar men's work wear was pretty low: "Being a guy, it's pretty hard to screw that up." If a man would simply "put on a white shirt or a blue shirt, and a tie . . . nine times out of ten, unless you start getting some crazy colors, it kind of just works." Other men, who might have differing views on ties (which may be seen as eccentric, for instance, in a casual or business casual workplace) concurred that dressing appropriately was less difficult for men. For women, the challenge came not just from the nebulous borders separating work and nonwork clothing but also from the available variety, as Caleb mentioned: "Women have so many more options . . . close-toed shoes or open-toed shoes. If you're wearing a dress or slacks, and if you wear a dress, how long [it should be]. For tops, all the different kinds of tops, jewelry, and . . . There's so many layers to a woman's wardrobe. I think it just requires a lot more thinking." Sean Albertson said, "I feel bad for women and all these fine clothes that they have to wear. My ex-wife, her dry cleaning bill sometimes, when we were together, was . . . I couldn't believe it, it was incredible." Men seemed to see both women's work dress and out-of-work dress as complicated and high-maintenance, and they also appeared to recognize some of the social pressures on women to wear "fine clothes." But not all the men I spoke with viewed this situation negatively.

Women's Dress Flexibility as an Advantage

Many research participants emphasized with amazement or envy the disproportionate degree of creativity and the range of options that they saw in white-collar women's work clothing. In the words of Travis Jones, who stated that the women in his company dressed much better than the men, "There's so much more flexibility in terms of their attire. . . . There's some [women employees] that you'd swear they never wear the same thing twice, just because of the . . . amount of flexibility and opportunities they have to accessorize or whatever." Both Louis Katz and Jeff Michaels, who represented different occupations, age groups, and ethnic backgrounds, saw women's clothing as more variable:

> Women's fashion is more interesting. Men's always just seems like a rehashing of stuff. It's only in women's fashions where you actually see like something innovative. (Louis, white, Jewish, fifty-eight, advertising)

> I think with men's clothing, there is gonna be trends, but usually every-
> thing is staying the same. It's not like with women; there's like these
> new, innovative things that are coming out. With men, you're not really
> gonna get too much—there's not like a huge gamut or spectrum . . . of
> different types of clothing that you could wear. (Jeff, black, twenty-five,
> sales)

These two interviewees, concerned with looking good and dressing well in and
outside of work, seemed open to the idea of innovation in men's fashion but did
not see evidence of creativity or expanding options. The style trends and changes
in menswear that they and other interviewees referred to were quite minor: for
example, the move to flat-front rather than pleated dress slacks, the increasing
popularity of slim-fit dress shirts, and the shift from single-vented suit jackets to
those with two side vents. Even the tailors I interviewed couldn't point to many
other recent developments in men's formal or business casual clothing.

Women were most often cited as dress code violators and sartorial trouble-
makers, yet some participants who argued that women had more freedom in
their work dress recast this freedom as advantageous rather than risky. Patrick
Flowers, who described the women in his business casual office as embodying an
"Ann Taylor Loft-type aesthetic," put it this way:[20]

> I think women, they have a little bit more leeway. . . . Some women wear
> sneakers, even though technically they shouldn't. . . . The expectations
> for the way men dress, it's a little bit more homogeneous, and so women
> sort of, you know, kind of construe flexibility as like, "Oh, I can wear
> some sneakers if they kind of fit in with everything else."

This doesn't mean that men never push dress code boundaries. I interviewed two
men who—like Patrick's female coworkers—wore forbidden sneakers to work.
Other interviewees complained about male colleagues' wearing nondress shoes,
especially on Fridays.

Domingo Sala argued that with women's work dress, as long as it was "suitable for the workplace . . . you can wear anything." Workplace suitability seems
to rest on a certain level of modesty and the avoidance of overly trendy clothes.
These are, as the participants themselves noted, unclear (and sometimes un-
written) standards that may apply differently to women. Only one man I interviewed seemed to take women's "leniency" as a sign that *he* could dress a
particular way. Jacob told me why he occasionally wore flip-flops to work in
the summer: "Girls wear flip-flops all the time in the office, so I feel like it's not
a big deal. . . . To date, I haven't seen any other [*laughs*] guys in my office wear

flip-flops. But, no one said 'don't wear them' to me, so 'til someone says, 'don't wear them' . . . I think it's fine." Jacob's anecdote upends the logic of "dress for success" manuals for white-collar women, which often advise them to take their cue for what to wear to work from men's dress.[21] Here he sees an opening created by women's seemingly greater dress options, and he walks right through it. (Though he walks quietly: Jacob told me that when he did wear flip-flops to the office, he tried to walk in such a way as to avoid the slapping sound of the sandal against his bare foot and thus not draw attention to his questionable choice of footwear.)

Even the men who viewed women's supposedly wider options positively remained in a privileged position in relation to the dress code. Although men sometimes described their work wear as constraining or hot, it was unlikely that they would get into trouble for it. Reinforcing the idea of men's embodied privilege, one participant boasted jokingly that "having to wear a jacket and a pair of [closed] shoes is a fair trade-off for being able to pee standing up."

Dressing for Women in and out of Work

Women are perceived as sex objects in U.S. culture, as things to be looked at, and many scholars argue that women are victimized or demeaned by the ways that men visually consume female bodies.[22] Feminists debate whether women can be empowered by using their bodies to attract or manipulate (heterosexual) men.[23] There is much less discussion about men as sex objects or the ways that men may present their bodies to be gazed upon by women. When participants listed the different audiences for their dressed bodies, however, they often mentioned their intention to attract or impress women, as in Al's quote from the beginning of this chapter.

While many men pointed to bosses or clients as the intended audiences of work dress, others mentioned women coworkers. Among guys who dressed "more flashy" for work, said Joseph Davis, a newlywed I interviewed in Cincinnati, "if I was a betting man I would say 99 percent of them are single." When you get married, he said matter-of-factly, "you start looking like everybody else. . . . You don't care. . . . It's not a big deal to you." Despite saying this, Joseph was interested in clothing and fashion and didn't show any signs of abandoning this interest now that he was married. Paul Massey told me he put thought into dressing for work, and that "there's an element, I guess, that I'm single and there are . . ."—here he paused for a couple seconds as he seemed to consider his words carefully—"attractive women that work in the office." He suspected that he was not the only man in his office who kept in mind this "boy-girl" scenario when deciding what to wear to work.

Joseph figured that some of his male coworkers strategically dressed to attract women colleagues, and Paul admitted to doing this. Aaron Levitt raised the possibility of becoming an object of women's attraction without meaning to. He said he'd recently heard that "some members of the female staff" at his new job had said that either he or his male coworker—the details of this secondhand story are obviously sketchy—"either way, one of us, or both of us, were considered to look great for the part, and one or both of us was commented [on] as being 'cute.'" As a man who was involved in a serious relationship and who wanted to be taken seriously on the job, Aaron seemed somewhat concerned by this development. Yet he told me that you can use being seen as attractive "as an advantage when you're working with all females" (he had many women coworkers). He concluded that such attention was a positive thing because "as much as you'd like to downplay that there are attractions . . . whether it's your superior or somebody you work with, if there's [someone of the] opposite sex, it's important to look nice." Although Aaron might not have been completely comfortable with being a potential sex object for his women colleagues, he seemed willing to accept any ensuing workplace advantages.

Other men mentioned dressing for women *outside* of work. Ryan Carter, a young, single, straight man who said he appreciated getting positive comments on his dress from women at work, told me, "If I'm looking for stuff to go out in, I'm dressing for women." When I asked Frank Miller whom he thought he dressed for, he quickly replied, "For women." He said this was "especially true of dressing to go out" and not so much the case at work, where "there are no young, pretty girls." Married men often claimed their interest in clothing and style faded after they began living with their wives. Some single interviewees seemed primarily interested in dressing well to attract women—that is, they wouldn't be interested unless they were, in the words of one young man, "thinking about eventually finding a wife." Both married and single straight men say that women's reactions to their dress matter, directly affecting their choices. As Caleb put it, "I've gotten signals from women, from girlfriends and friends. *You look good in that. You wanna gravitate towards that style. That's the style you wanna avoid.* We're getting that feedback." Caleb appreciated these interventions from "girlfriends and [women] friends." As I initially suspected and eventually confirmed through my conversations with partnered straight men, however, not everyone appreciates his wife's or girlfriend's input when it comes to dress.

Hostile Makeovers vs. Helpful Advice

About half of the research participants were married, and another quarter were in nonmarital relationships, most of them with women.[24] Married men were often seen by others—and by themselves—as no longer dressing to attract women. When I asked Jordan if he liked shopping for clothes, he told me that he used to.

> *Jordan*: When I was younger, fashion was more important to me than it is today. I enjoyed doing it more. I spent more of my income on it than I do now. It's just not a priority for me anymore.
>
> *Erynn*: Mm-hmm. Why do you think that changed? That before it was important, and now it's less so?
>
> *Jordan*: I think it's just life. My whole priorities on life have changed. I mean, we have kids now. I'm married and have a pretty demanding job and have lots of other commitments outside of work, and it's just not important to me in the grand scheme of things anymore. Back then I was single. Very interested in putting myself out there. I don't feel that need anymore. Maybe I should, but I don't . . . it's just not a priority.

When Jordan was younger and single, the focus was on "putting himself out there," presenting an attractive appearance to single women. Now, as a harried, married father, he doesn't care as much about style, beyond being appropriately dressed. Other married men expressed similar opinions, and many single men described their married male colleagues as utterly uninterested or unburdened by questions of dress.

Nigel, who was engaged, admitted to losing interest in clothing: "I've just gotten older and nobody cares as much." Committing to marriage or other long-term relationships also happens as men get older, leaving behind more trend-oriented youth subcultures. Like Jordan, Nigel saw changes in his shopping habits: "[Before] I probably would have gone out, bought new clothes on a more regular basis. . . . I can't be bothered anymore." Part of the reason Nigel felt less stress about what to wear was that his fiancée shopped for his clothes and gave him advice on what to wear:

> I think it's very useful having a partner. . . . You might say, "Hey, you know, what shirt and tie combo goes with this?" And so then I feel more comfortable in terms of what I was wearing. Whereas if you make your own decisions, you're a bit more like, "Oh, what do people think of these?" Luckily my partner is quite—she's very fashionable. So she basically made—threw out most of my old wardrobe. And you know, she's been very helpful with going shopping and stuff. 'Cause she likes that. . . . All her friends work in fashion. She loves to go to shops and, she actually likes sort of dressing me. Which is perfect for me, 'cause I can't stand it.

Ironically, as Nigel begins to care less about what he wears, he begins to dress more fashionably because of his fiancée's influence. She has taken on the stereotypical role of wife as consumer and, more specifically, the role of executive's wife, as described by sociologist Rosabeth Moss Kanter in the 1970s.[25]

Asking for Advice

A common thread in men's accounts of dress-related interactions with women at work and at home was that they positioned women as experts on clothing, fashion, and style. Women were seen as having more of this type of cultural capital (specialized middle-class knowledge), as being more interested in this area, and as just better at thinking about and doing dress. As I mentioned at the beginning of the chapter, research participants disagreed over whether this was an innate difference between the sexes or the result of harsher critiques of women's dress, bodies, and appearance. Like Nigel, many men seemed grateful—or was it relieved?—to have a woman partner to help with dress decisions. Many men would directly ask their wife's or girlfriend's advice about dressing for work or other settings. There was a certain comfort in getting reassurance from these significant others, and some interviewees described women's advice about dress as a form of caring (indeed, an act of caring once performed by their mothers):

> I didn't have a girlfriend for years and that was . . . okay. I loved shopping as a kid. My mom would take me all the time; I loved it. . . . Now, having a girlfriend . . . [you] have an opinion . . . you know, "that looks nice on you," or "that's a good color on you," or you know, I wouldn't have thought about that before. You have to learn.

Some interviewees, including Sean Albertson, who is quoted above, seemed to learn willingly from their wives or girlfriends.[26]

Other men did not exactly solicit detailed advice on dress but rather sought a thumbs-up or thumbs-down on their clothing before leaving the house. As Aiden put it comically, "I have a fiancée now and so sometimes, I tend to like throw stuff on and go 'huh?'"—gesturing with his palms turned up, eyebrows raised questioningly—"and then she will . . . adjust [my clothing] appropriately." Brett said his wife would tell him if he "happened to mismatch a jacket with a pair of pants," which can happen if he is in a rush or dresses in the dark. "She usually says, 'wait a minute,'" as he is walking out. "More importantly," said Brett, who had two small kids at home, "she usually tells me if there is child's snot on my jacket, which is typically the biggest battle . . . trying to make sure you have clean clothing that doesn't get snotted at the last goodbye hug as you're going out the door." Tom Marino said he wished for this kind of last-minute check of his appearance, telling me with a laugh: "[My wife] could care less what I wear, almost to a fault. . . . If I forget to comb my hair, she won't say anything . . . [and I'm] like, 'godammit, why didn't you say something?'" For Tom at least, his partner's *not* alerting him to something amiss with his appearance was a liability. Her obliviousness was incongruent with the stereotype that women are more aware of appearance.

John liked that his wife gave him feedback but did not pressure him to wear particular items: "If I ask her, 'Does this look weird?' she will tell me, but it's not like she cultivates a look for me." When I asked Eli Abrams whether he ever regretted making expensive clothing purchases, he told me,: "I usually don't take it back, but I usually need immediate reinforcement from my fiancée . . . that it was worth it and [that] that's what some people spend on clothes." Participants often described women not only as more knowledgeable about clothing but as superior consumers.

Asking a partner's advice did not guarantee that a man would act accordingly. Jack told me, "I'll ask my wife's advice as far as, what tie do you pick? And she gets upset, because I think I [usually] pick the one that she doesn't pick." Luke said he valued his fiancée's opinion "to a certain degree." Sometimes when she told him she didn't like an item he wanted, he would respond, "Well, I do, so too bad, I'm buying it." But even those straight men who claimed to frequently reject their partner's advice said that they respected and valued their opinions.

As many of us have learned through our own relationships, the line separating advice from criticism can be quite thin, and our interpretations of what our partner says can be affected by preceding interactions, our emotional state, and countless other factors. It seemed common for female partners' comments on their husbands' or boyfriends' dress to veer into the territory of negative and judgmental. One participant recalled a typical borderline statement that could be interpreted in various ways: "My wife believes that I'm not a type who should . . . wear stuff that is too light, given my complexion." While that remark may be relatively harmless, there was a harder edge to some of the comments that men attributed to their wives. Since dress is so close to the body, and is seen as an extension of the self, these comments could sting.

"You Look Like an Idiot"

Some examples of negative feedback from partners, as recounted by my interviewees:

- "She gives me [a] hassle about the amount of blue shirts I have."
- "'No, you can't wear that. You look like an idiot.'"

- "She'll say I have the most shoes she's ever known a man to have."
- "'Enough. You need a pair of blue jeans.'"
- "I'd buy things and they would end up going back more often than not, because my wife would say, 'Are you out of your mind?'"
- "And she said, 'Why do you wear that? It's horrific.'"
- "She's always like, 'those jeans are like [from] 1995.'"
- "My wife would say, 'Unh-unh, it doesn't work.'"
- "When I bring clothes home . . . my wife would say, 'You have that shirt already.'"
- "My wife always makes fun of me for [wearing so many polo shirts], being like 'Yeah, just put on a polo.'"
- "My ex-wife—when I started wearing pocket squares—didn't like it, and was critical."
- "My girlfriend said, 'Um, just so you know, if you keep wearing things like this, we are not going to be dating anymore.'"

These comments may not be verbatim quotes from the interviewees' partners, and may be exaggerated. Yet in the aggregate they reveal a couple of patterns. First, women seem to be shutting down men's dress decisions, such as wearing a pocket square or buying another blue shirt. Second, men feel that women undermine their knowledge and discount their ability to choose appropriate or attractive clothing. By doing this, women reassert their own expertise and stereotypical role as dress authority and primary consumer of clothes for the household. Third, in some cases, a man hits on a style or type of garment that he likes and feels comfortable in (e.g., polo shirts), but she implies that he should break out of this routine. Since dress is not something men are supposed to know or care about, they tolerate women critiquing their clothing choices openly. The men's ignorance is a badge of traditional heterosexual masculinity.

Here my analysis bumps up against the limitations of interviewing just one member of the couple, as opposed to interviewing both partners or observing them together. Since I didn't witness these interactions, I can't distinguish between good-natured ribbing, harsh criticism, and perpetual bidirectional nit-picking between spouses. A few more textured anecdotes show how men's interpretations of women partners' comments vary.

Trevor Robins was a tall, thin, white man in his late fifties working as an architect in Cincinnati. He had been married to the same woman for more than thirty years when we met for our interview in a downtown coffee shop. He was enthusiastic about my research and thoughtfully considered his answer to each question, sometimes going back to rephrase something to ensure his point got across.

When our conversation turned to how he dressed outside of work, he noted with a quiet chuckle that "one change recently is that my wife has told me that I need to wear my shirttails out as opposed to in, because my figure isn't what it was." According to Trevor, who said he tended to defer to his wife and children (and his fashionable brothers) in matters of style, his reply was "Okay, dear." I opined that Trevor's wife's tactic was "pretty direct," and he concurred: "I thought so, too. I'm sure she wouldn't say—well, she might have said it that directly . . . when I asked." Trevor's wife's advice related to changes in his body shape, a major concern of the men in my study (see chapter 6). She was apparently monitoring his overall look and giving him pointers on how to improve.

Clark was a successful salesman working in San Francisco's tech sector. He was in his early fifties, and his casual, friendly demeanor made me think of a sort of business casual surfer: indeed, he had grown up in Southern California (though I didn't ask if he surfed). He had been married nearly as long as Trevor and described himself as concerned with being appropriately dressed but not having much further interest in fashion or clothing. He was also thrifty and disapproved of his wife's tendency to buy clothing for him and for herself that he thought of as too pricey or unneeded. When I asked if she ever gave him advice on what to wear, he replied that occasionally when they were going out together, she would "comment negatively" on something he was going to wear. "But," he went on, "I rarely ask . . . I'm not *asking* for her opinion." I inquired about his reactions to this unsolicited feedback from his wife. There was a longish pause, and Clark said, "If I think it's appropriate, I'll respond, but usually I'm not in agreement, so I'll just kinda like smile and say something comical and keep on goin'." I wanted to know whether he would ever go and change what he was wearing if she said something about it. "I have," he admitted, "but it's rare." In both Clark's and Trevor's accounts, there is a moment in which the man decides whether to engage with his partner on the substance of her commentary or whether to blow it off. In marriages like these that last for decades, there must be many such moments of choosing one's battles and deciding to steer toward or away from conflict over something like dress.

Sometimes it doesn't take even a word from a man's spouse for him to know that she is not a fan of what he is wearing. When I asked R. J. if he sought his wife's advice on what to wear, he said that he did so "very infrequently." He told me there were pieces in his wardrobe that he knew she didn't like. "And I know that," he said, "because of the way that she looks at it when I'm wearing it. . . . She'll give me a disapproving eye, but that's the extent of it." I couldn't help but wonder whether R. J. and his wife, who were recently married when I interviewed him, might eventually fall into the pattern of more vocal wife-to-husband criticism that some of the more seasoned relationship veterans mentioned.

Fashion Pressures at Home

Whether or not partners critiqued their style of dress or complained about particular clothing items, about a dozen research participants mentioned feeling pressure from the women in their lives to become more fashionable. One man's wife persuaded him to wear blue jeans, and another's tried to get him to wear more form-fitting jeans. Hans Schroeder, who described his wife's dress as "very elegant," reported that the two of them had discussed pleated versus nonpleated (flat-front) trousers; he found the pleats more comfortable. "But she is pushing me hard," he said, "to buy nonpleated stuff [pants], because that's how you look today and how you would dress if you want to be a little bit fashion-forward." Hans identified as more of a classic dresser. Other men also felt their wives nudging them to be more adventurous in their dress, despite the constraints imposed by their corporate workplaces. According to Andy Lipmann, his wife influenced him to be more interested in fashion, to try new styles, and to look at fashion blogs occasionally.

In general, men approved of women partners' attempts to make them more fashion-forward or more modern-looking. Vince Lo, who labeled himself a conservative dresser both at and outside of work, said he had "become a little bit more fashionable" because of his wife. Although he said he was sometimes "stubborn" and did not let her "dress him up," he described his wife's efforts in glowing terms: "She is definitely artistic, and she kind of creates more color in my life, so definitely: my wardrobe, I want to involve her in that." Referring to his wife as "the origin of my current clothing standards," Vince recounted that he would often put something on and ask for her opinion, and "most of the time, her opinion is correct." George Wong, who thought of himself as a pretty good dresser, valued his wife's opinion on his clothes, although it sometimes took him a little while to come around to her point of view. "She knows the style," George said, "and she probably has a certain way she would like me to look, and so even if I'm not a fan right away, I'll wear it, try it, and usually it just grows on me." Wives' and girlfriends' campaigns to make their men more fashionable aren't always welcomed, as in the case of Daniel, who recounted a time that "she talked me into buying some colored striped shirts that had coordinated colored striped ties, and they were the most god-awful things I had ever worn." Fashions can sometimes become questionable when viewed in retrospect, especially if they weren't your own idea. There is also a whiff of hegemonic masculinity in Daniel's disgust for an outfit that looked too curated, too coordinated, and ultimately, perhaps too feminine.

Given the sartorial expertise that research participants attributed to women, it is not surprising that only a few men copped to criticizing their partners' dress directly. Nicholas, who was in a "creative" profession and described himself as interested in fashion, characterized his wife as not "particularly car[ing] about what clothing she wears." He told me that sometimes he would say to her, "I can't believe you're going out of the house wearing that." After hearing so many stories about men being taken to task by their wives and girlfriends for their dress, I wasn't sure I had heard Nicholas correctly, and asked, "Wait, she says this to you?" He shook his head, explaining that he was the one who said it to his wife, and then added, "I'm not meaning it in a bad way." Nicholas couldn't understand "how some people would leave the house wearing something that doesn't flatter their appearance." As some of the men inevitably did in confrontations with women partners over dress, Nicholas's wife defended her clothing choices by saying, "But I like this." Nicholas's sly reply, which I can't be sure he actually uttered in her presence, was "Yes, but it doesn't like you." When straight men positioned themselves as the fashion expert in the relationship, as a few of my interviewees did, women could either accept this claim and let their husbands influence their dress, resist, or get angry. Sergio, who was engaged to be married, was interested in dress and saw himself as a pretty fashionable guy. When I asked whether he gave his girlfriend advice about what to wear, he responded succinctly: "I do, and that's been a big issue between us." He especially disliked when she wore clothing that he saw as too big, not "fitting her body." Sergio said he reminded her of her "short torso and really long legs" and said that she should choose clothing with her bodily proportions in mind. He agreed vigorously when I said diplomatically, "It sounds like she might not always be receptive to a discussion" about what she should wear. Men who said their critiques of female partners led to conflicts and those who stated that they "dressed" their wives or girlfriends (doing all their clothes shopping), were a tiny minority of the interviewees.

Women as Coworkers, Women as Partners: Two Sides of the Same Coin?

When interviewees talked about women and dress, whether those women worked in an office down the hall or lay down in bed next to them each night, they tended to espouse a view of women as uniquely knowledgeable about, and invested in, questions of what (not) to wear.[27] This perspective fits with popular stereotypes in the United States that fashion is a woman's world—and a gay man's world—rather than the province of the red-blooded, manly, heterosexual male. Some men felt they had to struggle to get dress skills and acumen that women were seen as naturally possessing. Others devalued fashion and dress, thus associating women with something that was a waste of time and money.[28] They reminded me of some heterosexual men in sitcoms or stand-up comedy, always complaining about their wives' extravagant shopping or limitless wardrobe. These points of view were common among straight white-collar men of all ages in the three cities. Men's experiences and interactions with women in the arena of dress, however, were different in the workplace than they were at home. I see in these divergences substantive implications for gender inequality and embodied privilege in employment and in intimate relationships.

In describing dress code infractions or other instances in which a coworker's clothing raised eyebrows, men almost always gave examples of women colleagues. Since I did not conduct systematic observations in their offices, I can't know if the men's accounts match up with the facts—that is, whether it was actually women whose dress had negative repercussions. I was able to interview several men who specialized in human resources and had personal experience enforcing dress codes, and they also supported this view of gendered dress troubles. So accounts of women's violating dress codes more frequently than men probably do correspond to some objective reality. Since I'm interested in narratives and discourses, it almost doesn't matter whether women *are* more likely to be called out for their workplace dress. Their dress is *perceived* as more problematic by their male coworkers at all levels of the corporate hierarchy.

The greater variety in women's wardrobes and the fuzziness of the boundaries of their work clothing, especially when this clothing is compared with men's suits or business casual wear, imbue their dress decisions with greater risk. While some interviewees felt sorry for women because of these unique circumstances, others envied the blurry definitions and copious options that gave women more freedom to dress as they wanted and to express themselves through work dress. They viewed this flexibility as a plus rather than a liability. Yet if the corporate world is a man's world, a world run by business*men*, who see women as troublesome, as potential sex objects, or as not fitting the mold, this could have implications for everything from job interviews to promotions to layoffs. While women have integrated many white-collar workplaces, especially in the lower echelons, the image that we have of the white-collar worker in the for-profit sector is still a masculine one. Regardless of how men view women, they stand to materially benefit from a situation in which the ideal or default worker's body (or manager's body, or CEO's) is implicitly male. This cultural ideal of male workers, and the resulting "gendered organization," has been the subject of feminist scholarship for some time now.[29] I am encouraging us, on the basis of these white-collar men's accounts, to consider how the privileging of this ideal worker's masculine body makes it difficult for women to conform to appearance expectations in male-dominated work settings.

Participants communicated harsh critiques of women coworkers' dress in our interviews, thus maintaining their privileged position based on an accepted bodily self-presentation. Yet they were neutral or complimentary when talking about their wives' and girlfriends' style and the ways in which these women affected their (the men's) dress. It seemed that *these* women's willingness to play with styles and colors, to mix it up, to flex their fashion muscles could be an asset rather than a threat to conformity. Many men claimed to benefit directly from their spouse's influence on their dress in and out of work, and some spoke affectionately about intimate connections to their partners through clothing. Although no interviewee said this, I would imagine that a man's status could also be displayed or heightened by attending work or social events with a well-dressed woman at his side.

Though some men extolled women partners' dress expertise, I was surprised at the acerbic tone that came through when research participants recalled things that their wives said to them about their clothing. Image matters for these men, nearly all of whom deal with internal and/or external clients as part of their job, and these pressures are currently heightened because of the instability of employment and the greater exposure of idealized men's bodies in popular culture. Although interviewees laughed off some of the nastier comments from wives, fiancées, and girlfriends, their tone sometimes conveyed hurt feelings. Since women are seen as holding valuable information about dress matters, and traditional masculinity discourages men from caring about those matters, this is at least one small area of the relationship in which women can expect to wield power. Men did not seem particularly invested in challenging women's dress knowledge because they could benefit directly from partners' advice. Also, ignorance of this topic actually bolstered men's claims to masculine privilege (traditional, heterosexual masculinity). Men also gained from women's being seen as dress outliers at work and being judged more harshly for their dress, thereby preserving masculine privilege in the office setting.

It is crucial to look at men's interactions with and opinions of real-life women, as we have in this chapter, before attending to their tentative or conflicted relationships with fashion. Much of the discomfort that the "F word"—fashion—generates for these white-collar men stems from its association with women (a lower-status social group), with attracting the gaze of others, and with frivolity rather than manly seriousness.

Suspenders
Shoes with buckles
Short jacket
Linen
Dark clothes
Worn clothes
Ascot
White***
Speedo
Purse
Dirty shoes
High
Sweatshop products
Lace
Rubber-soled shoes
Shorts
Skirt
heels
Pleated pants
Capris
Crocs
Paisley
Bright golf pants
Spandex
Bra
White sandals
Thong
Jorts*
Cargo shorts
Ugly tie
Women's
Mesh
Lighter pants than shirt
Cape
Rolled-up jeans
underwear
White socks**
Anything that draws attention to himself
Big clothes
Women's clothes
Black socks with sandals
Silk shirt
Stripes with checks
See-through clothing
Knickerbockers
Tight jeans
Sweatpants
Pink
Colorful items
Fedora
A tie with short-sleeved shirt
Flip-flops

* Jean shorts

**Unless you're Michael Jackson

***Unless it's spring and you're on a boat

"A Man Should Never Wear _____." Interviewees' answers to the question of what a man should never wear. More frequent responses are in larger type.

THE F WORD
Men's Engagement with Fashion

Fashion, like language, is aimed from the outset at the social.
—Jean Baudrillard, "Fashion"

Erynn: Do you consider yourself a fashionable person? A stylish person?
Luca: I don't know. Maybe. Somehow.
Erynn: Why do you say maybe?
Luca: No, I don't know. And not in the sense that I pay attention—I go
   back and forth, I guess. On one side, I want to be one of those people
   that really don't care [about fashion] because I know that it is not
   that important. On the other side, once . . . I start looking at what
   I wear going out or whatever, then I obviously . . . try to see myself as
   like wearing fashionable (or whatever) clothes.
Erynn: Do you think the people who know you would say, "Yeah, he's a
   stylish guy; he's a well-dressed guy"?
Luca: Uh . . . I don't know. Um, maybe. I guess so. I don't know. Yeah,
   I think so. I mean at least in social meetings I try to wear different clothes, but I don't know if I would pop out as particularly . . .
   [*trails off*]

Excerpt from interview with Luca Constantino in New York

Fashion—the F word referred to in this chapter's title—is a slippery subject to define. In exploring men's ambivalence to the F word, I draw on sociologist Joanne
Entwistle's characterization of fashion as "a historically and geographically specific system for the production and organization of dress . . . characterized by an
internal logic of regular and systematic change."[1] This definition captures the two
intertwined ways my study participants used the word "fashion": as an industry
(driven by particular designers, publications, and brands) and as a set of trends
that could change at any moment.[2] Like Entwistle and the men I interviewed,
I separate the concept of fashion from its cousin, "dress," which I take to mean the
actual decisions and practices that people enact when they decide what to wear

each day. They may dress paying close attention to the current dictates of fashion, or they may dress with no regard to fashion as a system or a set of trends. Most men find themselves somewhere in between these two extremes.

In this chapter, I investigate men's uneasy relationship with fashion and the meanings they assign to being fashionable and following trends. I also include their frank and detailed assessments of their bodies. Their discussions of fashion often led to talk of the body. In fact, their sense of who fashion is for and who can engage in fashionable practices has much to do with the ideal body types they see the fashion industry as constructing and representing. These white-collar men strongly link fashion, the bodies prized in the fashion industry, and their own bodies as they experience and evaluate them. Their lay conceptions are thus more advanced than the academic literature on the body, which "has so far almost entirely ignored fashion," just as the "literature on fashion has generally ignored the body."[3] Men's feelings toward fashion are influenced by their views of ideal versus ordinary bodies and by whether they accept negative stereotypes that associate an interest in fashion with femininity. It becomes clear as we examine these men's narratives that the image of the ideal male corporate worker relies on a particular (fit) body type. This body type is similar to that which fashion designers apparently have in mind as they create clothing.[4]

Ideas of masculinity are shifting in the United States today, and as a result I found some variation in perspectives on fashion among the men I interviewed. When the discussion turned to fashion, I had no idea what to expect. A man I perceived as quite fashionable might tell me he didn't think of himself that way, or a man I thought dressed in a rather staid manner might claim to read fashion blogs religiously. On the basis of my conversations with white-collar men, the clothing logs kept by a subset of interviewees, and my observations of how they dressed for our meetings, I found it difficult if not impossible to divide them into a group that cared about fashion and a group that didn't. Research participants frequently expressed contradictory opinions, as in the case of the man who told me that he wasn't interested in fashion just a moment after he recounted emulating the styles of dress he saw on the television program *Mad Men*. Men's divergent and sometimes (to an outsider) downright perplexing relationships to fashion seemed to be influenced by several factors, including their sexual orientation, race or ethnicity, commitment to ideals of traditional hegemonic masculinity, income level, and the city they lived in. The firm bond in U.S. popular imagination between fashion and femininity—whether performed by women or by gay men—loomed over our discussions of fashion. What the men left unsaid was often as telling as the views they voiced. Starting with their stated opinions on fashion and trends, we'll progress from dress to the more intimate realm of the body.

Fashionable vs. Trendy vs. Stylish

The fraught question of whether men thought of themselves as fashionable is entangled with ideas of who fashion is for and whether men can or should participate in it. Most men adamantly denied being fashionable. Some expressed—as we'll see—a preference for words like "stylish" or "well-dressed" over "fashionable" or "trendy." A few men affirmed that they did see themselves as fashionable and that they thought or hoped others perceived them as fashionable. Yet research participants were nearly unanimous in their reluctance to claim "fashionable" status for themselves.[5]

One of the handful of interviewees who seemed comfortable calling himself fashionable was Jeff Michaels, a twenty-five-year-old black man from the New York sample. Jeff seemed to contradict his statement a few moments later when he said that he was "not looking for anything innovative or too creative" with his dress. Barney Nicks, a white thirty-nine-year-old in San Francisco, answered "absolutely" without hesitation when I asked him if he considered himself fashionable, and he also responded affirmatively when I asked whether he thought others saw him this way. However, when I later inquired whether he felt *knowledgeable* about fashion, he qualified his claim, saying, "Not in the sense that like I know who, like, Diane Von Furstenberg is, and who Michael—and you know, all these different designers. . . . I would say that I'm probably in the top twenty-fifth percentile. . . . And so the big difference [is] if you're in the top fifth percentile." Bryan Lee, a New York interviewee in his early thirties who identified racially as Eurasian, recalled being tagged as fashionable in his previous job. He also showed ambivalence:

> I'm certainly regarded as more of a maven when it came to dressing there. I pushed the boundaries a little bit. I wore skinny ties. Also like, the pocket square that I started wearing, a lot more people started wearing. I pushed the boundaries a little bit. I'm not going to say like I'm over the top. It's a very fashionable-looking suit. It's just the attention to the trims. And people knew that I was one of the—the best-dressed kid in the company.

In his old workplace, Bryan was seen as a fashion "maven" because of his on-trend accessories, which he said some of his coworkers plagiarized. But he clarified his maven status somewhat by saying that he didn't wear anything that was "over the top" and only pushed the boundaries "a little bit." Later in our interview he confessed, "I love to think I'm original, but I'm not." His dress details, innovative in his conservative office, were not things that he had come up with or that people who followed fashion would see as anticipating new trends. Bryan claimed that people perceived him as fashionable relative to the rest of the group. Given the degree of conformity required in most white-collar work settings, this does not place him at the cutting edge of fashion. Being more avant-garde would bring into question Bryan's professionalism and also his heterosexual masculinity.

Brett Mason, a forty-year-old white man working in New York, also claimed fashionableness and then hedged. When I asked if he considered himself fashionable, he replied, "I try, yes." He immediately added that he was not as fashionable as others but would like to think that people who knew him thought that he was in style. This was important to Brett because he worked in a creative occupation (advertising), in which he said that he and his coworkers needed to appear as "someone who's stylish and knows what's going on." There was thus a strategic bent to Brett's concern with being seen as fashionable; he wanted me to know that he didn't pursue fashion for fashion's sake, but to play his occupational role. This was increasingly a priority for him as he grew older, he told me.

When I asked Aaron Levitt, a Cincinnati interviewee who was white and twenty-four years old, whether he was fashionable, he told me, "I don't know if I would use the word 'fashionable,' but I would like to say that I care about my image. . . . I think I have *clothes* that are considered fashionable or trendy." So fashionableness could apply to a man's clothes without attaching itself to him as an identity.

Hans Schroeder was a fifty-eight-year-old man born and raised in Germany who maintained strong ties to that country. He told me, "I'm not fashion-forward." He went on to explain that he wouldn't wear flashy clothing that "just came to stores from—I don't know—a fashion show in Milan or Paris or whatever." Yet in the next breath, Hans said he felt he was "ahead of the mainstream." He attributed this fashionable dress to the fact that he usually bought his clothes in Europe. Hans said he thought that America, especially the Midwest region where he lived, was "a few years behind" European styles.

R. J. Logan, a white twenty-eight-year-old in New York, admitted to being "aware of big brand names," able to "sort of identify certain pieces," and capable of "obsessing over a piece of clothing." Yet R. J., like Aaron and Hans and most other men I spoke with, resisted calling himself fashionable. Despite being more cognizant of style trends than most, R. J. told me, "I don't necessarily think that I'm like a fashionista." The F word—when it implied extreme forms of dress or flamboyant attention seeking—was not something these well-dressed straight men of various ages were willing to embrace.

Men's reluctance to speak positively about fashion is rooted in the stigma of fashion as feminine, which, according to the gender-binary logic of hegemonic masculinity, means it is something men should avoid. When I asked Dave Baker, a white twenty-four-year-old in Cincinnati, whether he was knowledgeable about fashion, he replied, "Yeah. Well, above average, especially for males." Did he think others would agree that he knew a lot about fashion? Dave chuckled and said yes: "I don't know if that would be considered a compliment or not." He related that people who knew him would say he knew more about fashion "than most normal guys." Although he did not mention sexual orientation, I got the impression that the category of "normal guy" was reserved for straight men, but only straight men who—unlike Dave—didn't care about fashion. Whereas Dave's statements seemed to have implications for a variety of social settings, Joseph Davis, a thirty-two-year-old African American in Cincinnati, felt that fashion was particularly frowned upon in his workplace. When I asked him whether he would describe his work dress as fashionable, he said no, it was "typical." After a brief pause, he continued, punctuating his speech with laughs: "Anything I would consider fashionable, I leave here [at home]. . . . I don't wear it to work." Joseph and I talked about how he enjoyed shopping, was known for wearing bright colors outside the office, and owned a sizable shoe collection. When I ventured that it sounded like he was interested in fashion outside of work, Joseph concurred: "Oh, I'm very interested in it, and I would do it"—wear fashionable clothing at work—"but I don't think it would fit the [Company C] way." Joseph was one of a few men who conveyed frustration that his workplace dress norms constrained his ability to dress as fashionably as he would like.

Aside from the men discussed above, just a few others unequivocally proclaimed an interest in fashion. New York interviewee Travis Jones, a thirty-nine-year-old black man of Caribbean descent, said he knew enough about fashion "to be dangerous." He might not be able to discuss the history of fashion or the merits of particular colors, but "I think I can make the right guesses or recommendations as to what colors look best with your skin tone, or should you be wearing a lace-up oxford [shoe] versus a loafer with that, [or] is the cuff on those pants too big? Sure." Wilson Turner, a white thirty-seven-year-old interviewed in San Francisco, told me, "I like fashion; it's fun. . . . I enjoy shopping and I enjoy clothes." Nonetheless, he tempered his enthusiasm with the qualification that he was not a "fashionate" or a "fashionista"; he "wouldn't be able to track the season's color or whatever." Sean Albertson, a thirty-eight-year-old San Francisco participant who was also white, echoed Wilson's description, saying, "I enjoy clothes, I really do. I like looking at different types of . . . patterns, different colors, not your standard stuff. I experiment a little bit here and there." Sean worked in sales for a tech company and thought that his dress set him apart, particularly from the engineers, who were stereotyped as bad dressers in his organization (and others). I noticed that not many men explicitly characterized dress and fashion as sources of pleasure. Those who did, as we have seen, often hesitated to describe themselves with words like "fashionable" or the more extreme (and feminine-sounding) "fashionista." The fun or enjoyable aspects of dress were seemingly too frivolous for them to accept as part of their identity.[6]

Some participants were open to the idea that people around them judged their dress, but they objected specifically to the term "fashionable." For them, it meant faddish or trendy, indicating an extreme devotion to fashion. These men preferred to be considered "stylish." When I began discussing this topic in interviews, I soon realized that, while I subconsciously considered fashionable and stylish to be synonymous, most of these white-collar men did not. Our conversations about these adjectives fell into a predictable pattern: (1) I would ask a research participant whether he thought of himself as fashionable or stylish; (2) he would say he was stylish but not fashionable; (3) I would ask what the difference was; and (4) he would say fashionable meant trendy, which he was not. A typical explanation came from Patrick Flowers, a white forty-two-year-old from the New York sample: "Fashionable to me means somebody who follows the trends. Stylish is somebody who has taste . . . who has likes and dislikes that kind of reflect who they are to some degree or their aesthetic or something. And I think to that degree, I'm stylish." Other men also insisted on distinguishing fashionable, stylish, and trendy, including Sergio Rivera, a Latino in his midthirties:

> Well, stylish is personal. And then fashion is . . . is what is in style? [*Here he recognizes the seeming contradiction and adjusts his wording.*] Or is in fashion. Trendy. So I would say that I've always been conscious about wearing clothes that fit me well. And not just wearing . . . baggy clothes in college because I like hip-hop or whatnot.[7]

These statements and others like them from men of different ages, racial and ethnic backgrounds, and sexual orientations, show a distinct aversion to the "fashionable" label or identity and a desire to self-identify instead as stylish. Given the diversity of the research participants, I was surprised by this robust finding and common language for dress and appearance.

Sergio hit on something important when he said that *style* is personal and implied that *fashion* comes from outside oneself. To the extent that men want to be seen as autonomous, rational, and independent (values idealized in U.S. culture, especially for men), they must reject being fashionable. Richard Schneider, a twenty-seven-year-old white interviewee from Cincinnati, supported this self-society division, privileging personality and freedom from the dictates of fashion: "I feel like I have a sense of style, but I don't believe that society would feel I have a sense of style." This eschewing of fashion as external to the self and thus inferior to style, which is seen as internally developed "taste,"[8] recalls interviewees' claims that women were more eager to please, more outward-focused, and more invested in obtaining external approval of their dress and appearance.[9] Validation-seeking behavior is cast as feminine and thus linked with fashion through following trends. Fashion's connotations of superficiality and frivolity run counter to these men's accounts of themselves as serious, masculine, and professional. Avoiding or demeaning fashion (as both a concrete set of current styles and a sphere of activity or interest) emerged as a clear pattern in the interview data. This form of ritualized speech simultaneously expresses antifemininity and affirms traditional American masculinity. Even men whom gender theorists would see as excluded from hegemonic masculinity—members of racial minorities or gay men—engaged in this denunciation of fashion.

The distaste for fashionable (read: trendy) dress also materialized in interviews through the participants' praise of "classic" style. Daniel Moorehouse, a white man of "forty, unfortunately," works in human resources in Cincinnati. He went beyond dissing fashion and trendy clothing to spell out his theory of classic, timeless work dress:

> I mean, how can you go wrong with an oxford-cloth, button-down, long-sleeved shirt? I've never heard of that going out of style. . . . I try to buy stuff that—if the style changes tomorrow, does anybody really notice or care? With the clothes that I wear, I'd say probably not. I've never had to go out and change what I have based on the fact that nobody is wearing it anymore, because it's always been around.

Andy Lipmann, a white thirty-six-year-old New York interviewee, agreed with Daniel, sketching an image of growing and curating his wardrobe over time. Andy said he didn't qualify as a "trendy dresser" because he tended to "buy things and then wear them for years." He described a process of picking "the best" clothing items in his wardrobe ("what I feel are going to be classics") and "build[ing] on those." Andre Leung, a Chinese American in his thirties, described his dress as fitting into a "classic style . . . more traditional wear." This extolling of classic clothing raises the specter of conformity discussed in earlier chapters and reinforces ideals of traditional masculinity as excluding innovative or fashionable dress.[10] Place matters, too: Andre identified fashion risk taking with his friends who lived in New York but said their dress would seem out of place in the San Francisco Bay Area, where he lived. Whereas Daniel dismissed fashion as ridiculous and saw his own dress as merely strategic and appropriate, Andy and Andre were interested in fashion and style. Yet they all disparaged the label of "trendy" and described consciously choosing elements they considered classic.

Andy, Daniel, and Andre identified as heterosexual. Men who claimed gay identities also preferred classic to trendy, including Jacob Burstein, a white twenty-eight-year-old from New York. As we chatted in his living room early one morning, Jacob, who expressed enthusiasm for dress, style, and shopping, said, "I don't wanna be fashion-forward. I don't wanna be known as a trendsetter . . . [but as] someone who looks good [in a] very classic way." Pete Costa, a gay white man in his midthirties, shared this outlook and linked his preference for classic dress to the aging process: "I'm getting older and I'm trying to buy things that are sort of a classic, timeless thing that you can wear and it's not going to go out of style. I'm kind of not into as trendy things . . . [as] I used to [be] when I was a bit younger."[11]

Sam Wahl was a white man of twenty-eight who identified as gay and was engaged to be married. I interviewed Sam in San Francisco, near the office of the retail organization he worked for. Though he also refused the fashionable label, he told me that he was interested in trends and would participate in them if he felt they fit the personal dress style he had consciously developed over the past several years. However, he claimed that being perceived as trendy could be stigmatized and seen as a marker of homosexuality. "I do still think there's this misconception," Sam said, "that if you're like a trendy guy, you're probably gay." "The farther you tip on the trend scale," according to Sam, the more likely you'll be classified as gay, regardless of your actual sexual preferences.

The virtues of classic dress were espoused by participants born in the United States and those born abroad. Frenchman Pierre Molyneux had an interest in fashion, yet referred to the constraints of his employment sector:

> Fashion is always to be at the top of the fashion . . . like if there's a new fashion, I'm doing it [snaps fingers]. I'm not fashion, I'm more classic in my style. I love the fashion, I love to read it and stuff, but [just] because this is very fashionable to wear like a very thin tie [I'm not going to do it]. I'm not in the media, creative, advertising business.

Brazilian interviewee Luiz Rodrigues also favored a look that did not change in response to fashion trends. When I met with Luiz in his midtown Manhattan office, I asked him if he considered himself a fashionable person. "Not at all." A stylish person? "Far from that." Why not? Luiz responded, "Because I don't pay attention. I think if you pay too much attention to fashion you become a slave of yourself . . . and the brands . . . I never bought anything because of fashion." He bragged that the suit he was wearing (light brown, in a fabric pattern some might call Prince of Wales and others would call glen plaid) was twenty years old: "I can wear a suit for twenty, thirty years. . . . I have clothes that I use for more than twenty years that I feel perfectly comfortable with." Luiz saw this constancy as extending beyond clothing to grooming; for example, he had always cut his hair the same way. He implied that steadiness of taste was part of his personality.

Among the respondents, I noticed that black men were less dismissive of fashion and trends when compared with their nonblack counterparts. When I finished the questions on my interview guide, I asked Jeff if there was anything he wanted to add. His talk turned to race, and he suggested that "fashion in the black culture is . . . a higher priority, than [in] a lot of other cultures." No black interviewees were entirely disdainful of fashion (as were many men from other racial groups), and most expressed some interest in fashion, trends, and experimenting with dress. Not everyone felt free to enact this fashion sense at work, as Joseph's quote above shows. If fashion and style are more valued in their racial and ethnic communities, then it makes sense that men of color would accept these values and embody them, at least outside of work. Minority men are denied access to the privileged status of hegemonic masculinity, so they have less to lose than white men by engaging in potentially feminizing attention to fashion.[12]

Close to twenty men flat out told me that they did not follow or were not affected by trends. These men, and others who were less definitive in their claims about fashion's influence, expressed the view that fashion was not interesting to them for one reason or another. Fashion wasn't "for" these men:

> I don't think being hip and cool and fashionable would look good on me. (Ron Varick, Cincinnati)

> I'm pretty plain vanilla in terms of the stuff that I buy. I wouldn't wear like a flamboyant color or a shirt that had . . . some kind of hipster-type of pattern on it or anything like that. There are people that do that [who] work in my office. They want that hip look with like big dark [rimmed] glasses and stuff like that. But that's really just not me and it would look kind of silly on me, I think. (Tom Marino, New York)

Men from Cincinnati were more likely than New Yorkers or San Franciscans to describe themselves as existing completely outside the world of fashion. When I interviewed Ted Demetriou (white, twenty-eight) and Ethan Mueller (white, thirty-three) in Cincinnati, they both connected their lack of interest in fashion to their place-based identities. Ted employed his identity as a fan of Cincinnati's major-league baseball team as a symbol of traditional, nonfashionable masculinity: "I focus more on knowing what the Reds lineup is, as opposed to understanding the latest on fashion." Ethan told me he was "not an eccentric dresser . . . not fashion-forward." He went on to say, "I'm from the Midwest, so I would dress like . . . a typical Caucasian Midwest male in his early thirties." According to Ethan, this description is "stereotyping, but it's true." As someone who did not grow up in the midwestern United States, I was curious to know more about Ethan's claims. He explained that men like him from the Midwest were not going out and "buying whoever the latest designer is." He contrasted his "Midwestern" dress with media representations from another part of the country: "I don't wear tight Ed Hardy T-shirts like the guys on *Jersey Shore* do. . . . That's what I mean by Midwest, just . . . like what I have on today, a blue, button-up, kind of plain-looking shirt."[13] Ethan's comments illustrate my concept of local dress cultures. For Ethan, local and regional cultural norms discourage men like him from participating in fashion, even if they are aware of trends and designers. To be legible as a heterosexual, middle-class man in this setting, Ethan conforms to what he and other research participants think of as plain, understated, midwestern dress.[14]

Tracking Trends

Many interviewees rejected fashion (especially its more extreme elements) and claimed not to follow trends. It seemed that they used their dislike of fashion to signal their independence. Turning away from fashion also shored up men's claims to hegemonic masculinity. Yet a greater proportion of men admitted that fashion trends *did* affect them, whether they liked it or not. Considering the amount of verbal energy men expended to deride fashion, being fashionable, and trendiness, I did not expect that some of the same men would then turn around and say that they were affected by changes in fashion. Participants saw specific clothing styles as shaped by current trends, including "spread collars," European-cut suits and slimmer clothing in general, skinny ties, flat-front pants, pants without cuffs, and pocket squares.[15]

In their accounts of trends, men said they did not want to be forerunners, but they felt the need to pay attention to shifts in fashion so as not to be left behind.[16] Many discussed wanting a wardrobe that was seen as current. This position is summed up succinctly in the words of Ron, a fifty-six-year-old, straight white man from the Cincinnati sample: "I've tried to evolve as times have evolved; I've probably been on the trailing end of that [rather] than the leading edge." Other men expressed the same idea, saying "I'm not the cutting edge" or "I am not the first to try something new, but I'm the second or third—not the last." Adam Gerber, a white gay man in his midtwenties whom I spoke to in Cincinnati, said he was not the first person to try out a new fashion trend. His cautious approach was also used by other men: once a new style has "gained a little bit of traction, I'll join the bandwagon. . . . [but] I'll wait a little bit." Like Adam, San Francisco participant Tony Hirsch (a white fifty-year-old who identified as gay) was somewhat interested in trends. Tony told me, "If I see something new, I may wait two or three years to see if it sticks, then I might get it."

Men's goal in keeping up with trends, yet not being "avant-garde" or a "trend-setter," was to avoid looking old-fashioned. Several participants mentioned their age: they might be getting older but didn't want to look like "old guys." In the words of George Wong, an Asian man in his midthirties from the San Francisco sample: "I pay some attention to [trends]. . . . I don't want to get too old too fast." As Marc Hoffman, a white architect in his early fifties from Cincinnati, put it, "I think it's a constant effort to *not* be out of date. Particularly in a design field, [you can't] dress in a way that kind of looks like 1980. So, you know, I definitely don't want the dress to be behind. My own personal taste is not to be the first person with the new fashion item." Although Marc presented his stance as his "own personal taste," this waiting to see about trends, preferring the coziness of the bandwagon to the loneliness of the cutting edge, was common among many of his white-collar counterparts. They did not want to be seen wearing clothing that was outdated. For Sergio, the fashion don'ts mattered most: "I try to stay up on trends and pay attention to magazines, and what isn't fashionable at the time, what is out . . . what you shouldn't be wearing." Fabricio Silva, a thirty-one-year-old native of Argentina I interviewed in New York, said he liked knowing that his style was current. Laughing, he said, "I don't want to be looking like . . . from another decade." Laughing harder now, he added, "Lost in space." Men follow trends (if only from a distance) because they want to be part of the present time, the present space. They want to dress and feel like members of their social groups. Efforts to stay current, however, are sometimes undertaken grudgingly and are not always fruitful. Caleb Green, a white San Franciscan in his late thirties, expressed this frustration, saying, "It kinda pisses me off, that the whole fashion world changes up styles. . . . I try not to look outdated, but sometimes I do."

I wanted to find out where men got ideas about current trends. How did they know what was in or out at any given time? Vijay Singh, a thirty-one-year-old New Yorker who identified as Indian, claimed that he learned about trends by observing what types of clothing were available in stores. "When you go to buy something," Vijay said, "you tend to see a lot of something . . . [and] go in that direction." He employed the example of plaid shirts. Although he wasn't sure whether plaid shirts were still in or were already on their way out of style, he said, "I have like five of 'em now for *no* apparent reason, other than the fact that that's all they apparently sell anymore." Jeff said he read *GQ* magazine, explaining, "I just like to go through and . . . see what's new in terms of style of professional clothing." This is how he learns of trends in business wear, for example: "There has been this whole change from the huge double Windsor knot . . . to the skinny tie. *That* is something I will kind of customize to." Despite the fact that Jeff worked in a casual-dress office in Manhattan, he was interested in what he called "professional" clothing trends.

For participants from San Francisco and New York, the city itself was a source of information about fashion trends. When I asked Aiden Curry (white and thirty-two), "How do you find out about what the trends are?" his quick rejoinder was "I mean, I live in San Francisco." New York was identified both by its residents and by men from the other two cities as the origin of many dress trends. When Andre in California described his work dress as "a little trendier," he added, "I don't think it's *New York* trendy." Several Cincinnati men described their town as relatively unaffected by trends or claimed (echoing the Mark Twain quote) that trends got to Cincinnati late.[17] The fashion hierarchy of these three cities, agreed upon by most interviewees, was led by New York City, with San Francisco second and Cincinnati a distant third. This stereotypical ranking did not correspond to dress formality. As I showed in chapter 1, white-collar men in New York and Cincinnati dressed more similarly, with San Francisco the casual-dress outlier.

Although knowledge of trends could come from magazines, the Internet, store displays, television, and film, ultimately the arbiters of trends who mattered most were the men's work peers. Brad Jennings, in his late forties when we met, told the following story:

> I bought a sport coat a couple of years ago and it had a vent in it, and it was this time when sport coats had no vents, and I remember somebody commenting on the fact that they liked the sport coat that I bought. And I said, "Yeah, but it's got a vent." And they go, "No, no, no, that's coming back." And I remember the sense of relief, like, "Oh, good. Okay!" But then it made me think about all my other sport coats that don't have a vent in them, and should I be ditching those?

Because fashion is characterized by change and men want to dress in a way that is current, they risk being too far ahead or behind the trend for their social comfort. Sergio, who said he paid attention to what was happening in the fashion world, remarked, "I think you can't follow [fashion] too closely, because then you'll feel like you're always in and out, or like it's moving too fast for you." Many interviewees stated that they were affected by trends and were primarily concerned with not looking dated, with being stylish *enough* but not overly trendy. It is a balancing act particular to occupations like these, in which conformity is valued, but so is youth and appearing to be in the know.

Fashioning Bodies

In her novel *Jazz*, American author Toni Morrison writes that "a badly dressed body is no body at all."[18] Clothing is seen as communicating something about the self.[19] In order for that self to be intelligible to others, it must be dressed and dressed well—or at least well enough. While I anticipated that the men in my study would talk about their bodies and *the body* more generally as they discussed their decisions and practices, I was surprised by two things. First, their body talk was often directly connected to fashion and current trends in menswear. This makes sense if we consider how men's bodies are increasingly visible, even exposed, in U.S. popular culture and if we consider the movement toward more form-fitting clothing for men, including white-collar work wear. Second, men spoke in detail and apparently candidly about their feelings toward their bodies, including their physical shortcomings. In this way, they sounded a lot like women I've spoken with about their bodies, reminding me of Susan Bordo's statement cited in chapter 4: "I never dreamed that 'equality' would move in the direction of men worrying *more* about their looks rather than women worrying less."[20]

Most participants were aware that clothing styles for men have become more body-hugging in recent years. Aaron liked this development:

> I've seen it a lot in the last several years where people have started wearing clothing that's much more, uh, size-appropriate, especially within men's clothing. Women have always had sizes that fit them. But men's clothing . . . has gotten much slimmer, and it's become much more size-appropriate. You don't see the blousing [shirts] . . . like you used to. And I'm not sure if that's because men in general are becoming more conscious of that? Or, if they're—or if the industry, you know, the major marketers (even like the Men's Wearhouse) . . . has kind of become conscious of the fact that maybe men wanna wear something more size-appropriate as opposed to "one size fits most."[21]

While many women would argue that our clothing sizes are more idiosyncratic than Aaron presumes, he raises an intriguing question about whether the slimmer-fitting clothing trend is driven by male consumers or by retailers. Aaron emphasizes that this type of silhouette is now available to the masses in mainstream stores such as Men's Wearhouse. Luca, whose interview excerpt began this chapter, has also come to accept the new style. "I guess now tighter pants are back on," he told me, "and when that started, I was kind of suspicious; I didn't think it looked very good. But then I noticed myself more and more appreciating that." Juxtaposing Aaron's and Luca's comments, we see that the slim-down in U.S. men's apparel has been a top-to-bottom affair, encompassing shirts, jackets, and pants. Despite the recent changes, several men who were from Europe or had spent time there still found U.S. men's clothing to be too baggy, too loose in its fit. And some U.S.-born men had reservations about the slim look, which works against traditional masculinity's downplaying of the body and appearance. The desired balance was, in the words of one interviewee, to "accentuate the body in a positive kind of way without being overboard around that kind of stuff."

Age came up repeatedly in men's discussions of the trend toward closer-fitting clothing. Aiden told me that "younger men prefer" slimmer pants: "If you go into Banana Republic"—a midprice retailer not associated with avant-garde fashion—"they don't carry boot-cut [pants] anymore. . . . Most of their pants taper." This was a problem for Aiden, who preferred wider-legged pants. Pointing out the window of the San Francisco restaurant we were chatting in, Aiden said, "The skinny jean thing is what's in right now—like that guy who's just walked by, or that woman who's walking that way, and probably the next person who walks by as well." When I asked George, who had expressed a desire to not make himself look older with his dress, why he thought tighter clothing was more popular at the moment, he said he couldn't explain it but could only tell me why *he* liked this style:

> Well, luckily I'm not overweight or, or big, so I think it helps. . . . The style nowadays, I think everyone wants to show their figure a little bit more, so I think it fits me a little better, and it just suits me a little more not having loose-fitting clothing. . . . The baggy clothing is out, and people are wearing more thin, clean, less baggy clothes. It's more modern-looking.

George described this trend as modern, getting away from the dated styles sometimes associated with older white-collar men. Unlike other participants (including gay and straight men of all ages), he didn't say that slimmer-fitting clothing is only for young, thin, or fit guys.[22]

Several men evoked this form-fitting clothing trend to explain why they thought that fashion was not for them.[23] Marc admitted, "I don't think I've ever had the figure for a lot of the kind of cutting-edge, sleek clothes." Like George, Marc used the word "figure" to refer to the male form; this is a word typically applied to women's bodies. Ed Hatcher, a white man from the Cincinnati sample who was nearing retirement, told another story of the body defying fashion and rebelling against clothing. He was responding to my question of whether any item stood out as the ugliest thing he had ever worn: "I know exactly what it was. It was a Ralph Lauren sweater—a V-neck. . . . But it wasn't your grandfather's

V-neck, which meant it was like almost skin-tight. . . . And the damn thing was so [tight] . . . I looked like a fool . . . like ten pounds of something shoved in a five-pound bag." The greater visibility of slim-fit men's clothing over the previous five to ten years had made several interviewees wonder whether this look would work for their bodies. More than a few concluded that it wouldn't. The discussion of skinny pants (and other body-hugging clothes) often led to talk about body image more generally, and in many interviews, men revealed their assessments of and struggles with their body weight, proportions, and other aspects of their physiques.

Ideal Bodies

Fatness is stigmatized in modern society.[24] Two insights from studies of the body are especially useful for understanding white-collar men's narratives. The first is the rise of "body projects" as part of a larger cultural shift toward self-improvement.[25] Through body projects (e.g., cosmetic surgery, dieting), people attempt to bring their external appearance in line with their internal sense of self or in line with the moral or aesthetic values of their society. Relevant to men's discussions of looking current, body projects are entangled with the experience and expression of modernity in different countries and locales.[26] Second, although negative connotations of fatness in the United States are not new, stigma, prejudice, and discrimination against people who are perceived as overweight are on the increase, especially in light of the body-projects discourse that makes people fully responsible for how they look and represents bodies as infinitely malleable.[27]

While antifat attitudes are present throughout the United States,[28] the proportions of people classified as heavier than average vary by location. For my research sites, the percentage of people who would be classified as overweight or obese (by the Centers for Disease Control) in Cincinnati is 62 percent; in New York City it is 60 percent and in San Francisco, 55 percent. The "obese" category alone includes 27% of Cincinnati residents, 22% of New York residents, and only 18% of San Francisco residents.[29] A few interviewees mentioned this variation in the prevalence of different body sizes. For instance, Ron opined, "Cincinnati, I think, has an obesity problem. . . . Everybody knows that. You go to New York or San Francisco—I think there're people here [who] don't realize quite how big they are." Carlos Calle, from the San Francisco sample, remarked that "many areas of California . . . are very health-conscious. Like, weight is not very visible. . . . You're like, 'really, there's no overweight people in the world, right?'" Perhaps Carlos and Ron were especially conscious of average body size because they worked for clothing retailers.

Many research participants raised the issue of body size and shape in describing other people's dress.[30] Nicholas Georgiou, a thirty-nine-year-old white man interviewed in Cincinnati, favored slimmer-cut clothing for men. He complained that he saw many white-collar men in Cincinnati wearing clothes that he thought too big and baggy for them. When I asked why he thought that was, he said, "I think a lot of it comes to fitness level, frankly. When you're feeling overweight, you don't wanna wear stuff that fits your body. You wanna hide."[31] Nigel Peters also claimed to see this pattern in New York: "Those sort of larger guys would probably wear the more bulky suits and perhaps it wouldn't work, [or] look as slick as, say, some of the thinner guys, who are probably more in tighter-fitting clothes." Here it is unclear whether the bulky suits make bigger men look less "slick" or whether it's their heavier bodies. Nicholas and several others thought that heavier men should resist the temptation to gravitate toward looser clothing. For example, Hans told me, "I think a number of people believe that by buying more spacious clothes, they will look slimmer, which is obviously a misconception." Despite the common saying that men and women want to "look good naked," it seemed that these men associated being thinner with looking good *in clothes*. As one interviewee put it, "If you work out . . . you fit your clothes better, so you've got a better style." Here the links between body projects (e.g., working out), the fit of clothes, and fashion production and consumption are exposed. You look better in clothes—especially the fashionable slim-fit styles of the moment—if you are thin, and you get thin or stay thin by engaging in particular bodily practices.

Interviewees in all three cities made anti-fat comments in the form of social critiques, as Ron expressed in relation to Cincinnati. Seeing that Sergio was a fan of the new, leaner look of men's clothing, I decided to play devil's advocate, asking him if he thought that sometimes people wear baggier clothes because they feel too heavy to wear slimmer-cut items. Sergio replied, "Yeah, but . . . it's also something that's *allowed* Americans to be overweight, right? . . . So it's almost like, what came first, oversized clothing or big Americans?" This chicken-and-egg perspective paints fatness as a social problem and obscures the feelings of the men and women who choose to cover themselves with more fabric than may be fashionable.

Several participants told me that men should make decisions about slim-fit fashions as well as other dress items based on a deep understanding of their bodies and the image they desired to project. Dave spoke about variations in size as simple matters of fact that should be acknowledged and dealt with through strategic dress practices:

> If you know what you're doing, based on your face shape, or like how fat
> you are or how thin you are, you kind of know what kind of collar you
> should get and what kind of tie knot you should wear. So it's very obvi-

ous if somebody is, let's just say very overweight, and they have a very narrow collar, and they have a very fat tie knot, they're doing everything wrong. . . . It's going to accentuate how fat you are. . . . If someone's very thin and they have a very wide-collared shirt, it's going to accentuate how thin your face is.

Sean also highlighted the challenges of being thinner, saying, "If you're a really strong, athletic person, you can—some things can work for you very well. If you're very skinny, kind of scrawny, and you're wearing oversized clothes, it doesn't work very well." Barney complained that he sometimes saw "guys dressing for the guy that they wish that they were, but they're not even close to," and he said that "part of picking clothes is understanding that." Barney figured that you could either get to know and accept your body type, or else, "if you really want to be that guy, well then, you are going to have to starve yourself for like a year and go to the gym four days a week." I realized that, while the thin imperative is omnipresent for women, these men saw two options—do the best with what you've got, or change it. Hating and subsequently altering the nonideal body was not the only way to go.

In general, my interviewees upheld the thin, fit, or muscular ideals of men's bodies prevalent in the contemporary United States. One man said he liked the emphasis in metrosexual subcultures on fitness because it was good for your health. Another, Ian Geary, a white man in his late fifties from the Cincinnati sample, spoke at length about changing body norms:

> What I find interesting is: when I was in my thirties, men in their fifties were so out of shape and they were near death as far as I was concerned. . . . But now that I'm more close to sixty than fifty, there are more men my age that are still very athletic . . . work out and take care of themselves and watch their diet and are still climbing mountains and doing all of this stuff. . . . By my age, my dad had two heart attacks. There's a picture of him in his mid- to late thirties with all of his friends sitting at my grandmother's dining room table. They all have chinos on and white shirts opened up, T-shirts underneath. Half of them are smoking cigars; the other half have cigarettes. And they're playing poker, and they're all sitting about two feet away from the table because they all have at least a thirty-six- to a forty-five-inch waist. You know, just all these round, World War II veterans having a great time, and isn't that life? . . . Yeah, they're all dead by this point. I think a lot of men in my generation, having grown up with that, are just much more health-conscious and aware.

Ian's nostalgic yet caustic recollection highlights changing body ideals over time and shows the potential roots of body projects among men in his generation. However, Ian didn't mention that today's masculine body projects partly result from social pressures that did not exist to the same degree for the World War II veterans whose cigar-clouded poker games he vividly remembered. Contemporary ideals of masculinity are more bodycentric than those of the mid-twentieth century, and men's bodies are more frequently bared in media and more openly commented on in social interaction. Health and fitness have emerged as a sort of modern morality, which Americans reject at their own social peril.

Weight and Body Image

Body size and shape, as many research participants noted, can affect a person's engagement with fashion and trends. An individual whose body is far from the thin or fit ideal may feel that fashion is not for him or her. Fabricio told me that he had lost eighty pounds over the previous year and that this changed the way he thought about and shopped for clothes. "That was a big transformation," he said as we talked in a tiny meeting room at his Manhattan office. "After I started losing weight, I started looking into other clothes . . . [with] a little bit more design in the shape. . . . I'm going to experiment a little bit more." He now had more options and felt more license to play with fashion, something that he had been interested in when he was heavier but had hesitated to participate in. I mused that some people (including many interviewees) thought fashion was for thinner guys, and Fabricio responded, "I mean, it's true."[32]

Across age groups, participants talked about their weight, often in self-disparaging ways. For example, Daniel told me that when he shops for work shirts, "I make sure it's not an athletic cut, because I'm not so athletic anymore." Later he returned to the topic of weight, saying, "I've lost my great metabolism and I've gained some weight; I just would never have the audacity or gall to put on something that is form-fitting and go out in public." Jordan Simms, a white Cincinnatian in his late thirties, said that sweaters were his favorite piece of clothing; he regularly wore them over his shirts. "I will be really open and honest with you," Jordan said. "I've put on a few pounds over the last few years." Jordan felt that (though "it's probably not even true") the sweater "hides some of the weight. . . . I do not feel comfortable in things that are really tight or form-fitting. . . . It emphasizes how much weight I've put on." The current trend in men's fashion is form-fitting, and Daniel and Jordan felt that their body weight and shape prevented them from participating in it even if they wanted to.

Several men lamented having gained weight in recent months or years and talked about how weight and clothes shopping related to each other. One interviewee told me that if he gained any more weight, he would have to stop buying clothes at Express, a midprice retailer of both men's and women's clothing, which was his favorite store. Another said his last shopping trip was precipitated by the fact that he was "eating out a lot more and gaining a little weight." A third said that he bought new shirts as soon as the ones he was wearing started to get tight around the neck. These weight fluctuations that many men claimed to experience could also cause them to avoid slim-fit clothing. Luke Gottlieb, a white man in his thirties, explained this in reference to a particular brand associated with traditional-fitting rather than slim-fitting clothing: "Brooks Brothers [shirts are] . . . kind of like the American staple of men's corporate wear. And the *cut* is the same on all of 'em. So whether I'm up ten pounds, down ten pounds, I can fit into it, I can button the collar." These men seemed to be following the advice of interviewees Barney, Sean, and Dave: they were aware of their body size and shape. One especially blunt research participant called himself "heavy-boned," built "like a nightclub bouncer," and "thuggish" in appearance. Thin men were often also self-critical, calling themselves such names as "tall, skinny bastard."

Not surprisingly in this age of body projects, weight-loss surgery, and television shows like *The Biggest Loser*, many interviewees who felt they were overweight engaged in bodily practices designed to slim down. In fact, Ed was engaged in an office-wide weight-loss contest when I met with him in Cincinnati. When I asked him to describe what he was wearing to work that day, he told me that he had purposely chosen lightweight clothes because it was the day of his weekly weigh-in. "Unbelievably complex planning goes into" that day's clothing selection, Ed told me, adding with a smile, "It's not working, by the way." Dave had reached a tipping point:

> These [shirts] are actually getting a little tight at the moment because I lost a lot of weight and then I had a bunch of shirts made, and . . . I am in the middle of a tough thing for work and so I'm not as active as I used to be and so they're starting to [get] a little tight. So it's kind of encouraging me to work out a little more. I'm like, okay, I'll have to back into a whole new wardrobe here if I don't get this under control.

Control over the body, social scientists tell us, is associated not only with masculinity but also with middle-class norms.[33] People who are seen as unable to control their own bodies—for example, women or the poor—occupy lower status than those who are thought to master the flesh, as Dave hopes to do. Controlling the body begins with monitoring it. Dave noticed when his shirts got tight and knew that he had gained exactly eight pounds since he had the shirts custom made.

As much as men complained about their weight and discussed needing to lose what they saw as extra pounds, there were also stories of victory over the fat body. One of the clearest indicators of this victory was a change in the way clothes fit or, more dramatic, the need to buy a new wardrobe. Frank Miller, a white twenty-four-year-old, had recently undergone gastric bypass surgery, subsequently losing nearly one hundred pounds. Gesturing to his shirt, he said somewhat apologetically, "I've had it for a while. . . . This is obviously too big." Jack Harrison told me he had lost "a sizable amount of weight" in the past year. He now had to try on clothes rather than just picking up something in his usual size. He reflected on his feelings after the weight loss and his changed relationship to dress:

> It's exciting because I'm like, oh wow, I can fit into . . . the thirty-four [waist pants] and have room, or I'm wearing a large versus an extra large. . . . I can get a fitted shirt versus just a regular shirt. So yeah, I mean there's—I guess there's a certain amount of pride about the appearance now because I feel like, I don't know if it's more popular, but . . . it just feels like you have a little more pride about being able to fit into things that maybe you didn't fit in before. You know, everyone likes to put that pair of jeans on that they're like, "oh, I won't wear those" and then all of the sudden you're like "wow, these fit great."

For Jack, the validation that came with wearing a smaller size led to feelings of pride and affected how appealing ("popular") he felt he was to other people. Other men also recounted big shopping trips after losing weight or being able to buy slim-fit clothing because they had shed some bulk. The reactions of coworkers and others were a meaningful reward for the men's investment in reducing their body size.

Frank recounted that since his surgery-induced weight loss, his colleagues had been teasing him, telling him, "Hey, good job" but also advising him to get some new shirts. Vince Lo, a man in his midthirties who identified as "American-born Chinese," was trying to lose weight with some success, and had also gotten positive reinforcement from his workmates. "They will say, 'Hey, your clothes are getting baggier. . . . They just want me to know that they are noticing" the weight loss, Vince said, adding that it "makes me feel good." He wanted to buy some new clothes, but he was waiting for his "weight to stabilize" before spending the money.

Vince was not the only one to view weight loss as an ongoing process. Tom, a thirty-six-year-old interviewee from the New York sample who identified racially as "just white," described his relationship to body weight and dress over time:

Earlier in my life, I was very overweight. I am now too, but not like I used to [be]. . . . I wore all dark colors because I felt they were more slimming. . . . I never really had a reason, like an incentive to actually buy nice clothes. It's like nothing's really going to look good on me, so, what the hell's the point, you know? But after I took off the weight, I did start buying nicer clothes. I would be like, hey, I'm actually excited about buying dress shirts because they look good on me.

Body projects are never really done. The path to self-improvement through altering the body has no finish line. Tom's body was no longer "ridiculously *fat*" (his words), but: "until I'm back to the weight I really want to be—I still want to lose about twenty more pounds—I'm not going to invest in any shirts that cost more than thirty or forty dollars: cheap. It just doesn't make sense." For Tom, further weight loss was not only desirable but inevitable. Other men also connected their weight-related aspirations to clothing, such as the participant who told me he had been hanging on to clothes that no longer fit him because if he lost ten pounds they would fit. Luke had bought a bunch of expensive new suits a couple of years before and then had gained weight and could not fit into them. Laughing, he told me, "That's my goal, to lose weight" so that he could get back into the pricey suits.[34]

Idiosyncratic Bodies

Weight was at the center of men's discussions about how their clothes—and other men's clothes—fit. Having a trim silhouette was a key component of the ideal image of the corporate worker's body and was seen as the necessary foundation for wearing fashionable items: slimmer shirts, pants, and suits. Men also expressed concerns about their height and other physical attributes. Scholars have shown that women tend to think of their bodies as a set of discrete, fragmentable parts.[35] Rather than assessing the whole, they zero in on parts of the body that they like or despise. This is even how psychological scales of body image work—they ask questions about the body as a whole, but also about people's feelings toward the different pieces that compose that body.[36] Men displayed this mind-set, splitting their bodies up and scrutinizing their component elements, sometimes harshly. As these comments were idiosyncratic rather than falling into easily identifiable patterns, I'll present a list, and then discuss what I think these bodily complaints mean.

- "I have an awkward size. . . . I'm bigger in the shoulders. . . . If I try to buy a shirt that's the right size for the rest of my body, it tends to be tighter through the shoulders, and that's very uncomfortable."

- "I'm kind of an odd size. . . . My torso is pretty long."
- "I'm also kind of unique too, because I'm a little shorter. It's harder to find stuff that fits. . . . I'm not like a cardboard cutout of a medium or a small."
- "I have big legs—thighs—because of [practicing] kung fu, so especially pants often don't fit me."
- "I'm not exactly an off-the-shelf kind of size either, so I tailor almost everything that I buy."
- "Suits here are made for the typical American male, who is bigger than me. . . . When I lived in Japan, I had an easier time finding clothes that fit."
- "Tucking in a polo shirt . . . makes me look about two feet tall."
- "I have a skinny neck for somebody of my gender [so I don't wear ties]."
- "Because of my height, I can't really buy very stylish clothes in my size. . . . I actually learned how to do my own altering 'cause I really can't afford to constantly be doing that and almost everything—every pair of pants I get have to be hemmed. So I've got my own sewing machine."
- "I happen to be large-shouldered, and I like my things to fit fuller."
- "I have a long torso; it means that my legs are shorter. So I won't wear baggy pants, because it'll just make my legs look that much shorter."
- "I have a preference for boot-cut jeans. . . . I have really oversized feet for my height, so there's like a logical reason for that."
- "Despite my somewhat normal appearance, I have fitting problems in pants. . . . I'm built—I have long legs and a short torso."
- "I'm a bigger dude; skinnier guys can wear like the straight leg [trousers]. . . . I need the fold on the bottom [cuffed pants], and then the bigger shoes."

Taken together, these comments argue for the uniqueness of each individual's body, the way that it can't just be put into clothes that are then expected to fit perfectly. Each body is seen by its inhabitant as quirky, odd, strange: definitely not generic.[37] Yet the clothing available to men is described as unyielding, not customized to their bodies. They want to conform to dress standards, but their bodies get in the way. Getting clothes tailored is one possible (if expensive) solution to this problem.

Interviewees' discussions of their proportions and bodily idiosyncrasies further distance them from dress practices that they claim to avoid, such as the blind following of trends or submission to fashion dictates. In these statements, they argue that they choose their dress because of the pressing material needs of the flesh rather than more abstract stylistic considerations. The association of

fashion with femininity and frivolity is upheld, as these men affirm their masculinity by stating the reasons they *need* to dress a certain way. Ironically, in the
very same comments, they describe their bodies in ways that we would typically
associate with women's body image and body talk.

Fashion, Fitness, and White-Collar Embodiment

Men's ideas about fashion and their feelings about bodies (their own and those
of others) are often linked. Why is this? Can we attribute the fashion-body link
to the rise of slimmer-fitting men's clothes in recent years, which has ironically
coincided with an increase in the number of Americans classified as overweight?
The timing of these two shifts may make it more likely that men will talk about
their weight publicly and decide whether to follow trends based on their self-
evaluated body type. But there is more going on here.

Through the anti-fat attitudes interviewees espoused, the ideal for the corporate worker's body becomes more—forgive the irresistible pun—fleshed out. I've
shown how men talk about dress, but here they're delving deeper, going beyond
the surface to reveal their feelings about the body that's wearing the suit, the
Dockers, or the jeans. Being fit, working out, and taking care of oneself are all
body projects and practices associated with the U.S. middle and upper classes
and supported by the research participants. They ridicule white-collar men who
do not approximate this ideal body shape, as with the research participant who
cracked up when describing his 280-pound boss squeezed into skinny jeans for
Casual Friday. They also, as we saw in Tom's narrative of being "ridiculously fat,"
berate themselves when they fall short of this ideal.

Men's body image struggles, as they emerge through these discussions, are
perhaps more like those of women than we previously assumed. They lament
their long torsos, large feet, and big shoulders. Some of these supposed flaws
are actually exaggerated forms of stereotypically masculine traits. For example, a
man may prefer overly large shoulders to slight, waif-like ones. (And we all know
what they say about big feet.) Yet we do see the progression of what surprised
Susan Bordo twenty years ago—men's slide into the land of body anxiety—and
these cultural shifts are especially pronounced in white-collar occupations, in
which image matters and men are required to "sell themselves."

Given the newly augmented social pressures on men to look good, dress well,
lose weight, and so on, why do they roundly reject fashion (by associating it with
extreme rather than classic styles) and hold their nose when they speak the word
"trendy"? As I see it, three interrelated factors act as obstacles to men's engagement with fashion: traditional or hegemonic masculinity, corporate conformity,

and the repudiation of frivolity. The first of these is self-explanatory: the idea still persists in the United States, despite the headway made by the metrosexual phenomenon, that real men aren't interested in fashion and don't worry too much about looks or clothes. One research participant put it this way: "If a bloke takes longer than a girl to get ready," that's a problem.

Corporate conformity is also an antifashion force in these men's lives. The oft-stated goal of fitting in in the white-collar workplace is seen as incompatible with being a trendsetter or taking fashion risks. The style to which men are expected to conform is generally conservative and subdued, adjectives not usually applied to cutting-edge fashion. As we've seen in other chapters, these workers are also concerned with being taken seriously and exuding professionalism.

Embodying seriousness requires a rejection of frivolity in dress and manner, which is not to say that play does not form a part of some office cultures. I found that it is often the most formally dressed offices that have the most boisterous workplace hijinks. Frivolity can happen once the work is done, but can still not be expressed through dress. There is a "safe zone" within which men can be seen as caring enough, but not too much, about their appearance and dress.[38] Too trendy is dangerous, but so is dress that's out of date.

Let's consider how these specific versions of antifashion corporate masculinity intersect with men's identities. Given scholars' claims that gay men have a more negative body image than straight men, I was surprised that gay and straight respondents spoke similarly about their bodies (e.g., pointing out specific flaws or problem areas).[39] Across lines of sexual orientation, participants also generally denigrated trendiness, aiming for stylish or classic rather than fashionable dress. The main difference in views on fashion emerged between black men (African American and immigrant-descended) and nonblack men. Black interviewees seemed to feel fewer qualms about using the F word or admitting that they kept track of dress trends. This speaks to the greater value placed on fashion and style in black cultures, as expressed in the lay theories of Jeff and other black participants (and in the academic literature). Men of color and immigrant men may already see themselves as being excluded from the dominant image of masculinity identified with white, U.S.-born men. Associated with marginalized masculinities no matter what they do, these immigrant and minority men don't forfeit any privileges by embracing their racial or ethnic groups' values regarding fashion.

In all demographic categories, men frequently used the language of body projects. They aimed for self-presentation through clothing that strategically conveyed identity and worth in the work world. They felt obligated to know their body type, to identify their physical flaws, and to maintain or work toward a fit body that was seen as under control and thus easy to dress.

COMFORT

'Cause I'm built for comfort
I ain't built for speed
But I got everything
That a good girl needs

From "Built for Comfort" by Willie Dixon

Describing his personal dress philosophy, Ron Varick, a fifty-six-year-old human resources executive in Cincinnati, brought up the blues. "You know, there's an old blues song: that 'I'm built for comfort, not for speed.' . . . I would say that's kind of how I view clothing. I much prefer to feel comfortable than to be stylish." He mentioned his weekend blue jeans, "probably two sizes too big." Ron had successfully resisted his wife's ongoing campaign to get him to wear more fitted jeans, because "it's more about comfort than it is about anything else with me."

Other men echoed Ron's desire for clothing that fit comfortably on the body, for *physical comfort*. Frank Miller's favorite item of clothing was a pair of Under Armor brand sweatpants, and he detailed their sublime physical comfort:

> They fit me perfectly. . . . They never shrink. . . . They don't cling. They're just all around the best thing. And I can sleep in them perfectly. If it's really hot out, they're cool. If it's really cold out, they're warm. I don't know what their deal is, but they're my favorite. . . . It's the most comfortable thing that I own.

Richard Schneider, who served as the one-man IT department at his small company, privileged physical comfort in his work clothing:

> I'm trying to keep myself as comfortable as possible, so you know, I'm not going, "man, these pants are itchy" or, you know, "my shirt's cutting into my—" . . . I don't want any of that type of distraction. I want to be able to focus and be comfortable, so I tend to do better work when I'm like this [*gestures to his T-shirt, khaki cargo pants, and multicolored sneakers*]. . . . At some point I just decided that it's more important to be comfortable than anything. And you're going to do better if you're comfortable. . . . As long as it's comfortable, then let's focus on if it looks good later.

Domingo Sala worked in accounting, spending the bulk of his often-long work-days at his computer, and he tried to maximize physical comfort: "I like to be comfortable, so I keep my slippers under my desk." He said he would remove his slip-on dress shoes and use "little Bath and Body Works roll-y things" to massage his feet. Other men reported preferring slip-on or loafer-type shoes because they appreciated being able to kick them off at their desks.

What's the connection between physical comfort and style? Is opting for physical comfort always a fashion death sentence? Aaron Levitt believed that comfort and a professional look could go together for white-collar men, but *style* was another thing. "Maybe if they're older and they're a little bit heavier, they wanna wear something that's more comfortable than it is stylish," Aaron—himself a young, thin man—hypothesized. "That's why they buy the items that are still appropriate, but they're larger, they're more comfortable." Eli Abrams, who preferred a slimmer fit in both shirts and pants, admitted, "I definitely think it looks better. . . . I question whether it feels better." He had become more comfortable wearing tighter clothes, but it took time. Andy Lipmann connected the physical comfort found in loose, casual clothing to a spirit of rebelliousness or independence unique to the United States:

> I think that there's kind of this like weird construction that Americans have towards clothing . . . that if you wear something that fits, then it's going to be *constricting*. You know, but it's like, if I put on something that feels too baggy now [that I wear slim-fit clothing], I feel like a blob. . . . It doesn't feel right. . . . I think it's just like . . . if they can't wear their Tevas [a brand of casual sandals] and like, khaki shorts to the office that [*deeper voice*] The Man's out to get them and he's keeping them down. It's like, no, it's actually 'cause it just looks really sloppy.

In Andy's cultural-historical framework, some American men's distaste for fitted clothing resonates with our nation's motives for westward expansion, purchasing big SUVs, and space exploration—bigger is better, and we need room to move around.

The more men I spoke with, however, the more I sensed that there were multiple meanings to the word "comfort."

Social comfort involves the relationship between self and others as mediated by dress. People feel socially comfortable when they are conforming to existing norms. Ted Demetriou, who worked in advertising, aimed to dress in a way "that doesn't make . . . the people around me uncomfortable." Richard also referenced others, saying, "Sometimes my comfort level is other people around me who I'm working with knowing that I'm dressed to the occasion; that makes me feel comfortable." Marc Hoffmann said his firm's mantra was to have fun doing good work and making money. "So, some of the things that we do are [about] how you encourage people to interact and to relax," Marc explained, saying this environment would be difficult to achieve "in a dark suit and a pressed shirt." For Marc, the relaxed image and easy interactions were a result of a collective decision that "we can do our work dressed in a way that's comfortable to us." He thought his employees were both physically and socially comfortable in such a setting.

People also feel comfortable if they're dressed in a way that seems congruent with their sense of self. I call this *identity comfort*, and some interviewees described it as feeling "comfortable in their own skin." Cincinnatian Paul Massey provided an out-of-work example. "We'll go out," he said, referring to himself and a male friend, "and I'll put on a sport coat, and he goes, 'Why are you wearing that? It makes me look bad.'" Paul would reply that "it just makes me comfortable, 'cause I'm not comfortable just going out in a T-shirt like some people are. . . . I feel like, uncomfortable, like I'm not putting my best [*pause*] person forward." Paul, despite his casually dressed friend's objections, wears a jacket because it makes him feel comfortable, feel like *him*. It's not about how the clothing feels on his body (physical comfort) or what others are wearing (social comfort) but about attempting to convey his individuality—his best person—through dress. Social comfort and identity comfort can go hand in hand, as for Luiz Rodrigues, who opined, "I think it's a statement of self-confidence, the way you dress. . . . When I dress appropriately, I feel much more comfortable with myself." Luiz is speaking the language of the self, yet the context is appropriateness, being dressed as others are. In contrast, Sean Albertson prioritized identity comfort, saying, "I definitely dress myself, and what makes me most comfortable is what I like, and I roll the dice." Rolling the dice means not being able to predict how others will react.

These different meanings of comfort were interconnected. When I asked Tony Hirsch, who was in human resources, about common mistakes job candidates make during interviews, he mentioned "wearing clothes that they don't normally wear." You could tell if someone was physically uncomfortable, for example, if he was pulling at the collar of his shirt. Such physical discomfort (*ties are not for me*) could reflect a deeper sense of identity discomfort (*this job is not for me*). When asked what advice he would give to a young man entering the corporate world, Caleb Green said, "More than anything, go with your gut and what you feel comfortable in, both in terms of what you feel physically comfortable wearing, and what you feel kinda psychologically comfortable in, in terms of appearance."

Comfort: two simple syllables that carry multiple meanings in this white-collar world. It's physical, in the way that clothes feel against the skin and the frame of the body. It's social, in the way that we fit in with others, feel and look like we belong. It's about identity, in the way that we choose our dress to express our personalities, hoping to be appreciated or at least accepted by others or simply not caring: "Dressing for yourself, and fuck everyone else," in the words of one unusually nonconformist participant.

BEING/BECOMING THE BOSS
Office Hierarchies and Dress

Despite the attention that innovative management structures have received in recent years, nearly all for-profit companies in the United States are organized hierarchically.[1] The person or people at the top bring home bigger salaries (and bonuses, in some firms), and hold more status both within and outside the workplace. In this chapter, I argue that dress and appearance play a role in not only representing but also maintaining this corporate hierarchy. Their dress is something that these white-collar men feel they can control, which is meaningful given the instability and unpredictability of employment in today's corporate world. The strategic crafting of a personal image that communicates competence and success is particularly important for those who aspire to move up in business. But how do the links between status and dress get forged, and how do men learn who can and should wear what?

A new hire will look to his peers to help gauge the level of dress his position requires. The office is a place to see and be seen, a simultaneously public and private space.[2] This looking happens in all directions. People notice what the boss is wearing, and bosses also assess subordinates' appearance. By boss here, I mean anyone who has people report to him or her within the company.

There are almost always multiple bosses in an office, and their titles may vary widely (e.g., *manager*, which is typically lower than *director*, which is lower than *partner*, etc.). The person at the very top—usually a man—may be the most visible individual in the organization, and his self-presentation reflects some aspects of what my interviewees call "company culture." His wardrobe is expected to communicate high class status and power, and I found that employees can become critical or perplexed if it does not. To ask people about hierarchy and their position in an organization is also to ask implicitly about mobility—can they see themselves moving up or (God forbid) down the so-called corporate ladder in the future? How does clothing, or appearance more generally, relate to status and mobility within a business organization? Using dress as an entry point, I examine what it means to be the boss, to become the boss, to relate to the boss, and to look at corporate leaders from afar. From these stories, we learn about men's expressed opinions on workplace power dynamics and their identities as bosses and employees.

One interviewee told me a story about his office's "front desk guy," who was wearing a T-shirt at his post one day. The CEO of the relatively small company "sent him home to put on a shirt and tie, and he said, 'That's how I want you dressed.'" This anecdote was worthy of recounting to an academic researcher, not just because of the overt display of power but also because it narrates a face-to-face encounter between the low man in the corporate hierarchy and the man at the top. More often in my interviewees' workplaces, these two ends of the chain of command are separated by many levels of managers and bureaucratic barriers. Yet workers at lower levels are not ignorant of what's going on in the upper levels of the corporate structure.

White-collar men routinely talked about their boss, even without being asked specifically, and also about their "boss's boss," "executives," or "the leadership." Many mentioned the man (it was always a man) who ran the organization—that is, the CEO or president of the company. In this chapter, I use talk about bosses' dress to understand men's identities as members of hierarchical organizations. Nearly everyone in this study had a boss, and more than three-quarters of the research participants had people reporting to them, either currently or in previous positions, so they had also been someone's boss.[3] This allowed me to learn about relating to bosses *and* relating to subordinates, about being *and* having a boss, and about the ways that looking *at* the boss is connected to looking *like* the boss or being looked at *by* the boss. Here too my findings show that privilege is associated with conforming to bodily and clothing norms.

Boss as Audience

I asked interviewees who was the audience for their work dress. Some rejected the framing of the question entirely, perhaps because of the association of heterosexual masculinity with men doing the looking rather than being looked at (gender scholars call this being the agent of the "male gaze" as opposed to its object).[4] These men told me that there was no audience, or that the audience didn't matter: they dressed for themselves or to be comfortable or appropriate. This claim fits with traditional notions of masculinity in the United States, in which men are the lookers rather than the ones looked at, directing their gaze at women. The next most common answer, however, referenced hierarchical office interactions: the audience was the boss or other people who "outranked" the interviewee.[5] Daniel Moorehouse, interviewed in Cincinnati, told me that he thought men dressed for their boss "or their boss's boss." He said he considered these audiences when dressing for work: "In my role, you know, it's not unheard of to be in the Vice President's office at a drop of a dime. . . . You don't want to have to be worried about what you're wearing if that happens. So, you just always think about it beforehand." Another Cincinnati participant, Adam Gerber, expressed similar thoughts: "I'm dressing . . . to appease my manager, [and] my director. I want them to know that I'm taking it seriously." Adam figured that his boss and boss's boss would be looking at his dress as an indication of the seriousness of his commitment to the job.

Other interviewees concurred, saying that they dressed for "people up the ladder" or "to present myself to the higher, the upper management." Femi Banjo, who worked in IT in New York, opined that "some IT guys, they feel like, 'hey, I'm in the back and nobody can see me,'" leading them to think that their appearance is unimportant. He went on: "And that's *true*, buuuut,"—dragging out the word—"it's also not, 'cause the CIO [chief information officer] has to see you." The power dynamics are clear: (1) men dress in particular types of work clothing; (2) that dress is viewed by men and women located above them in the corporate hierarchy; and (3) some sort of evaluation is made. This power is also gendered, as subordinate men present themselves to be looked at by bosses, taking on a stereotypically feminine position by becoming the object of the gaze. Since most research participants' bosses were men, there is a potentially homoerotic component to this self-presentation and the act of looking that it assumes.[6] As San Francisco interviewee Caleb Green put it, when it comes to whom men dress for, "often, in male-dominated workplaces, it's for other males."[7]

Just a few weeks into his job at a New York real estate firm, Bryan Lee had caught the eye of the top man in the company: "The CEO commented that I dress as well, if not better, than he does, and I should teach the rest of the guys how to dress." Yet looking less than put-together may sometimes be the goal. Brad Jennings, whose job in San Francisco involved handling labor union negotiations, explained:

> Seriously, sometimes I want to look disheveled; I want people to think, "Oh my God, Brad's really harried; he's got two big negotiations going on." . . . So sometimes I actually intentionally appear a little disheveled. Now I may not necessarily [do anything] with my clothing, but I'll walk in holding a book or my pen, you know, and what little hair I have all, you know [*mimes mussing his hair*].

Brad told me he anticipates being looked at by higher-ups and peers, and clearly he thinks strategically about how to visually communicate that he is working hard on weighty company business.

In chapter 1, I discussed the importance of the job interview as a magnified moment in which a candidate's appearance is scrutinized. In that scenario, the audience for a job applicant's dress is the potential boss and perhaps potential future coworkers. Once the candidate is hired, there may be other magnified moments in which the boss wields great power and appearance matters more than usual. Brett Mason, who worked for a Manhattan advertising outfit, told me about one of these instances:

> *Brett*: I did have a designer who was fairly slovenly, who came to me and my boss and asked for a raise. And he was wearing slippers . . .
> *Erynn*: In the conversation about the raise?
> *Brett*: In the conversation about the raise. . . . Some people say—you know, think it's fine. I mean, if he's doing the right work and he's a valued designer, because we are all about the product. . . . you can wear whatever you wanna wear, if your product is great. Um, but at the same time, I think I need, as a [*laughing*] older person in the studio, to tell these guys that you might be able to get away with it here, but if you're not doing a great job—and he wasn't doing a great job—then going in and asking [for] a raise while wearing slippers probably isn't a great idea.

This anecdote shows the importance of boss-as-audience during critical career moments, such as a meeting to request a salary increase. In Brett's office, dress expectations were much less formal for designers than for directors or account representatives. After all, the employee wasn't sent home for wearing his slippers. But there were limits to the tolerance for casual dress in moments during which employer-employee obligations and relationships were being renegotiated. Wilson Turner, who ran a business services office in San Francisco, mentioned another of these moments: "If you are going to see your boss for your yearly appraisal, then yeah, you might wear jeans and a T-shirt, but that jeans and T-shirt might be a little bit smarter" than usual. Though Wilson's office had a business formal dress code except on Fridays, he imagined that even employees in a casual-dress workplace would want to dress up a bit for a performance evaluation.

Many men at different levels of their organization's hierarchies agreed that the boss was an important possible audience for work dress. However, the boss is also looked at by others, from both above and below (except for CEOs or presidents, who usually have only people below them).[8] Interviewees often said that, in their companies, the higher up a man was, the more he dressed up. Participants had a lot to say about how bosses' dress differed and how it could affect the dress of subordinates.

Boss on Display

Participants often associated more formal dress with higher-level positions. Lev Asgarov, a New York interviewee who worked in finance, specifically saw suits as the distinguishing dress, telling me, "The higher-up managers and directors wear suits and ties, but no one else does." Though most people at Sean Albertson's big technology company (based in the San Francisco area) dressed casually or at most in business casual, he said he saw a difference with the top brass, who wore suits and ties more frequently: "Upper management in the big jobs, they play role model, if you will."

Sean also noted that he saw older men, regardless of whether or not they were executives, dressing more formally. Ethan Mueller, who worked in the marketing department of a large company in Cincinnati, also mentioned age and status as determinants of formal dress, and wondered about the relationship between the two:

> Our executives wear suit[s] and ties at work, so at a certain level and above, and all those men, and you know, the women too, the women obviously don't wear suits, but they're dressed much more formal than probably the standard middle-management employees are. And I've always been curious, is that a function of the fact when they were here kind of . . . starting out, it was more formal, and they've just carried that throughout their career? Or if it's because they feel like, "I'm a vice chair of the company, now I should be wearing a suit and tie?" If I had to guess, I would say it's probably a little bit of both.

So workers like Ethan not only are looking at the higher-ups in the company, but are also interested in how and why they dress differently than lower-level employees. Many executives in U.S. companies are older than Ethan, who was thirty-three when I interviewed him. This makes it difficult to separate their status in the organization from their membership in generations that were socialized into more formal dress norms.

Not all dressier bosses from the men's accounts were older. George Wong, a San Francisco interviewee in his thirties, often found himself the most dressed-up person in the room when visiting clients in Portland—known for its relatively casual local dress culture—with a salesman who worked under him. He thought they might "discount" him for being dressier than the laid-back norm in the Portland business world. But he surmised with a shrug that "I'm just his boss and they're like, 'okay, maybe this guy dresses up a bit more because he is the boss."

Al Elkin, an HR executive in New York, reported wearing a suit to his business casual office nearly every day. He made this choice precisely because he was the boss and felt the need to dress more formally than the official dress code:

> If I'm going to be responsible for the enforcement of policies and proce-
> dures, than I have to be *above* them. So, while I'm not *solely* responsible
> for the dress code policy and procedure, I *do* have to, on occasion, ad-
> dress it. And if I'm the one who's going to address it, or the people who
> work for me are, then we cannot *violate* it.

It matters here that Al Elkin supervises a team of employees and that his job is
in human resources, the arm of the organization tasked with setting and enforcing the dress code. He was just one of many bosses who told me they purposely
dressed up more than their subordinates.

Several interviewees pointed out that bosses' more formal dress was due to
their different material conditions. A common sentiment was "They have more
money than we do, so of course they dress better." According to Pete Costa, in his
corporate retail office in San Francisco, dress "depends on what your position level
is." While most were wearing casual or business casual, upper management, which
he defined as directors and above, tended to dress up more and have a "higher
price-point outfit" from what he could tell. Others agreed that higher-ranking
folks could "afford more" and "junior people don't make as much." Timothy Stein
characterized his boss at a Manhattan hedge fund as a fashion-conscious lover
of shopping with expensive tastes. Timothy's explanation: "I have a budget constraining my life; he doesn't." When Louis Katz told me that the only people in his
office who seemed like they dressed up or put thought into their dress were the
bosses, I asked him why he thought that was. "They're more vain," he replied flatly,
adding, "and they have more money to spend than we do."

A couple of interviewees said that in their workplaces bosses were not always
more dressed up than folks on the lower rungs of the company ladder. For example, Marc Hoffman, who ran a Cincinnati architecture firm, said "You earn
your ability to be casual" as your status increases. Pierre Molyneux, who often
dealt with high-ranking corporate officials in his job, repeated a saying he had
heard, that "the higher you are on the hierarchy, the less suits you wear," with the
exception of what he called "very formal" organizations such as IBM. In these
accounts, power has the effect of loosening restrictions on dress, as bosses are
protected from some of the criticisms leveled at lower-ranking employees.

People who lead teams or groups are more visible than those who constitute the
rank and file of those groups, and they may interact more with outsiders. Travis
Jones, who had experienced significant upward mobility at his Manhattan advertising company, reflected on what it means to become the boss:

> You're playing the role. . . . Dressing the part is just as important as being
> true to who you are. When you get into more senior levels . . . you spend

more time in front of clients, and . . . you're a bit more prepared on a daily basis to play that role, so there isn't sort of the natural flip back and forth, where one day you're gonna wear jeans and T-shirt because you know you don't have a client meeting, and then the following three days, suit. What ends up happening [is] you're just gonna start wearing a suit [every day]. Right, you either naturally fall into that role or you just become more conscious [that] the lion's share of your time is spent in what might be the uniform of a more senior person.

What Travis described was not an overnight transformation in dress when he began managing others, but a subtle realization that a new role might mean dressing up more often. Eventually it becomes easier to just dress more formally for the whole workweek. Travis's statement shows the tension that some men experience between "dressing the part"—in this case, embodying the social and structural role of the boss—and wearing what you want, "being true to who you are." The theme of conformity versus individualism was also present in other men's narratives of being the boss.

So bosses are looking, assessing the self-presentation of those who work for them, but they are also being looked at. This bidirectional visibility is crucial for understanding how bosses affect the dress and other behaviors of subordinates and how bodies are constrained and privileged in business organizations.

Boss as Influence

Most research participants agreed that the people above them in the corporate hierarchy, especially their direct supervisors, influenced their work dress to some degree. They mentioned direct forms of influence, such as explicit enforcement of standards and simple communication of expectations, but also indirect forms, such as employees' emulating the boss's appearance and the boss's setting a tone for dress in the group.

Direct Effects

It's easy to see a boss's influence on employees' work dress when he or she en-forces rules in a strict or harsh manner or punishes dress that is seen as out of bounds. Some bosses go beyond written rules or official dress codes to proscribe their personal pet peeves regarding clothing or appearance. Men shared several examples of such enforcement behaviors. An anecdote from Nigel Peters, men-tioned in an earlier chapter, is worth revisiting here for what it says about the boss's power. Nigel told me that on his first day on the job at a New York recruiting firm, he went out for drinks with some members of his team after work. His dress shirt had a pocket on the chest, and, according to Nigel, "My boss came up to me and ripped it off." In the interview transcript, my reaction of *"Really?"* is italicized because of the degree of surprise in my voice. "In a pub, yeah," replied Nigel. Was it a new shirt? He confirmed that it was. This is the most dramatic example I encountered of a boss's enforcing dress norms (I use the word "norms" rather than "rules" because pocketed shirts were not explicitly prohibited by the dress code). In this case, the company culture was based on competition among salespeople, playful ribbing, and one-upmanship, so this action by the boss was less shocking than it might have been in other settings.

More often, bosses used words rather than actions to bring attention to dress violations. In some offices, such as Ken Wetzel's financial services firm in Cincinnati, this verbal correction of dress is seen as part of the company culture. As we chatted in my campus office, Ken told me that in his workplace, "it is very common for people's superiors to call them out if they are dressed in a way that they [the managers] don't like." He described one "woman manager" who was especially straightforward about her preferences for employees' clothing beyond the dress code requirements. Ken recalled hearing her say that "anyone who wears brown shoes to work doesn't deserve to move up in the company." Jon Harper from New York didn't remember seeing many instances of enforcement in his office, but he did recount, "My old boss grew out a beard while on vacation, and someone told him to get rid of it, like, immediately." Jack Harrison managed the local office of a national business services firm in Cincinnati. When I asked him how he would handle dress code infractions, he answered: "If you don't fall in line, I might not send you home, but I definitely make a comment like, 'You're going to see a client. It's inappropriate that you're in a golf shirt.' Or 'It's inappropriate that you don't have a jacket on.'"

Other bosses were reportedly a little softer in their critiques of workers. Timothy recalled the time he "was dressed casually [and] not on a summer Friday," when such dress would be common in his office. He encountered the CEO and founder of the company, whom he described as an "old guy." When he saw Timothy's dress, the CEO asked, laughing, "Are we comfortable?" Because of the organization's structure, this high-status person didn't have direct control over Timothy's day-to-day work. Still, he said, "I noticed it, and remember it, obviously."

Some bosses may allow for dialogue when there is disagreement over dress practices. Consider the following anecdote from George, who managed a national team of salespeople:

> So my guy in Portland, he dresses always very casual to meetings. . . . He wears almost sneaker-looking things . . . they're pretty much sneakers.

And a polo shirt or a short-sleeved shirt or short-sleeved button-up shirt. Casual, and then just jeans. He can get away with it because, I think for him, you know, he's also older and more experienced. And, I actually called him out on it once. . . . I told him, "Can't you dress up a little bit more?" I tried to give him a hard time and he told me, "This is how the customers dress, and this is how it is up here." And I was like, okay, fine, we'll let it go; unless there's an issue with it, I'm not going to bother with it.

George's usual work dress when visiting clients consisted of a button-down, long-sleeved dress shirt, dress pants, and dress shoes. When he tried to get his "guy in Portland" to adopt this more formal dress, the employee pushed back. George relented, given the salesman's age, experience, and knowledge of the local dress culture.

Communicating dress norms more subtly took other forms as well. Dave Baker, an investment consultant in Cincinnati, noted that the president of his company gave out Brooks Brothers gift cards at the holidays, which he saw as an understated way of encouraging a particular style of white-collar dress.[9] Clark Landon, who worked in sales in the San Francisco area, was frustrated with what he described as the sloppy, "dumpy" style of a new hire in his department. While Clark confessed that he would love to say to this employee, "Dude, you're at work!" he was also considering a kinder, gentler technique:

(a) Because I'm over fifty, and (b) because he's working with me and for me, I'm a lot more comfortable to say, "Hey, you know what I think? . . . Let's go together, I'll buy you a pair of slacks. . . . I think you're gonna look better and feel better if you do this." The interesting thing is, the guy's thirty-one, so you'd think he'd have it figured out by now, but . . . I'm thinking about havin' that conversation.

Another boss in his early fifties, Carl Adelman, took a similar paternalistic approach to what he saw as substandard dress. If one of the guys he managed came into the office with shoes that looked "horrible or a mess," Carl told me, "I'd say, 'You know, listen, let's get a shine' . . . offer to go with him to take him to get his shoes shined. 'Cause I think that's important." These milder interventions are still clear, direct messages from the boss about which aspects of appearance matter and about the value of conforming through dress.[10]

Indirect Effects

Men described bosses' indirect influence on subordinates' dress in two ways: (1) employees emulate the boss's style or level of dress; and (2) the boss sets the tone for dress within the company, office, group, or department.

Some participants said that their boss had a workday look that they would like to or should emulate. For example, Vince Lo recalled asking his manager where he bought his clothes. When the manager told him that he shopped at Jos. A. Bank, Vince said, "I intentionally went to that store and bought clothes from there."[11] When I interviewed Brett, he mentioned that his company's new CEO was "fairly casual." He thought this noteworthy because "everyone's sort of looking at their boss and what they're wearing, and trying to emulate that." Emulation can also involve people who are more senior in the company but not a man's direct supervisors. John Wentz, with a Bay Area tech firm, said that when he attended important meetings, "the heads of state"—high-level executives—"are essentially in work-out clothes. . . . There's really no guidance . . . that you should wear this or wear that." Since the big bosses didn't seem to feel dressing up was a priority, John figured that his relatively casual dress was fine. Likewise, Daniel claimed to look at what the head of his department was wearing, telling me that if he employed a similar level of dress, he thought, "Okay, well, I'm dressing like they dress, so I must be in the right ballpark here."

Aaron Levitt, a new employee of a Cincinnati-area healthcare company, affirmed this strategy, observing that imitation went beyond appearance:

> If you wanna be an executive—It's kind of like when you go out to dinner. And you know, you've never really been out to dinner with a boss before. You don't order alcohol unless they do first. You don't touch your food until they touch theirs. You kind of mirror their movements, because you're assuming that, not necessarily that they're right, but that's what's gonna make them the most comfortable. So, same thing with your attire. It's—you follow the leader. And then, later if you find yourself in a leadership position that allows you to deem what's appropriate and what's not, then you tell your employees, or your team . . . those who report to you, "This is what makes me comfortable."

While newer hires like Aaron may be hyperattentive to the behaviors of their bosses, since they need to learn the ropes and find ways to fit in, more senior workers also talked about looking to their boss as a model. These accounts illustrate how bosses' power is experienced in everyday interactions in and beyond the physical space of the office. Interviewees linked emulation of the boss to upward mobility within the organization, as with Aaron's aspiration to one day be emulated by his own employees.

Nine men used the exact phrase "setting the tone" to define a less direct type of influence. When I asked Carl, the top man in his office, why he didn't often participate in Casual Friday, he said "I kinda like to set the professional tone." Jack Harrison, who held a similar structural position, agreed:

> I feel like I set the tone. . . . The folks that I would take direction from, the leaders within our company, you know, when they come to town, I try to emulate that same type of appearance and I think it does, it sets the tone for the new hires, [and] the folks that have been here forever, you know, they all just fall in line.

Jack's tone, then, originates above him, with the leaders of the company. His statement delineates a chain of influence in which he is the middleman between the corporate overlords and the lowliest new hires. Tone may also include the degree to which bodily self-presentation matters in a work group. Adam noticed that at his workplace, "the hot button for some managers is appearance and dress . . . [and for] others it's not." Jim Shaw, who led a human resources team, agreed, remarking that "if the boss has an expectation, and the boss is tightly wound, I think a man would be a little more tightly wound in the way they appear." Knowing how high appearance is on your boss's list of priorities is seen as indispensable for making a good impression.

If bosses set the tone for dress and other aspects of group culture or practice, then a new person at the top can change that tone. Brad recalled a time that this happened at his company:

> We had a CEO back in the nineties who was very anti-business casual, he hated it. And this was when business casual was becoming the rage; it was the dot-com era and all that. . . . The minute we knew he was retiring, everybody, there was this buzz going on and [people saying], "The minute he's gone, it's business casual," and that's exactly what happened. It was interesting. It really did have an impact, impacted all of us.

When Brad talks about the tone set by corporate leaders, he highlights the role of these leaders in shaping the relationship between individuals and organizational structures. Expectations for dress (and other work-related practices) can be introduced by a particular boss or CEO, and people beneath him or her will adapt to those expectations, which get translated into directives. In contrast to what happened at Brad's company, the tone set by a previous leader can be carried on by subsequent managers or presidents because "it's the way we've always done things."

Moving On Up

One version of the American Dream evokes the image of a white-collar worker beginning at the bottom of a corporate organization and gradually working his way up to the top. Many of the younger men I spoke with seemed to envision for themselves this unbroken path of increasing success, pay, responsibility, and status. Upward mobility within a company or field appeared in the men's accounts in a few different forms. First, they saw a connection between rising up through the ranks and changing dress. Second, they related personal dress to career aspirations, often repeating the cliché "Dress for the job you want, not the job you have."[12] Third, several men expressed concern that overdressing could be seen as threatening and could be poorly received by upper management.

Some participants assumed that as a worker's status increases, his or her dress will change. This is one possible explanation for bosses' supposedly more formal style. As Rohan Mehta, an early-career corporate accountant in Cincinnati, put it, "I can totally see somebody moving from a manager position into a director-level position and he would start wearing a tie. . . . You know, you would be dealing with the CFO or whatnot. So you would want to make sure you dress, even if it's too much, it's—too much is never bad. . . . It's bad when you are underdressed." Domingo Sala said that the higher-ups at his healthcare company dressed more formally and told me, "Maybe I would be like that if they moved me up." Evoking the idea of an audience for work dress, Domingo reiterated that "in the corporate world, a guy dresses for whoever's on top. I think so! So the people above will notice, right?" He saw putting effort into dress as an indicator of ambition; people who try to dress well for work "are dressing for the higher-ups and they want to present themselves as someone that they can move up on the leadership scale." Domingo's thinking is typical of the corporate world more generally. Just as looking good in a suit is taken as a predictor of career success or a signal of a candidate's fit during a job interview, dressing well once he has the job can be seen as signaling potential for upward mobility.

In his previous job, when Eli's boss took maternity leave, he assumed some of her duties. He recalled, "I made a conscious decision to stop wearing a hoodie and sneakers and wear a collared shirt and a jacket." While Eli didn't notice a change overnight in his status at work, he felt that "over a couple of months of dressing that way, people took me more seriously." He related that wearing more formal, professional clothing made him act differently and feel that "this job actually is important, and I'm important to the company." When he dressed more formally, people "responded to that," giving him more respect. Even if a higher-status role is temporary, as in Eli's case, it can trigger changes in dress and transform relationships with others in the workplace.

In recounting his ascent in the company, Brad emphasized care and attention to dress:

> I think when I was early in my development as an executive, I was very conscious of [dress and appearance] because I was moving up . . . in the company, and I wanted to get into future positions, and I knew that that had an influence. I'd seen other people who perhaps didn't care as much about that, and you know, if I'm in a room and if there are people who outrank me, for lack of a better term, who might have influence on my future career, I certainly want to stand out from everyone else, and dress is part of that.

Ironically, Brad "stands out" by conforming—conforming to the expected dress of a soon-to-be executive. Those who cannot embody this stereotype may hurt their chances for promotion. Now having achieved a relatively high position in the company, Brad feels less pressure regarding dress and appearance. He is thoughtful about his self-presentation, telling me that "looks are important." But today, "having been with the company so long," when he is just working in his office, Brad says he doesn't care too much about what he's wearing: "There's not people here I need to influence, so whatever, I mean, they know me, I know them, kind of thing." In this conception, the importance of dress fluctuates not only depending on the immediate situation but also over the course of an individual's career. Dress was a pressing issue for Brad when he was a young executive trying to get promoted, but now that he has gone probably as far as he will up the corporate ladder, he feels less motivated. In his view, the importance of dress diminishes once you meet a certain level. Here he is in disagreement with many other interviewees.

A well-worn adage in the U.S. corporate world dictates that workers dress for the job they want rather than the job they have. Nine interviewees repeated this saying verbatim in our conversations, many expressed the same idea in other words, and I've often heard it when talking informally to people about my research on work dress. Rohan said, "I always dressed a level above . . . where my position is" because this strategy "shows how mature you are, how much responsibility you're willing to take, and how much you're willing to contribute." Ryan Carter, who worked in the accounting department of a large Cincinnati-based company, said that dressing "a grade above the environment" of his business casual office was something that he and his peers in accounting all did. Lev reported only recently hearing this axiom around his office. He attributed it to "newer managers" who "want people to dress up more." Lev was concerned that this push for more formal dress predicted a shake-up in his company's structure (it turned out that he was right, as he was laid off shortly after our interview). Ted Demetriou reported receiving this advice directly from his supervisor at a Cincinnati advertising firm: "You want to dress to that next level. You want to dress to the next rung on the ladder. . . . If you want to be seen as a junior person, you dress down. If you want to be seen as . . . a little bit more sophisticated, then you'll dress up." Ted took his boss's counsel to heart, and his dress in a mostly casual office tended toward business casual. Dressing above your current position, in this view, is evidence of ambition and what we might call promotability—the potential for upward mobility within the organization. Domingo extended this concept to behavior, saying that if you want to "step up," you should not only dress but also "act like you are in that role already."

Several men countered or questioned the dress-for-the-job-you-want mantra. Ryan was a younger guy who liked dressing up and would be happy wearing a suit to work every day (which would be "unheard of for someone in [his] position"). He reflected on appropriate dress when meeting with higher-ups: "As an analyst . . . if I were to go into the meeting with a sports coat [on], I would be looked at as snooty or I'm trying to be a bigger deal than I am. . . . I think that's acceptable for more senior-level people." Ryan mentioned that age figured into the process of deciding what to wear to work. He felt that men who were younger and newer to the work world were more likely to be seen as overdressed if they wore clothing more formal than that required in the dress code. R. J. Logan, a twenty-eight-year-old in marketing in New York, characterized his dress decisions as "a little bit tricky" because he preferred dressier work clothing than what his bosses wore but didn't want to show them up or be perceived negatively.

Barney Nicks, a San Francisco interviewee, offered the most evocative account of the dangers of overdressing in his employment sector, finance.[13] When I asked him what advice he would give to a young man just starting out in his field, he replied,

> Be cautious about wearing too many flairs or embellishments or whatever. I think that you need to be at a certain level before you can pull off a pocket square. . . . I think that stuff that's kind of flashy or whatever is not what [you should wear]. . . . Your first job, in the first few years, you are supposed to stand next to and one step behind one certain man or woman [the boss] and you are not supposed to stick out. *They* are the star.

I mused aloud that this way of thinking contradicted the admonition about dressing for the job you want. Barney emphasized that his advice was specific to finance, which he described as "full of predators" with a "high prevalence of attractive men" who "may be innately jealous" of each other. For these reasons, he said people just starting out must avoid being flashy dressers, which could lead to their being labeled as "posers." His caution was based on personal experience: "That was an issue when I was in my early career. . . . I got some razzing about how I was dressed." It makes sense that concerns about outdressing the boss would be most pronounced in finance jobs, where workers' clothing is seen as an index of what they earn (according to Barney and other finance professionals I interviewed).

Even Rohan, who claimed to dress up more than he needed to for his position, drew the line at wearing a suit to his business casual workplace. If he showed up in a suit, he said, "I'd be like, challenging the upper management, you know? I mean, threatening, or—I guess that's the right word." These remarks show the significance of outward appearance for legitimizing, visually representing, and symbolically maintaining organizational hierarchies. If workers and managers are already differentiated according to salary, responsibilities, and authority, it would seem that clothing couldn't possibly threaten the established order, yet some interviewees accorded dress decisions this dangerous power.

Do men explicitly think about altering their dress when their role in a company changes? Yes. Clark exemplifies this strategic approach to communicating one's position through dress. When I met him in the summer of 2012, he had recently received a promotion and was thinking about changing his wardrobe to reflect this.

> Now when I go to a meeting, and I introduce myself as director of sales [*pause*], do I need to present myself differently? And so I'm definitely thinking that I'm probly gonna buy some new shirts that are more expensive and look a little crisper, I'm probly gonna wear a sport coat some of the time, and try and upgrade my dress to match the title. And so, I don't exactly know what that looks like.

It was important to Clark that his work clothing look better and more expensive, and fit his new, more authoritative title. The timing of our interview, on the heels of his promotion, was opportune. I was able to hear Clark's thinking as he planned changes to his image, changes that he thought becoming the boss required:

> When I fly out to Texas, and I'm going on sales calls with our national account manager there, and I'm bein' introduced as his boss . . . am I gonna intentionally dress nicer than him? So, I'm tryin' to figure that out and—part of that makes sense, so that when you see the title, and then you see the person, they go together, that there's, uh, a *hierarchy* here. So I'd like to message that in a way that's appropriate.

As we can see, Clark wants not just *to be* the boss but also *to be seen as* the boss, particularly when he is outside his company's offices. The label of sales director and the fleshy, clothed embodiment of that label should be congruent. Clark is imagining his dress and appearance being weighed against that of his subordinate as they stand, sit, or enter a room together, and he wants to come out on top. Several other interviewees shared Clark's sentiments, recounting how they reevaluated their work wear when taking a new position either with a new firm or within their company.

The Man

In conducting this study, I spoke with dozens of white-collar men. Some had just joined the corporate workforce, some were close to retirement, and most were located somewhere in between. Through these conversations, I noticed that because company hierarchy led to a concentration of authority in individuals, an almost mystical aura of power became associated with these individuals.[14] This happened at the very top, with the larger-than-life figure of the CEO or president, yet it also happened at lower levels, as there was generally one person responsible for each region, office, department, and so on.[15] Although the men I interviewed didn't use this term, they sketched a profile of a powerful and sometimes intimidating figure that I came to call *The Man*.[16] In participants' accounts, not every manager or director fits this often revered and uniquely powerful profile, but many vice presidents (VPs) do, and nearly all CEOs and presidents, chief operations officers (COOs), and chief financial officers (CFOs) do. Rank-and-file workers' level of contact with these influential individuals varies with the size and structure of the company, but even those who have never met or spoken with The Man have heard tell of him or seen him in person, in videos, or in photographs. I interviewed men at all levels of the corporate hierarchy, and nineteen of them fit most of the criteria I have laid out here for what it takes to be The Man. Many others spoke about The Man, most in glowing terms and a few less respectfully. Here are some typical descriptions of The Man from interviews. I have left out interviewee pseudonyms, name of The Man if given, and city of interviewee to protect confidentiality.

- "He's very tall, very thin. He always wears suits, dressed to the nine[s], but that's his responsibility. I mean, we're a [retail] fashion business, that's what he should look like. He's supposed to be the fashion plate for our company. When he is here [in the office] that is how he is dressed. I mean, I've never seen him without a suit on with the coat on. Never with even his coat off."

- "The current CEO and the previous one, they're very conscious. And when they stand in front of a room . . . they command the room. But their appearance is equally a part of that, in our [advertising] business. So, a CEO who stands up to speak to our organization, who's not only charismatic, intelligent, [or] whatever, but is also well put together, that's just another layer on top of his, sort of—his presence."

- "Very conservative, but very well dressed. . . . He'll always wear dark shoes, solid ties, probably a white shirt . . . very simple, yet very powerful. And you can tell he's wearing very nice stuff. Very well fitted, so it's probably all custom, I certainly noticed that."

- "[The president of the company is] a very big guy, so he has a big presence, and the way he dresses enhances that."

- "The [investment] firm, it was started by an older fellow called Richardson [pseudonym] from wealthy circa two generations ago. He believes that Wall Street is done in a suit and tie."

- "Our CFO is a sharp dresser. But you know, ya gotta look good for the clothes to look good on you, I think. He's like a taller guy. He's um, he's got like a good build and he um, he has a shaved head and . . . He just looks very professional and very sharp, I would say."

Even a quick glance at the above quotes turns up intriguing similarities in the ways that men from different employment sectors and different sizes and types of companies describe The Man. These idealized descriptions show—as in Clark's anecdote—the conflation of the person-as-title, person-as-wearer-of-clothes, and person-as-body. As I argued earlier, in the corporate world, subordinates inspect their superiors' appearance carefully, noticing things like their body shape and how current or expensive their clothing is. The last speaker's copious "ums" imply that perhaps some men are hesitant to talk about other men's physiques, as this suggests interest and attention to such matters, something that goes against ideas of traditional masculinity.

We see the effusive use of superlatives; for example, one interviewee used the word "very" a total of six times in his brief description. These hyperbolic characterizations communicate the idea that The Man is extraordinary, larger than life, a towering figure of competence, authority, and well-defined style. Another example of hyperbole is the frequent use of "always" or similar blanket terms.[17] The CEO *always* wears this or that. The CEO *never* removes his suit jacket in public. Such consistency is made to seem superhuman, or, less charitably, abnormal. Some of these descriptions also highlight the cost involved with maintaining such an impeccable professional image. The Man can afford more expensive, more fashionable, and higher-quality clothing than those who toil in the lower chambers of the corporate pyramid.

The consistent embodiment of his powerful role is what most strikes admirers of The Man. Dave saw his company president—"always very well dressed . . . very classy, very well put together"—as typical of other high-ranking corporate leaders in that he was "the whole package." As we chatted at a glossy conference table that seemed to go on forever, Dave explained,

> Whether that's [the] colors or, the clothes fit right or . . . the whole thing. . . . You know, you can't have a thousand-dollar suit, custom shirts . . . nice ties, and then a ten-dollar pair of shoes on. It just doesn't work. It's like, you know, which one of these things does not belong? And so you just kind of have to have the *whole deal*. Same as, you know, you can't have all this stuff and then you like hand [someone] a Bic pen [*light laugh*]. You know? It's like, it's weird. If there's one thing missing, it doesn't work. He has the whole—And he can afford it too. So he's kind of got the whole package. And in a hundred different ways.

Frank Miller's description also showed detailed attention to appearance, expressed through hyperbole. Frank got his job with an investment firm after meeting his future company's president at a social event. According to Frank, they struck up a conversation after he approached the man (The Man) to compliment his cufflinks. Frank told me that upon seeing these cufflinks, he thought to himself, "If I had cufflinks like that one day, you know what, I'd be really happy with my job." When I asked what was so special about the cufflinks, which Frank had described as "really, really large and thick," he replied,

> Just the size, and they were made of gold. There were gold coins and they were about as big as half dollars and I was just like [*correcting himself*]—you know what, that's a little large. Maybe a little smaller. Bigger than—Little bit bigger than a quarter though. And I was just like, wow, those are *such* nice cufflinks.

Now he sees the president regularly around the office, and Frank is still impressed by him: "I think he sleeps in suits," he told me, smiling.

The Man is characterized by his material position as a high-earning, high-ranked executive. And he dresses the part. These two elements appeared together in the men's depictions. His is not the only way of performing masculinity in the business world, however, and not everyone is equally in awe of The Man.

Sticking It to The Man

The idealized depictions of The Man as flawlessly dressed, perfectly presented, and never-changing obscure the instability and unpredictability of corporate work today.[18] Anyone who reads the headlines knows that The Man may be just one board-of-directors vote or one hostile takeover away from being out of a job (though we get the sense, from some study participants' breathless odes to The Man, that he'll land on his feet and get an equivalent position somewhere else). But positive characterizations are not the whole story. The Man is not universally loved and admired.

Patrick Flowers discussed one of the highest-ranking men in his office in a markedly irreverent tone, saying, "The head of sales is a multi-multi-million-aire. . . . I think he drives a Ferrari and blah blah blah." Patrick highlighted the difference between The Man's salary and his own, adding, "His clothes are all tailored by like the fanciest tailors in London. So of course he looks fancy." Nicholas Georgiou, who worked in design, was similarly unimpressed by his CEO, who "always" (again, note the hyperbole, despite the disrespectful twist) "wears this stupid tie or just dress pants and a sport jacket . . . but he's also a finance guy, so it's totally different." Given his nondesign background, how could The Man, in this case, be expected to dress in a manner pleasing to the designers, whose work lives—and possibly, their personal lives—revolve around aesthetic trends? As in Nicholas's office, in Aiden Curry's previous job, employees poked fun at the CEO's predictable, bland self-presentation. This CEO wore simple long-sleeved shirts and khakis, "to the point where one Halloween, about fifteen people got together and dressed as him, and they wore light blue shirts and light khakis." I asked Aiden, "So they knew exactly what [clothing] to pick to impersonate him?" "Exactly," he replied. It is worth noting that all three of these men who held less worshipful opinions of The Man worked for smaller firms or in smaller offices where everyone saw each other almost daily. Perhaps familiarity breeds . . . not contempt exactly, but more realistic or more negative assessments of The Man's professional image.

Sensitive to these potential critiques, three participants who held positions of power in their workplaces seemed especially conscious of their demeanor and appearance. They considered how they might be perceived by people in lower-ranking positions in their companies and by clients or other outsiders to the organization. Trevor Robins was a white architect in his late fifties who was doing pro bono work for a community nonprofit organization when we met. When discussing appropriate, professional dress in our interview, he reflected on this and other work experiences, saying, "In a multicultural setting, well, maybe we dress differently." He spoke of work-related interactions "where people are coming from different backgrounds, and maybe my khakis and white shirt look like 'the boss.'" I equate Trevor's term "the boss" with the figure I call The Man. Aware of the historical and political connotations of such a label, and the weightiness of being a white man in a racially mixed group, Trevor was concerned that embodying this authoritative stereotype could be counterproductive. Whereas Clark wanted to look like the boss, Trevor wasn't sure that this was always best for his coworkers and clients, even if he was the one in charge of a project. Similarly, Brett, who held a director-level position at his advertising firm, said,

> I don't really aspire to be one of the "suits" in the office. . . . I try to stay away from being too dressed up and really distancing myself too far away from [other employees]. I don't have the ego issues of looking like the boss. There's another creative director in another one of our offices who *always* wears a suit; even when we've had meetings on Saturdays or offsite, he was wearing a suit. I think he has . . . an ego issue that he has to look like the boss to everyone else and use that as a signal of power, rather than being casual and seeming like you're one of the [design] studio.

Brad, the retail executive, tried to convey an image antithetical to that of the unapproachable, pedestal-occupying Man when he visited his company's stores. He did this consciously by dressing in business casual, avoiding dark suits and ties, and engaging in friendly behavior: "I just like to interact with the [store employees] and . . . knock off all the bad guy image, you know?" Brad, who you'll remember conducted negotiations with employee unions, comprehended the potential of The Man to be seen negatively, as an oppressor of the company's workers. He strategically endeavored to counter this by dressing in a down-to-earth manner and behaving in unexpectedly open and informal ways. It is impossible to know whether this self-presentation strategy affected the way low-level employees viewed Brad, but he felt that it could create more positive interactions.

The Anti-Man

High-ranking officials who take The Man image less seriously, or who try to avoid embodying The Man's undesirable or off-putting traits, make up another pattern I found in participants' accounts. Several described a foil to The Man, whom I dubbed the *Anti-Man*. The Anti-Man's existence seems to trouble interviewees' depictions of The Man as a force for good, as someone to be esteemed and emulated. But unlike the critiques I've just summarized, the figure of the Anti-Man does not challenge but rather strengthens the hegemonic position of The Man in white-collar workers' imaginations. The Anti-Man is often seen as a failed version of The Man, the person who performs The Man's role wrong or inadequately, thus leaving himself open for criticism.

Ian Geary, who had worked at a few different companies, compared the CEOs of two of them. Emerging from these contrasting descriptions were the figure of The Man and his seeming opposite, the Anti-Man. The first CEO "got his hair cut every two weeks . . . wore a gray suit and a striped tie, and had his shoes buffed by the guy downstairs three times a week." Ian, who was not a CEO, still compared his own dress and appearance with this embodiment of The Man, remarking, "I'm not that guy; I also don't have his money or his background, either, so . . ." The second CEO, according to Ian, "was a very nondescript guy." Here the person-as-title and the person-as-body did not seem to match up: "Everyone knew his name, but if you saw him in person, he's like one of these little short guys, that you would never guess he was [the CEO], and he frankly dressed very badly for a person of his . . ." Ian trailed off, then went on to describe this CEO's dress as "plain," saying that he tended to wear "a polyester navy blue thing [jacket] and gray slacks and loafers . . . one of those invisible, security guy kind" of outfits. Ian judges the self-presentation of these two CEOs—their clothing, their shoes, even their height—and the Anti-Man comes up lacking.[19]

Aiden's boss at his former job in San Francisco fit the Anti-Man type:

> My direct supervisor was the vice president, and on the executive team, and he was obese with a ponytail, with like jeans and a T-shirt. He was just that kind of dude. He would put on a button-up [shirt] and a jacket and have nice pants and shiny shoes when he's going to meet clients, but generally speaking, he was a fat guy with a ponytail. He calls himself the fat hippie. He's comfortable with who he is, that's for sure. Um, but, that really took that pressure off, right?

The value placed on thinness or fitness is especially pronounced in the corporate world, as gauged by my informants' accounts in the previous chapter. Slimness is also strongly associated with The Man. It's as if he can be trusted to control the company's fortunes in part because he can control his bodily impulses and dominate his body, as evidenced by being in shape. The executive Aiden describes can never be The Man because he lacks the expected grooming and body shape, even when he does dress up. Consistent with the idea that high-ranking company men affected the dress of their subordinates, the Anti-Man was seen as having a trickle-down effect on dress and image requirements for employees.

Jeff Michaels linked his Manhattan business services firm's casual dress code to the appearance of the CEO, another Anti-Man, who "comes in [to the office] in shorts and a golf shirt on a day-to-day basis. Flip-flops. Sneakers. So I think with that being the example there, everyone else kind of follows from that. I've never seen anyone be called out on what they're wearing at work. So, [it's] very lax." In Jeff's portrait, the CEO is an unlikely bearer of power and an implementer not of dress rules but of dress freedom. It seems he consciously chooses not to be The Man—to set a different tone, in the words of participants.

The Anti-Man image can result from intentional rejection of business dress norms, unintentional sloppiness, or lack of dress know-how. Yet the question of whether he is projecting this image on purpose does not seem to matter for how employees perceive him or for his material conditions. The fact remains that the Anti-Man shares a lofty socioeconomic status and prestigious organizational position with The Man, despite differences in their appearance.

The Anti-Man was more commonly spotted by my interviewees in tech and creative organizations, showing that occupational sector affects how executives present themselves. Even for men who worked in these types of companies, the way the Anti-Man looked (and, sometimes, behaved) could come as a surprise. R. J., a few years into his marketing job in New York, confided, "There's always a disconnect for me to see someone that's like an owner or a partner . . . wearing just like a polo shirt and a very casual outfit." He said that his bosses, who dressed in this way, did not fit his mental image of a company owner or a rich man. R. J. expected that such a person "would sort of present themselves in a very important stature all the time." He went on to say that this different type of authority figure made sense in his company, which was a "down-to-earth environment" and lacked a "sense of corporateness." In marketing, advertising, and other creative sectors, being cool is its own form of power. Whereas in other fields embodying the Anti-Man might be a liability for a high-status executive, in these areas it could be a strength. (This is not to say that The Man was absent from creative workers' accounts of their companies' leaders.) It seems that some high-ranking businessmen who enact what I call the Anti-Man self-presentation see themselves as purposely challenging the accepted routines of the corporate establishment (à la Marc Zuckerberg). This symbolic refutation of traditional modes of doing business can be a performance aimed just as much at external audiences—say, clients or the media—as internal audiences composed of employees.

Beyond the words that participants used to describe the Anti-Man, I noticed the tone of disdain or amusement. Clark described his CEO as "pretty casual," which is not too surprising for a tech company in Northern California. The outfits Clark described this boss wearing fit business casual dress norms. But in assessing the CEO's clothing, he remarked that "none of it looks very new; none of it looks like he's bought it at Brooks Brothers or someplace expensive, it's just kind of middle-of-the-road." Clark's disappointment was audible and visible. This CEO could and should do better: "He's a *rich dude.*" The Anti-Man is thus not always accepted as a legitimate alternative to The Man, and his leadership of the company can be subject to question (and was, implicitly, by some participants). There was a great deal of criticism of bosses' dress in the interviews, especially when they embodied the Anti-Man prototype. This complaining, of course, took place behind bosses' backs in private, confidential interviews with a researcher who was unlikely to ever see or interact with CEOs who were not themselves interviewed. Such surreptitious criticism is unlikely to ever upset power relations in these organizations.

Both The Man and the Anti-Man, because of their high position, are generally protected from direct criticism of their dress by subordinates or people with similar status. One interviewee, who was not a CEO but fit the category of The Man because of his powerful position in a large company, told me that when he receives comments about his dress at work, they are usually positive. "I'm also the boss," he added matter-of-factly, "so it would be hard for them to say, 'Boy, you look like crap today.'" Another who embodied The Man (and occupied the most prestigious post of anyone I interviewed, as one of the top leaders of a huge international corporation), put it even more bluntly, saying he didn't "think anyone would dare to make a negative comment" to him directly. Because of their similar material position, regardless of the way they look, both Man and Anti-Man are shielded from negative feedback about their appearance. The outcomes for workers at lower levels of the organization are the same regardless of which cultural type high-ranking executives embody. Whether he wears a hoodie or an Hermès tie to work, the man at the top is still profiting more from the business than his employees.

One final note about The Man or the Anti-Man: he is male. The truth behind the stereotype of the male CEO is depressing for those of us who care about gender equality in the workforce. Top officials at most U.S. companies, despite their size or specialization, tend to be men. Only twenty-three of the five hundred firms that make up the Fortune 500 (4.6%) are headed by women, and if we consider the Fortune 1000, only twenty-three more women's names would be added to the list.[20] At lower levels of corporate management, where women are better represented, the word "boss" still conjures up mental images of men.[21] Most of the time, when the men in my study talked about their direct boss, he was also a man. In fact, the language of emulating the boss's appearance assumes a same-gender boss and employee. As one participant put it, "My direct supervisor is a woman, so obviously I can't compare what I wear exactly to what she wears." Only one interviewee mentioned a woman CEO, though I wonder: If others had talked about such a figure, would she have embodied the characteristics associated with The Man? Could she have? The Man is also, as the political use of this term in decades past implied, usually a white man rather than a minority: 73 percent of members of the boards of directors in Fortune 500 companies are white men.[22]

Dress, Hierarchy, Power

By asking about work clothing, I learned much about men's relationships with and opinions of their bosses and other organizational leaders. Of course, these relationships and opinions encompass much more than dress and appearance. In the men's narratives, an individual's workplace image is embedded in dynamics of respect, emulation, gossip, mocking, and power that characterize corporate life. I learned of men's complex, strategic decisions about whether and how to embody the role of the boss (and for a privileged few, The Man or the Anti-Man). Regardless of the rung of the corporate ladder on which a boss was perched, significant commonalities emerged from the accounts of the core group of seventy-one interviewees.

The role of the boss, at every level, is tied up with visibility and acts of looking. Many participants described higher-ups—especially their direct supervisors—as an important audience for workplace self-presentation. They felt bosses were constantly looking at them and assessing their appearance and dress. This looking took on added meaning during key, possibly career-changing, moments: interviews, evaluations of work performance, and asking for a pay raise. Bosses were also looked at by people located both above and below them in the corporate hierarchy. This constant, multidirectional surveillance that managers experience helps explain why many of the men, whether they were bosses or not, described bosses as dressing more formally than those laboring beneath them.

While the boss's degree and sphere of influence over subordinates' dress seems to vary widely across companies and offices, most participants agreed that bosses had the power to affect the dress of the people they managed. Control could be direct, as in explicit instructions and rules, or punishment used to enforce such rules. Or it could be indirect, with the boss setting a tone for workplace dress and behavior. Another mechanism of indirect control was emulation of the boss by his or her employees. Emulation should not be taken to indicate deeply felt motivation or positive evaluations of the boss, though. While some workers emulated their boss because they liked and respected him (it was usually a "him"), others did so purposefully, wearing or doing things that they did not personally care for but that they thought would help them keep or advance in their job. Deferring to bosses' dress preferences is another way that white-collar men strategically embrace conformity.

Ideas of mobility within the capitalist organization are also at play in the men's discussions of dress and hierarchy. Brad and other executives could provide accounts of how they had moved up.[23] Young people like Rohan and Ted focused on the future, and positions they aspired to, rather than the ground they had already covered. Most interviewees who were not managers aspired to rise in the company and had usually given some thought to how they could make this upward mobility happen. Some discussed the trickiness of balancing aspirations and "dressing for the job you want" against the danger of upsetting bosses by overdressing. Dress must be a powerful social force indeed if it can be perceived as a threat to the existing hierarchy and channels of control. When a man received a promotion, as in Clark's story, he encountered a new set of considerations: How do you physically embody and thus visually represent the role of the boss?

In the corporate world, biological *sex* and socially performed *gender* are wrapped up with dress practices and standards. Most business leaders are born male, and the boss role is perceived as a masculine one.[24] The Man, as an idealized image of a high-status corporate boss, is the epitome of white-collar masculinity. He doesn't just wear a suit. He always wears a suit, sleeps in his suit, is called a *suit*. It is not just any suit, but a conservative, expensive, expertly tailored suit. Not just anybody—any body—can wear these suits in this way. It matters that his body is stereotypically masculine: he is tall and slim and clothes invariably look good on him. (Even one CEO's shaved head could be seen as a positive measure of his masculinity.) Despite differences among research participants in occupation, class, racial or ethnic background, and age, The Man was someone nearly all of them would recognize. Whether he was respected or despised, his power and influence were unquestionable.

The Man's foil, the Anti-Man, had similar power but embodied it differently, strengthening the original type even while rejecting its characteristics. Participants viewed the Anti-Man as cool, amusing, or pathetic, but these views did not rock the hegemony of The Man in the corporate world. Neither did they challenge the power and wealth of the Anti-Man, who's laughing all the way to the bank as he snubs corporate conventions of self-presentation. These are just two modes of corporate masculine embodiment, which my interviewees could view from afar, try on, or reject. There are other options, and the same man may make different choices in different scenarios, within the constraints of the dress code. Today's business masculinities—shaped by hierarchy and status—are multiple and shifting. Typically, only a limited range of masculine embodiments are on display in the vitrine of the office each weekday.

Conclusion

> **Work, once regarded as a (relative) certainty and a central aspect of personal identity, especially for men, has itself become a fluid, multiple, and uncertain performance.**
>
> Linda McDowell, *Capital Culture*

Throughout this book, I've argued that U.S. white-collar men accept conditions of constraint and conformity in their work clothing because they get something in exchange. That something is the privilege associated with being a man who is a member of the middle or upper class, with a job that is assumed to call for brains rather than brawn. Many of the men in my study also have privileges associated with being heterosexual, U.S.-born, and white. Regardless of their salary or rank in the companies that employ them, these men all have a degree of social and economic power. Yet the research participants often feel powerless to influence the dress expectations in their offices, instead adapting their self-presentation to written and unwritten rules in order to blend in and be accepted. The pressures that men feel stem from the entrenchment of unstable, precarious employment and from the heightened attention to men's bodies in contemporary U.S. culture. Exploring white-collar men's occupational habitus in the context of these new social and economic realities, *Buttoned Up* picks up where last century's classic sociological studies of corporate America left off. Through a focus on dress, I bring attention to workers' bodies, which this previous research largely neglected. White-collar men's dress and professional appearance extend beyond the walls of the office, shaping the ways that they are viewed and treated in their families and communities.

Because there was so little descriptive research on my topic, I chose to interview men across companies and business sectors, designing a comparative inquiry rather than an in-depth study of one or two workplaces. This approach uncovered common patterns in the stories of men who might otherwise seem quite different. Yet we also need ethnographic research on how dress and appearance are managed in individual white-collar workplaces. We could gain incredibly rich data from in situ observation, capturing conversations about clothing in real time. Here popular culture—especially television—is outpacing academia. We know more about what it's like to work at Dunder Mifflin and Sterling Cooper than we do about what it's like to work at real U.S. companies. The field of body studies, originally focused almost entirely on women, is changing, but we need more research that examines what it means to be and have a particular type of male body in a particular time and place.

Urban location matters for men's work and leisure dress in ways that they are conscious of and that they reflected on in our conversations. I argue that region and city permeate decisions about clothing through *local dress cultures*. Assumptions that Cincinnati is conservative, New York is dressed-up, and San Francisco is laid-back were borne out when I analyzed the men's accounts in aggregate. Urban researchers should take these assumptions and lay explanations seriously and view them as a rich source of data about what it means to be from, and live in, a particular place. Middle-class people are often studied in suburbs, but they are engaged in meaningful interactions and embody their social status in city spaces as well. Given the surging interest in urban living among professionals and well-documented processes of gentrification, we'll miss out if we plan to encounter and study middle-class people only in the suburbs.

This study has real-world implications and applications. In speaking to human resources professionals, I have found they are interested in the ways that employees perceive and navigate dress codes. Yet there is precious little sociological analysis of workers' perspectives on dress. Corporate leaders must decide whether they want their organizations' dress codes to reflect company culture, employee preferences, particular values, or a combination of all three. My research participants' accounts can help these leaders consider the balance between uniformity and self-expression, between formality and comfort, that they want to foster in work spaces. I've shown that the dress regimes under which men labor can affect how they feel about themselves as workers. Seemingly trivial standards for work clothing also influence relationships with colleagues, bosses, and clients and can visually signify and justify corporate hierarchies.

The phrase *white-collar masculinity* invokes assumptions about biological sex, gender performance, and sexuality. Men's sense of masculine identity and others' perceptions of them are tied to their ability to earn a living wage and the prestige of their paid work. My main argument in this book, that white-collar men accept constraint in order to maintain their privilege, invites the question: privilege over whom?

Privilege over women and gay men. For the most part, research participants accepted our culture's view of traditionally masculine men as the default (or ideal) corporate workers, a view that casts women as deviants and outsiders, beginning with their dress. I was surprised that in the second decade of the twenty-first century, women—even in low-level positions—were seen as not fitting in at white-collar workplaces. While judging their women coworkers as overly concerned with dress and fashion, many men simultaneously relied on and appreciated the sartorial expertise of women in their private lives. Some straight men also had gay male friends who took on this fashion-maven role.

Traditional (or what gender scholars call hegemonic) masculinity idealizes men who look good without trying and do not admit to any conscious preoccupation with their appearance. Trying too hard to impress others through dress, in and outside of work, is perceived as unmanly. We now see hybrid masculinities that selectively incorporate the different orientations toward fashion and the body common among some gay and minority men. Real men, Americans increasingly believe, *are* allowed to care about their image, especially in the image-conscious white-collar world.

In a new employment reality, characterized by unstable work even in high-status occupations, men must always be ready to interview for a new position. Engaged in service work, with its fuzzy measurements of success, today's business organizations increasingly use men's appearance and self-presentation to assess the quality of their work. Employee evaluations may not explicitly mention dress and appearance, but the men in my study feel that they are judged on these aspects of performance, and they strive to get them right.

Metrosexuality as a cultural phenomenon has expanded the options for men in the areas of grooming, dress, and gender performance, but its impact on the structure of U.S. society is limited. The interviewees' accounts suggest that the existence of metrosexuals does not challenge the hierarchy that privileges straight men over gay men and men over women. It simply broadens the socially acceptable performances of masculinity by straight men. Metrosexuality's intense focus on men's appearance, coupled with its inability to unseat hegemonic masculinity and entrenched homophobia, helps explain a paradox. Men vehemently reject fashion yet simultaneously engage in anxious, self-deprecating talk about their bodies. Not only are men now subject to appearance-related worries along the lines of what U.S. women have typically experienced (though less intense), but they still must balance those concerns with the lingering idea that men should not fret over their bodies. This is a cultural conundrum brought on by shifts in gender norms, idealized media depictions of men, and expanding consumption.

Rather than looking at conformity in business organizations as a top-down, coercive process, I argue that (while there are elements of coercion) men manage their appearance at work through a *strategic embrace of conformity*. What are the costs of men's conformity to workplace dress expectations? For individual men, dressing and presenting the body in a way that is comprehensible in white-collar settings can lead to a sense of belonging and acceptance by colleagues. For smaller groups or work teams, dressing alike can have the same effect as wearing other types of uniforms, promoting esprit de corps and uniting disparate personalities in the service of common goals. At the level of the organization, though, the benefits of conformity may be less clear. Are there advantages to having a uniform company look? Is it good or bad for an organization to have members who question and challenge its policies? The skeptical social critics of the twentieth century would remind us of the potentially damning consequences of silently going along with what's asked of us. Most of the men I interviewed decide to conform because they think it will help their careers; they are not unthinking drones but thoughtful actors. This thoughtfulness, however, may not keep unethical or illicit practices—such as those at the heart of recent banking crises—from taking root at the organizational level. There could be other outcomes of conforming, more difficult to pinpoint than Enron-sized collective moral failures.

Esteeming conformity as an organizational value (either implicitly or explicitly) can discourage dissenting opinions and lead managers to hire people who dress, look, talk, and act like them. Could appreciation of diversity in dress lead to greater openness to diversity in gender, race, sexual orientation, and social class background? Men of color in my study felt extra pressure to dress well for work since they already stand out in other ways. Some felt stifled by work dress codes but saw themselves as powerless to change this and other aspects of the white-collar work world. Men from working-class or poor families saw a need to assimilate middle-class habits, including dress practices. Success in this endeavor lay in the judgments of men who were raised middle class.

These discussions of conforming to white-collar masculinity have made me curious about the outliers. There are men who throw caution into the paper shredder and do their own thing, experimenting with colors and patterns and accessories and—why not?—medieval chain-mail shirts in the office. Most of the men in my study don't do this, but I wonder how these more daring dressers fare in their careers. Does standing out rather than blending in help or hurt them? I couldn't identify any differences in men's accounts of their career trajectories based on their personal dress philosophies and practices. The more creative dressers didn't seem to be faring better or worse than their more conformist counterparts. We still need more research on outcomes, but I suspect that taking chances with their work fashion may just be less risky than white-collar men fear. It is true that most of the men who engaged more in fashion and unconventional looks were younger, so their belief that dressing for corporate work can be fun may become more widespread as they rise in seniority. Alternatively, this creativity in clothing may be squashed as they ascend the corporate ladder and learn by experience the value of conformity.

Might there be other organizational approaches to dress that would facilitate the social, physical, and identity comfort that men crave? Could companies' stated respect for diversity extend to workers' appearance? What would happen if organizations that claim to value innovation and creativity in their work products also encouraged innovation and creativity in employees' bodily self-presentation? There are reasons that utopian social movements usually propose radical changes to people's dress. What folks wear can represent and perpetuate the existing social order (by signaling their place within that order) and maintain long-standing ways of thinking. To employ dress in other ways could revolutionize social interactions—and the organizations where they take place.

Acknowledgments

To Henry	For brainstorming in tandem, cracking me up when I need it, loving me unselfishly since grunge was new, and for sometimes just not buying it. No hay nadie como tú.
To my parents	For inspiring me to get a highfalutin degree and write books (even though I'll never make it to Oprah's Book Club) and for teaching me that sometimes life's simplest joys are the sweetest.
To my children	For being a couple of beautiful hilarious wise-asses with highly developed sociological imaginations.
To my UC colleagues and friends	For never asking, why a book about clothes?
To the Taft Research Center	For research support and chances to try out new material.
To my writing group aka Team Tenure	For reminding me to put clarity above cuteness, and for reading every damn word.
To Tamara	For strength, wit, and friendship of the elusive BFF variety.
To Tish	For being the nosy office neighbor and generous work spouse I never knew I always wanted.
To Amanda, Emily, and Scarlett	For enduring the tedium of transcription and keeping me abreast of what all the kids are wearing.
To Fran Benson	For embracing the weirdness of this project, and being not just an editor but an advocate.
To the interviewees	For trusting me enough to talk—I hope you think I got it right.
To everyone I forgot to thank	I'll buy you a drink to make up for being an ungrateful jerk.

RESEARCH METHODS AND DEMOGRAPHIC PROFILE OF INTERVIEWEES

To engage in research on dress is to place oneself at the fringe of academic respectability.

—Efrat Tseëlon, "Ontological, Epistemological and Methodological Clarifications in Fashion Research"

Research Methods

The stories and quotes in this book are drawn from semistructured interviews that I conducted with seventy-one white-collar men (one retired, and the rest employed, at the time of our interviews): twenty-six in Cincinnati, twenty-five in New York City, and twenty in San Francisco. The interviews began with questions about the type of work the interviewee did and how he felt about the different activities his job involved. Subsequent questions explored early experiences of dress, including family influences, school and military uniforms (if applicable), and changes in personal style over time. The bulk of the interview guide addressed men's opinions and experiences of presenting their bodies at work, including topics such as dress codes, shopping for work clothes, and interactions with coworkers, bosses, and clients. There were also questions about gender and dress and about relationships with women and men inside and outside the office. My aim with the interviews was to get a holistic picture of individual men's views on white-collar work clothing, specific dress practices, and the image they wanted to present professionally. In addition to recording the interviews, which lasted from just under an hour to nearly two hours, I completed fieldnotes immediately afterward, describing the setting, the participant's demeanor and dress, and anything that stood out about our conversation and interaction.[1] Fifteen of the interviewed men completed a weeklong clothing log detailing what they wore to work each day, why they chose the clothing they did, what responses (if any) they got on their attire that day, and any other dress-related interactions they observed in the office. To get different perspectives on men's work dress, in addition to the seventy-one interviews with white-collar men, I interviewed three men affiliated with tailoring businesses and three military veterans, all in Cincinnati and New York. All names of research participants and their companies are pseudonyms in order to keep their identities confidential. This methodological decision is related primarily to the issue of access to this elite population. While some men would not have minded using their real names, I am certain that others would not have agreed to be interviewed without my promise of confidentiality. At the end of this appendix, I provide a demographic profile of the core group of seventy-one interviewees.

I began recruiting using my personal networks, beginning with people I knew who worked in corporate or white-collar jobs in the three cities. I mostly interviewed people whom I did not previously know, and by the end of the study, most of those I spoke with were several degrees removed from people I knew or had met. My goal in recruiting research participants was to obtain a diverse group of men employed at for-profit companies.[2] Rather than seeking a random sample from which I could generalize to all U.S. men in white-collar employment, I set out to interview men who worked in a range of occupational sectors, at different levels of seniority, and who differed in what sociologists call ascribed characteristics (age, sexual orientation, race or ethnicity, nationality, appearance, etc.). The fact that common patterns emerged in responses from such diverse corporate workers shows that there are aspects of white-collar embodiment that are shared across job and social categories.

Although I had planned to use snowball sampling, in which research participants recommend others to take part in the study, this proved nearly impossible. I asked every man to recommend others whom I might contact for an interview, and in the end only two put me in contact with a coworker or friend. Of these two men, only one was eventually interviewed. I see this stalled snowball as an important data point: a typical white-collar guy won't suggest to his male friends that they talk to a researcher about dress. Traditional ideas of heterosexual masculinity discourage men from talking with each other (or with anyone) about their bodies, clothing, and fashion. It is telling that the two men who did recommend a friend were both gay; already excluded from hegemonic masculinity, perhaps they had less to lose by admitting their participation in a study about dress.

Because I lived in Cincinnati when I began the research and had lived in New York for seven years before that, locating participants in those two cities was easier than it was in the San Francisco area, where I had relatively few contacts. The Cincinnati interviews were conducted throughout 2011 and 2012. Most of the New York interviews took place in the summer of 2011, when I spent approximately three weeks in Manhattan, and most of the San Francisco interviews took place in the summer of 2012, when I stayed in the Bay Area for about the same length of time. On a particularly busy day, I might crisscross these cities to interview four or five men.

Recorded interviews were transcribed by me, a research assistant, or a professional transcription service. I checked over all the transcriptions. Once the interview transcriptions were completed, I used NVivo software, not to code the data for me, but to organize the data as I coded it manually. I first used directed coding based on themes drawn from the scholarly literature and theory, then open coding to allow other themes to emerge organically from the data. This is a typical data analysis method for interview-based qualitative social science research.[3] The chapters that structure this book are built around clusters of related codes; for example, chapter 3 mostly discusses patterns found in the codes *uniform*, *school uniform*, *military uniform*, and *conformity*.

Reflexivity and Rapport

My own ascribed characteristics—being a white, heterosexual, female, middle-class professional, neither old nor young—may have made many of the potential research participants more willing to speak with me.[4] We shared a similar social class location, though I learned the limits of this similarity when one interviewee estimated his annual work wardrobe spending at $5,000 more than my yearly salary. Nearly all the men were college-educated, so we had that in common as well. My relative familiarity with the business world, developed through reading relevant books and my long-term participant observation of one businessman who happens to be my husband, also ensured that we shared at least some common language. Business norms of reciprocity and relationship maintenance helped me gain access to men who were quite busy: in some cases, I got the sense that the interviewee had mostly agreed to speak with me because I was recommended by someone he knew (often a woman). This was helpful, as it enabled me to talk to men who were not overtly interested in fashion or dress. In this way, I avoided interviewing only men who volunteered because they were especially interested in my research topic. It was important that I speak with those men, but also with men who claimed no interest in fashion or said they didn't put much thought into dressing for work.[5]

My biggest fear at the outset of the project, which literally kept me up nights, was that men simply wouldn't talk to me about the things I wanted to know. I dreaded one-word answers or meaningless responses to my earnest inquiries. After being married for a long time—as I like to joke, since God was a baby—I wasn't in the

habit of talking to men one-on-one, and I was concerned about my ability to effec-
tively carry on these relatively informal conversations, which were a work activity
for me but not really for the interviewees. While the interview meetings with men
did sometimes feel like extremely chaste blind dates (at which I always insisted on
picking up the check because I had some research funding), I needn't have worried about whether they would talk. Many of these men talk for a living, and even
those who declared no interest whatsoever in dress and said it was not a priority
for them—that they just threw on whatever was clean—had strong opinions about
what should be worn to work. I was pleasantly surprised that our conversations
probably produced enough data for two books. I am hesitant to overstate the rap-
port between me and the research participants; we spent only a short time together,
and no researcher can ever know for sure what her subjects really think of her.
However, most interviews went smoothly. I was sometimes surprised by the men's
apparent candor, and some of them told me that they found the interview "fun," a
nice change of pace from their everyday activities.

In previous research I have tended to "study down," that is, study people
whose social and economic status is below my own. That was not usually the case
here. The men sometimes made sexist comments or grouped me together with
all women in ways that reminded me of their gender privilege. Many of them
also had a higher economic status than mine, as I learned when I was told to
make appointments with their secretaries or when they talked about their clothing or other expenses. Some, perhaps unknowingly, used spatial arrangements to
convey their status, as with the man who sat behind his large, high desk as I sank
into a low-slung sofa that required me to gaze up at him from afar. Even though
I was more educated than most of the interviewees, they used their knowledge
about research to question me on everything from my sampling methodology to
how I would guarantee confidentiality to my take on the writings of postmodern
gender theorist Judith Butler. They suggested new lines of questioning, which
I sometimes adopted, and asked me about my plans for publishing my results.
One interviewee noted that in many social scientific books, people's race was
mentioned only if they weren't white. I felt that he was implicitly asking me to do
better, to recognize the power and meanings of whiteness and not to single out
respondents of color. These types of demands and status differentiations were a
new experience for me.

On the other hand, I believe in some ways my presumed difference from the
participants worked in my favor. I think that I was seen as nonthreatening in
a way that a male researcher would not have been, especially when it came to
talking to men about their body image and straight-up asking them whether
they identified as gay, straight, or something else. Male researchers asking such
questions have sometimes found themselves in uncomfortable, confrontational
situations.[6] Given many men's assumption that women cared about dress and

fashion, it seemed natural that I would be interested in these topics. My asking about sexual orientation as a piece of basic demographic information was not interpreted as a threat or a challenge to one's manliness, although it was met with resistance by a few men who self-identified as straight.

Limitations and Strengths of the Study

As with all research studies, there are limitations to my findings and the conclusions we can draw from them. It was more challenging for me to recruit participants in San Francisco, given the time and resources available. Thus, I interviewed twenty men there but twenty-five in New York and twenty-six in Cincinnati. San Francisco is the only city studied in which I have never lived, so my knowledge of its local dress culture is less developed. Nevertheless, my observations in combination with the interview accounts identified some real differences between the sites in terms of work dress expectations.

My reliance on first-person interview accounts is both a strength and a limitation. The dress scholar Efrat Tseëlon wrote, "Since most research output on clothing is gathered through language, what we are studying is actually discourse about dress" rather than dress behaviors.[7] I chose interviews because I was interested in how men thought about and experienced dressing for white-collar work. I wanted to hear their stories about what they did, why, and what they thought the consequences were. I was intrigued by the idea of how one presents oneself in the corporate work environment, yet I did not lose sight of the fact that an interview is also an opportunity for an individual to present himself to the interviewer and, ultimately, to the potential readers of the research findings.[8]

Trained as an ethnographer, in other studies I have conducted I've been interested in the gaps between what people say and what they do. The contradictions between people's accounts and the way they behave in the social world produce in-depth knowledge about identity and interaction. Yet in this study I wanted to access *accounts* of many different men; since I wanted to compare across work sites, it was not realistic or desirable to spend long periods of time observing in a few offices. In addition, it is more difficult to obtain access to corporate offices for extended periods of observation than for less time-intensive interviews. Conducting a comprehensive survey of what men wore in white-collar workplaces wouldn't do, as this method of data collection can't get at decision-making processes, men's identities as workers, or strategies for self-presentation. Interview accounts are just that—accounts. They represent men's explicitly stated ideas, thoughts, and opinions, and they offer narratives that are constructed to be shared with others (in this case, with me and you, readers). These may or may not be the same stories that men tell themselves about themselves. But the stories are meaningful, as the interviewees choose them to express their identity, to present themselves as rational and intelligent human beings. These discourses of gender, work, and dress are themselves my object of study.[9]

As with all studies based on purposive rather than random samples, mine does not claim to be representative of an entire group of people. There must be other ways of experiencing and thinking about embodiment and work dress among U.S. white-collar men that are not included here. However, despite their different positions, backgrounds, and locations, there was agreement on many issues among this diverse sample of seventy-one professional men. They saw appearance and dress as mattering in the business world. They saw it both as structuring interpersonal interaction and as being influenced by the hierarchical structures of companies and by relationships with coworkers, bosses, and family members. They believed that clothing could communicate messages but that these messages were not always intended or received as intended. They expressed the opinion that today in corporate America, most men were thinking about dress and self-presentation rather than viewing this as women's work. I would expect to find similar perspectives even in a larger, geographically distinct sample of urban white-collar men in the United States. Beyond that, however, it is the particularities as much as the commonalities of these accounts that make them fascinating explorations of contemporary white-collar subjectivity.

A Note on Language

Much qualitative social science research engages in "studying down." Studying down involves particular ethical and representational challenges, one of which is how to present the language of research participants whose ways of speaking may be stigmatized in the wider society.[10] Qualitative researchers who study down must balance a commitment to accuracy with a desire to avoid reinforcing stereotypes. For example, Tamara Mose and I have criticized a tendency among researchers to present black participants' speech using phonetic spellings while portraying the researcher as using fewer nonstandard pronunciations or grammar but instead speaking the King's English.[11] Such practices, when used uncritically, can reinscribe the difference and distance between researcher and researched rather than troubling or at least uncovering these power dynamics.

For this book, I was "studying up," exploring the everyday lives and beliefs of people who are privileged by their gender, social class, and occupation (and often because of their heterosexual identities and whiteness).[12] There were certainly moments in interviews when I was reminded of the higher status of my interviewees vis-à-vis myself in subtle and not-so-subtle ways. Given the issues of language in research methodology that I mentioned above, it was important to me to represent participants' speech accurately. So I kept the places where interviewees—and I—used nonstandard pronunciations or grammar. If a man said "gonna," I did not change this to "going to," and if he said "probly," I did not add an extra syllable. These educated, high-status men departed from the King's English in our conversations, and so did I, and I wanted to represent that faithfully. To present an overly standardized, sanitized version of their speech—as researchers studying elites may be tempted to do–would reaffirm stereotypes about who uses which kind of language in the United States. I did remove some of the times that men said "uh," "um," and "you know," in order to make quotes easier to read. Where I felt, given the context, that these utterances signified that an interviewee was struggling to find the words to answer a question, I kept them; where they seemed to be just verbal fillers, I took them out. Ellipses in the quotes indicate omissions for clarity or brevity; pauses in speech are indicated by the word "pause" in brackets. In general, the men did not speak in the grammatically standard, non-slang, mildly accented American English of Walter Cronkite and other anodyne news anchors, and I thought it would be a methodological misstep to make it seem that they did.

Demographic Profile of Interviewees

Participants ranged in age from twenty-four to seventy-one, with a median age of forty. Figures 1 and 2 show the educational levels and racial or ethnic

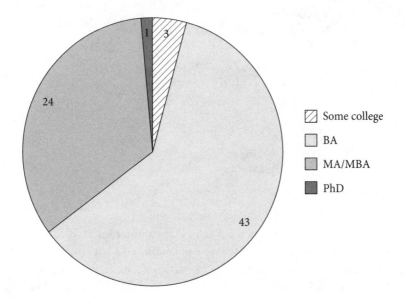

Figure 1   Education level

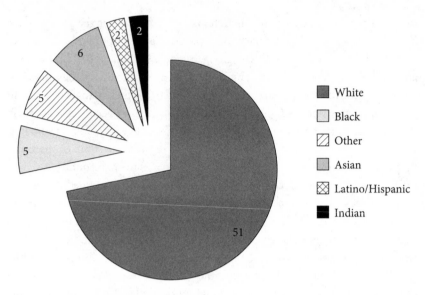

Figure 2   Race or ethnicity

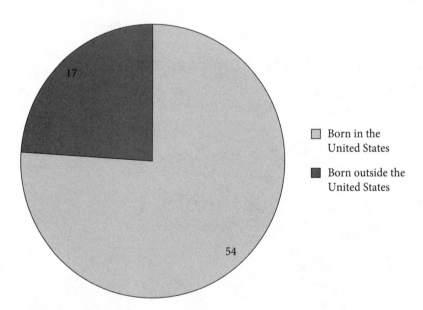

Figure 3   Place of birth

identifications of the interviewees. A total of forty-three out of the seventy-one men in the core group of interviewees had completed a bachelor's degree, and another twenty-four had a master's. One participant had a PhD, and only three had not completed college. This fits with popular assumptions that white-collar jobs require college degrees.

The picture of race and ethnicity is a bit more complex. I asked about race using an open-ended question ("In terms of race or ethnicity, how do you identify yourself?"), and I received a dazzling variety of answers. Figure 2 somewhat simplifies this complexity for the sake of having categories that more or less fit popular understandings of race in the United States. For example, the Black category (n=5) includes men who self-identified as African American, black, Afro-Caribbean, and "African. American.," a label coined by a U.S.-born black participant who was the son of African immigrants. The Asian category (n=6) includes men who identified as Chinese American, Filipino, Asian, and an Indian man who identified racially as Asian. Interestingly, two South Asian Indian men identified their race as Indian; this suggests that Indians may be racialized differently in the United States than other Asian-origin people are and that they see themselves as racially distinct. (Further research on the racial self-identification of Indian Americans and Indian immigrants in the United States is warranted.) Two men identified as Latino or Hispanic. The Other category (n=5) is a fascinating catchall including Eurasian, Brazilian, "half Native American and half (mostly) Irish," English, and "Jewish/Lithuanian and Ukranian." Three of the five men in the Other category almost certainly would be considered white by people who encountered them on the street; this would bring the total number of white men to fifty-four if we moved them to the White category. I decided not to do this in order to respect their self-identification and nonuse of the word "white."

As for the White category (n=51), which is often seen as an undifferentiated mass, even in racial and ethnic studies, there was diversity in men's responses. Many men who were Jewish included this modifier along with calling themselves "white" or "Caucasian." (There were ten self-identified Jewish men in the core group of interviewees.) Other men who identified as white plus something else included a self-defined "white South American" (from Argentina) and a man who said "I guess I identify as Caucasian, even though I'm mostly Latin in my background." As readers can see, I made some tough judgment calls in assigning men to one category over another. The portrait of the American middle class that emerges when we consider these self-classifications is one in which the vocabulary of race and ethnicity is expanding and new racial group identifications (e.g., Indian) are emerging as significant for social interaction and personal identity.

Figure 3 shows the number of participants born in the United States and the number born in other countries. Although most participants (76%, or fifty-four men) were born in this country, nearly a quarter (24%, or seventeen men) were born abroad. This significant portion of foreign-born men in the sample is certainly affected by the fact that I conducted research in large and medium-size cities, but it is also related to trends in transnational migration and the increasing globalization of U.S. corporations.

Figures 4 and 5 and table 1 provide information about the personal and family lives of the core group. Most participants identified as heterosexual or straight, with a sizable minority (14%) identifying as gay. I received two ambiguous answers to the question of sexual orientation. Although participants often made jokes when asked this potentially uncomfortable question, one man said in all seriousness that he was "mostly straight." Another said that he rejected the need to label oneself, and instead of choosing a category, he insisted that he was married (to a woman) and was a father. These two men, since they were married to women and did not identify as gay, were included in the "straight" category.

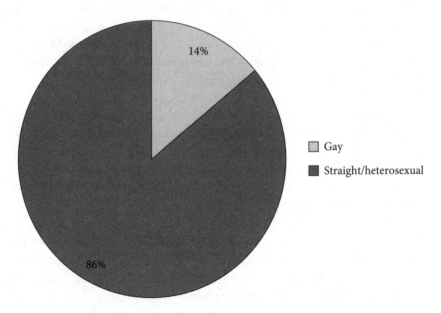

☐ Gay
■ Straight/heterosexual

Figure 4 Sexual orientation

TABLE 1 Marital/relationship status

	NUMBER OF INTERVIEWEES	PERCENTAGE OF TOTAL
Married (all heterosexual)	34	47.89
Single	18	25.35
Single and in a relationship	6	8.45
Living with partner	2	2.82
Engaged (most live together)	6	8.45
Divorced	4	5.63
Separated	1	1.41
Total	**71**	**100**

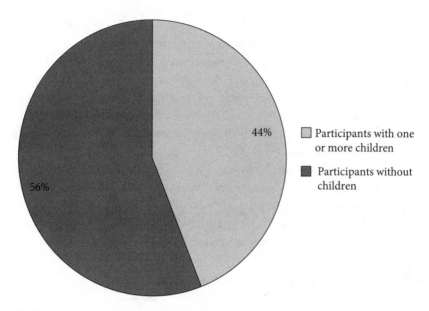

44%   ☐ Participants with one
         or more children

         ■ Participants without
56%   children

Figure 5   Children

As with the question of race and ethnicity, the issue of marital status has become increasingly tricky for researchers to navigate over time. I started with simple categories such as "married," "single," and "divorced," but it quickly became clear that these classifications were inadequate. This inadequacy pertained mostly to men who were not technically married but were in a committed, long-term, monogamous relationship: hence the added categories of "single/in relationship," "living with a partner," and "engaged." As scholarly literature on family formation shows, cohabitation prior to or in lieu of marriage is increasingly common in the United States.[13] I have not seen a scholarly discussion of the phenomenon of unmarried men rejecting the label of "single," but to many of the legally single men, it somehow seemed wrong not to mention their attachment to a partner (whether that partner was a man or a woman). Still, traditional marital status categories have not disappeared; a full 73 percent of the participants identified as either "married" or "single." There is no way of knowing (and I did not probe further) whether some men who self-identified as simply single were also in live-in or long-term relationships and did not disclose that fact. The late comedian Mitch Hedburg joked, "I don't have a girlfriend; I just know a girl who would get really mad if she heard me say that." Perhaps some men find themselves in this situation. Finally, the sample of interviewees was about roughly split between fathers and nonfathers, with 44 percent having at least one child (figure 5).

Another demographic variable worth mentioning is military service. A total of six men in the core group of seventy-one interviewees (about 8.5%) had served in the military, and of these men, one was still a member of the reserves. Half of these men (n=3) had served in military forces of countries other than the United States. Aside from these six veterans, one man had been in the U.S. foreign service, and another had served in the Peace Corps. To get more input from military men, I interviewed three former servicemen who were not included in the main group of seventy-one.

In sum, my interview sample looked a lot like the white-collar employment sector: they tended to be U.S.-born, white, heterosexual, relatively educated, non-veterans. However, I incorporated many men who fell outside this demographic profile in order to understand how social differences matter for men's identities and self-presentation as corporate workers.

TABLE 2 Jobs and departments in which interviewees worked

JOB/DEPARTMENT	PERCENTAGE (NUMBER)
Human resources	12.7 (9)
Sales/account representative	11.3 (8)
Technology	11.3 (8)
Recruiters (including managers and directors)	11.3 (8)
Creative work/design	8.5 (6)
Analyst/research	7 (5)
Architects	7 (5)
Financial advising/trading	5.6 (4)
Accounting	4.2 (3)
Training	4.2 (3)
Marketing	4.2 (3)
Upper management/executives	4.2 (3)
Other*	8.5 (6)
Total	**100 (71)**

* "Other" includes public relations, commercial real estate acquisition, merchandising, internal communications, and loss prevention.

TABLE 3 Type or sector of companies in which interviewees worked

TYPE OF COMPANY/INDUSTRY	PERCENTAGE OF INTERVIEWEES WORKING IN THIS SECTOR (NUMBER)
Corporate retail	21.1 (15)
Business services (including recruiting)	17 (12)
Technology (including software and hardware)	15.5 (11)
Banking/finance	14.1 (10)
Advertising/marketing/public relations	14.1 (10)
Architecture/design	7 (5)
Health care/medical equipment	5.6 (4)
Consumer Products	4.2 (3)
Publishing	1.4 (1)
Total	**100 (71)**

In tables 2 and 3, I provide information about the occupations and jobs that participants held and the types of companies they worked for. Although I did collect information on job titles, these were not consistent across organizations and often do not represent or indicate what the research participant actually did in his daily work. Instead I group jobs by function and/or the department in the company in which the individual worked, which is a better index of the types of tasks he performed. I also provide information on the specialty area or economic sector of the interviewees' companies. In an extra step to protect participants' confidentiality, I have decided not to list position, company, and city together in table form, as is often done in studies like mine. Since some of my interviewees know each other, this seemed the safest bet for trying to keep identities private. These two tables help place the accounts of research participants in context and underline the fact that, as with all nonrandom samples, we should be cautious about generalizing from this group of white-collar workers' experiences. My goal was to collect interview accounts from a varied group of workers rather than draw a representative sample, and the tables show that indeed, the group is quite diverse in occupation and industry. There are certainly white-collar occupations and business sectors that are not represented in the core group of interviewees, and as we can see, the men in this sample are more diverse in their job functions than in the types of companies where they are employed. Perhaps future research can include more types of jobs and industries or focus more narrowly on the habits and habitus of a smaller group, such as IT professionals or architects.

Notes

INTRODUCTION

1. One of these exceptions is Rosabeth Moss Kanter's landmark 1977 work *Men and Women of the Corporation* (which is as old as I am).

2. I define embodiment as the experience of being or having a particular type of body in a particular time and place. This experience is both phenomenological and social, and a focus on embodiment often emphasizes individual people's feelings, identities, and perceptions.

3. According to anthropologist Carrie M. Lane, "The average U.S. worker now changes jobs at least ten times over the course of a career," and half of the families in the United States have experienced one or more layoffs of income-earning family members (2011, 39, 41).

4. See Harvey 2005.

5. Bordo 1999.

6. Scholarly writings often present "the body" as a metaphor or abstract concept rather than flesh and blood; as sociologist Chris Shilling puts it, "The number of sophisticated theoretical works on embodiment has yet to be matched by sufficient substantive investigations of the significance of the body to people's daily lives" (2007, 13).

7. As gender scholars demonstrate (Carter 2014; Halberstam 1998; Pascoe 2007; Schilt 2011), bodies that are not assigned male sex at birth can also perform and embody masculinity. And of course, male bodies can perform femininity. This book focuses on people for whom sex and gender line up: biological cisgender males who identify as men and engage in performances of masculinity (some scholars prefer the plural term masculinities). Studying boundary crossers and bodies that are marked by their otherness is important, but it is equally critical to study bodies that are usually unmarked and viewed as "normal."

1. PLAYING BY THE RULES

1. The *American Heritage Dictionary* (2000) defines "white-collar" as "of or relating to workers whose work does not involve manual labor and who are often expected to dress with a degree of formality." Other dictionary definitions include references to working "in an office" or "professional environment." Today, the "degree of formality" in dress varies considerably, as this chapter shows. The term "corporate" obviously denotes people or things related to the corporation, a legal entity that is often assumed to be large (in number of people affiliated) but does not need to be. In this study, I associate "corporate" with for-profit companies in the private sector, regardless of size. As we'll see, the men in the study have mostly similar understandings of "white-collar," but some reject the "corporate" label despite their employment in the for-profit business world. Dress is a point of encounter between self and society, "an activity of clothing the body with an aesthetic element" (Entwistle 2000, 28); on dress, see also Barthes 2006 and (1967) 1985; Corrigan 2008; Eicher and Roach-Higgins 1997; Keenan 2001.

2. This book was later made into a movie starring Gregory Peck as the title "man," but in my opinion the novel is superior to the film treatment. And yes, I am one of those people who almost always think the book is better than the movie.

3. Janus, Kaiser, and Gray 1999.

4. All names of research participants in this book are pseudonyms. The first time an interviewee is mentioned in each chapter, I use the false first and last name; thereafter I use just the first name. For more information on this study's methodology, see the appendix.

5. Textiles scholar Linda Boynton Arthur details the process by which "aloha shirts" became acceptable business dress in Hawaii (2008, 300–301).

6. See Balestri and Ricchetti 2000 or Janus, Kaiser, and Gray 1999 for the historical particulars. Corrigan argues that Casual Friday, which allows people to wear their weekend clothing during the workweek, represents the blurring of the spatial and temporal separation between the public self (producer, at work) and the private self (consumer, at leisure) (2008, 53).

7. Janus, Kaiser, and Gray 1999.

8. These statements also recall the old adage that as U.S. women's hemlines rise, so do the country's economic indicators. Such explanations link personal dress decisions, collective fashion, and economic conditions.

9. This is a situation that search firms are aware of; one recruiter said he would tell candidates going to interview during a normal workday that they could come change clothes in his office first. Another recruiter said that he would prepare the interviewing employer for the fact that the interviewee worked in a business casual office and would thus not be wearing a suit to the interview.

10. Lane 2011, 47.

11. Rucker, Anderson, and Kangas 1999.

12. I borrow the term "magnified moment" from Hochschild (1994).

13. I take these terms from the work of sociologist Gerald Suttles, who argued, "Some places have a lot of such culture: songs that memorialize their great streets or side streets, homes once occupied by the famous or infamous, a distinctive dialect or vocabulary, routine festivals and parades that selectively dramatize the past, novels, dirty lyrics, pejorative nicknames, special holidays, dead heroes, evangelical moralists, celebrated wastrels, and so on" (1984, 284). I believe that Cincinnati, New York City, and San Francisco are places like this. Even in Cincinnati, which is the smallest and least nationally prominent of the three, this description evokes local cultural elements such as the pioneers of industry Procter and Gamble, whose company's international headquarters resides downtown, and the opening day parade for the Cincinnati Reds, which many Cincinnatians skip school or work to attend. I am grateful to Mitch Duneier for pointing me toward Suttles's article.

14. To illustrate this formality, New Yorkers discussed wearing suits on weekend outings (dinner, drinks, etc.) or to baseball games. The baseball game example may say as much about long work hours and physical distance between home and office as it does about dress formality.

15. Who the company's clients are also matters, as Sánchez Voelkl (2011) points out in her study of corporate executives in Colombia and Ecuador.

16. Hall 1994, 299. See also Dellinger 2002; Ho 2009.

17. Information technology workers and engineers were also likely to mention the physical aspects of their jobs—crawling around under desks to reach cables, for example—as reasons why they dressed casually.

18. Janus, Kaiser, and Gray 1999.

19. Mills (1951) 2002, 81.

20. I must have gone overboard in this probing technique with at least one interviewee, who had no sooner uttered the word "proper" in describing expected work dress than he teasingly questioned me, chuckling, "And now you're going to ask me what 'proper' means, right?"

21. See Dasgupta 2010 on how appearance is seen as reflective of work performance and abilities for businessmen in Japan.

22. In a quirky book entitled *Why Do Architects Wear Black?* one response to the title question is "Black is timeless, like architecture should be" (Rau 2008, n.p.).

23. Several men whose work dress regime was casual or anything-goes joked that, in their office, "Every day is Casual Friday."

24. Mills (1951) 2002, 74.

25. In the past, because the suit was more widely used, it didn't have such power to represent a particular class or type of person; when mass-produced suits became popular in the United States in the late nineteenth century, they were used by men of all classes (Kidwell and Christman 1974).

26. Seventy-one individuals comprised the core group of white-collar men I interviewed. However, one of these interviewees was retired, so in some places where it is important to understand current employment conditions or the perspectives of men still in the workforce, I refer to the seventy interviewees who were employed at the time of the interview.

27. Simmel (1904) 1957.

28. Entwistle 2000a.

29. For at least two centuries, the business suit has represented "hegemonic (bourgeois) masculinity" (Kaiser 2012, 127), which can have a sexual dimension as "a symbol of male sexuality in terms of broadening shoulders and chest and connecting larynx to crotch through collar and tie" (Edwards 1997, 3). For more on the phallic characteristics of the necktie, see Huun 2008.

30. Holliday and Thompson 2001; Wolkowitz 2006.

31. These accounts underscore the oddness of the interview as a moment of contact between employer and future employee. In the experience of many research participants, what they wore to their initial interviews was not what they wore to work on a daily basis once hired.

32. Two men who had people reporting to them mentioned that it was especially difficult for them, as men, to correct women's dress (see chapter 5).

33. Kanter (1977) showed that human resources is often seen as an area of the corporate organization in which women predominate. In Aiden's small company, one woman *was* the human resources department. Perhaps the fact that HR is represented by a woman, or is seen as a feminized line of work, factors into some workers' resistance to dress codes.

34. According to Mills, "The salesman's world has now become everybody's world, and, in some part, everybody has become a salesman. . . . The bargaining manner, the huckstering animus, the memorized theology of pep, the commercialized evaluation of personal traits—they are all around us; in public and private there is the tang and feel of salesmanship" ([1951] 2002, 161). Hochschild (1983) and Kang (2010) use the term "emotional labor" to refer to this practice. Recently scholars have begun discussing appearance together with emotions, coining the term "aesthetic labor," which is most often applied to service work (Warhurst and Nickson 2001; Witz, Warhust, and Nickson 2003; see also Adkins and Lury 2000; Wolkowitz 2006).

35. See Wolkowitz 2006 for a review of this literature.

36. Casanova 2013; Monaghan 2002a, 2002b.

37. Even some scholars reproduce this dichotomy: e.g., McElhinny (1994).

38. Some interviewees (e.g., an auditor who works with various departments, a corporate trainer) had "internal clients," and others talked about dealing with vendors, who were similar to clients in that they were external to the organization. Most of the clients mentioned here are external clients, but in some cases I include comments about internal clients and vendors. In all these cases, the employee is representing the company in some way.

39. See Kaiser, Freeman, and Chandler 1993 for a comparison of men's and women's narratives about their favorite clothing.

40. The ego boost gained from dressing well can also be activated in adversarial contexts, as Dave put it: "If you're an opponent of mine in a way . . . I think I'll instantly have more confidence knowing that you're kind of dressed like a schmuck."

41. Survey respondents in Kang, Sklar, and Johnson 2011 also reported this.

42. This is also discussed in Kang, Sklar, and Johnson 2011.

43. Goffman 1959.

44. Elias and Beasley 2009, 286; Connell and Wood 2005.

45. Berebitsky 2012.

46. Edwards 1997; Hollander 1994; Kidwell and Christman 1974; McDowell 1997.

2. JUST LIKE DAD?

1. Hochschild 1989; Gerson 1994.

2. Damaske 2011; Stone 2007.

3. Kanter 1977.

4. Blair-Loy 2003; Gerson 1986; Hochschild 1989, 2001.

5. Kaiser Family Foundation 2014.

6. One supplemental interview with a man who worked for a custom-clothing business presented a relatively deterministic view of the effects of background on work dress: "It's what you are exposed to, 'Hey, I was raised in the Bronx, we grew up in the streets, we didn't wear no clothes. My father was a worker in a steel mill.' Well, that guy's not gonna have the same as, 'Well, my father was a banker in New York City and his father before him was a banker . . . and we always wore tweed and the finest linens and wools.' . . . That person, his whole heritage is that he's been exposed to fine dressing all his life, but I think if you haven't been, you can—it can be a learned skill."

7. However, one scholar of dress has examined the exchange of clothing within the family unit, including hand-me-downs, which I discuss later in the chapter (Corrigan 2008).

8. Forty-four percent of research participants reported being fathers.

9. Bourdieu 1984; Bourdieu and Passeron 1990.

10. I use the term *embodiment* to refer to the experience of having or being a body in a particular social environment. I am interested in both bodies (that is, the material substance of human beings, the ideas that circulate around bodies, and the ways that they are perceived by others and represented in culture and media) and embodiment (the everyday subjective or phenomenological experience of the body by an individual, which involves social, physical, spatial, and psychological aspects).

11. Rutherford 1987, 55.

12. I discuss uniforms more in chapter 3.

13. Working in the same field as your father could provide advantages—consider Carl's anecdote at the beginning of the chapter—but not always. The time lapse between father's and son's careers, along with changing dress norms, stamp an expiration date on some advice. Timothy Stein, a hedge fund manager, also had a father in finance, but recounts, "I was told by my father, like, he, for example, always wore a button-down collar, and you know, after a few years of opening my eyes, I realized that no, spread collars are actually standard, and so I actually realized that he was wrong."

14. Glen paid is a fabric characterized by "pattern mixing" and "an alternating 'boxes' motif, incorporating stripes and cross-sections." It is also known as Prince of Wales check because of a famous historical wearer who held that royal title (GQ 2013).

15. Phil was the only interviewee who was retired at the time of the interview (to my knowledge, only one other interviewee has retired since our interview). I thought that it would be advantageous to have the perspective of someone who had begun working longer ago than the majority of the participants and who had left the workforce.

16. Blum 2005; Casanova 2011; Kaiser 2012, 112.

17. Bordo 1999; Coad 2008; McLeod 1996; Rucker, Anderson, and Kangas 1999.

18. This finding echoes a 2008 survey that found the greatest interest in fashion and appearance among African American respondents; white men were the least interested (Kaiser 2012, 87).

19. See Harvey Wingfield 2013 and McLeod 1996 on African Americans; Rucker, Anderson, and Kangas 1999 on Hispanics.

20. Military veterans' feelings about their uniforms are discussed in chapter 3.

21. Dickies is a brand of heavy-duty work clothing, most known for pants (which Andy is referring to here). Most Dickies pants are priced in the $20–$30 range (www. dickies.com). Ben Davis is a brand that offers similar types of items that are pricier, with its trademark jacket costing $76 (www.bendavis.com). This clothing is best described as unadorned, sturdy, and functional.

22. White-collar men's reminiscences about their blue-collar fathers' work dress brought out their feelings on other issues as well. Aiden Curry explained to me over Mexican food at a cozy hole-in-the-wall in San Francisco's Mission District that his father had worked in a warehouse, where the standard dress was jeans and T-shirts. He referred obliquely to his dad's being overweight, saying that he had a "size difference" due to lack of physical activity. Aiden conflated his father's casual work dress with his being out of shape, invoking stereotypes of U.S. blue-collar or working-class men as heftier than their better-off counterparts.

23. Timothy prefaced these statements by saying that he was partially of Italian heritage himself (perhaps justifying the subsequent negative comments). For a discussion of the "Guido" fashion associated with Italian Americans in the northeastern United States, see Tricarico 2008.

24. I won't overgeneralize from these cases, but nearly a quarter of U.S. Latino/a families live in poverty today (Krogstad 2014).

25. For some interviewees, these two values run counter to each other. Espousing the importance of "quality" in clothing, they stated that you need to spend more on items in order to be able to wear them over many years. In some cases, the emphasis on quality had been passed on by parents, and in others, the men had come to this opinion on their own, often connecting it to their rising salaries and ability to pay for quality.

26. See Pugh 2009 on contemporary patterns of children's consumption, in which parents see their progeny as needing rather than simply wanting what other kids have.

27. Hochschild 1994.

28. On occupational habitus, see Wolkowitz 2006.

29. Although Aaron didn't define "power tie," many online style forums, in which posters ask questions such as "What is a power tie?," point to a full Windsor (wide) knot and bold solid color such as blue or red as the defining features of a power tie, supposedly worn by people who either hold or aspire to powerful social, economic, or political positions. For a definition of the related term "power suit," see Heti, Julavits, and Shapton 2014, 217.

30. On heightened attention to men's bodies, see Bordo 1999; Gill, Henwood, and McLean 2005; and Moss 2011. On marketing to men, see Coad 2008; Moss 2011; Rinallo 2007.

31. Barry 2014; Rinallo 2007.

3. PUTTING ON THE UNIFORM

1. Even if people in a social group do not resist mandated dress, material facts such as limited or unequal resources among members or different sizes and shapes of bodies may challenge regulations requiring similar dress and appearance.

2. The United States is different from many other countries, both rich and poor, in that many public and private schools do not mandate uniforms for students (although

nearly all schools have some dress guidelines). Research participants who grew up outside the United States seemed to think it strange that I asked whether or not they liked wearing school uniforms. Since all the children they knew did it, and there was no choice involved, they seemed not to have developed a preference one way or another. On the purpose of school uniforms, see Craik 2008.

3. As recently as 2008, one scholar wrote that the suit is "the international work uniform" of men (Corrigan 2008, 54).

4. One interviewee, a native Cincinnatian now working in New York City, told me, "When you walk around downtown Cincinnati or you walk around Hyde Park or Kenwood [two upscale neighborhoods in which corporate offices are located and many white-collar workers live] and all that stuff, people are—they've just come right out of Brooks Brothers. There's a white button-down shirt or blue button-down shirt. There are khaki pants or there're navy blue pants. They've got a blue sport coat, and that's it." He followed this portrait of white-collar uniformity with the disclaimer, "Obviously, I'm making huge generalizations here."

5. A recent study of corporate men in South America found similar uniformity. One participant stated, "Everyone dresses the same . . . with a super-similar look, almost identical people . . . dark blue or khaki pants with a shirt" (Sánchez Voelkl 2011, 71).

6. This attitude is similar to that of another interviewee, a New Yorker working in finance, who disparagingly called a subset of his coworkers "the uniform guys" because they often dressed alike. He recounted advising a younger, newer employee who was emulating this style of dress to "mix it up more."

7. Dockers are a brand of casual (sometimes khaki) pants, considered slightly dressier than jeans by many of the participants.

8. One San Francisco interviewee, who worked in the tech field, described choosing to wear dressier clothing than what was required because putting on this self-appointed "uniform for working" got him mentally ready to do his job.

9. Vans are a brand of flat-soled sneakers popular among skateboarders.

10. Many participants agreed that dress was most uniform in banking and finance. As one man I interviewed in Manhattan put it, if you go downtown at lunchtime, you'll see "dude after dude in cornflower [blue] shirts, suits, and pleated jackets."

11. Thomas Pink is a pricey brand of dress shirt that was popular among many of the New York interviewees and/or their business contacts. As I learned from my visits to the company's website and Pink store located near the Chrysler Building in Manhattan, most shirts range from $100 to $200, though I saw a couple on the sale rack for around $80.

12. For example, participant Pete Costa remarked, "In this day and age . . . you can pretty much be yourself in the corporate environment to a certain extent." He saw this as a liberty afforded by business casual dress codes.

13. Merton 1961, 48, 53.

14. Marcuse (1964) 1991, 1.

15. See Matthew Gill 2009 for an insider account of how occupational cultures, through shared business practices, facilitate and justify (to the participants) such collective deceptions.

16. Simmel ([1904] 1957, 548) remarks that even in rejecting fashion, an individual still uses fashion as the point of reference. That is, the group norm is delineated or reified in its very rejection. Social theorist George Herbert Mead concurred, writing, "Perhaps one says that he does not care to dress in a certain fashion, but prefers to be different; then he is taking the attitude of others toward himself into his own conduct" ([1934] 1967, 193). The mainstream (and its dominant tendencies) is still the point of reference for the fashion rebel.

17. Simmel (1904) 1957, 542.

18. Sapir (1931) 2007, 39.

19. Blumer 1969, 284. The French sociologist Pierre Bourdieu similarly argued that people reject that "from which they are anyway excluded," and embrace that "for which they are in any case destined" (2002, 95). In short, people are conditioned to want the lives that they will most likely end up with; this is how social classes remain cohesive and enduring.

20. Blumer 1969, 289 (emphasis in original text).

21. Mills (1951) 2000, xii.

22. Ibid., xvii.

23. Whyte 1956, 46.

24. Ibid., 155.

25. Wilson (1955) 2002, 272.

26. Kanter 1977, 47. Of course I disagree with Kanter that workers' appearance is a "trivial matter." IBM's infamously strict dress rules (e.g., all but mandating sock garters for men, even in recent decades) were mentioned specifically by several interviewees.

27. See Harvey Wingfield 2013; Rivera 2012.

28. Kaiser 2012.

29. Joseph 1986, 2.

30. Craik 2003, 127.

31. I did not specifically ask each interviewee about sports uniforms. However, some men brought this topic up on their own, and seemed to enjoy wearing these uniforms, as they represented team spirit, fun, and leisure.

32. See Craik 2005 for an explicit link to masculinity; also Craik 2003 and Roche 1996.

33. For this definition see Joseph 1986, 144.

34. Simmel (1904) 1957, 543. Another Cincinnati participant offered up the Simmel-esque axiom, "Make your own statement, but don't stand out too much."

35. Ed worked in a business casual office in Cincinnati, so a suit would have stood out in that setting.

36. Dreby 2009; Rosnow and Fine 1976.

37. Bordo 1999.

38. For more on "looking important," see chapter 7.

39. For more on local dress cultures, see chapters 1 and 4.

40. Compare Luke's comment with this one from Claude Whitfield, interviewed because of his military experience, who was not currently employed full-time in a corporate office: "I like to walk into a room and make people stop. . . . I don't have to have someone say [anything] to me, but it's more the reaction I get when I walk into a room and people do a double-take. That's what I go for. Yeah. I just want a reaction . . . 'Cause there's no—to me there's no such thing as bad publicity." This is a very different take on dress than most of my white-collar interviewees expressed.

41. U.S. Department of Labor 2011.

42. U.S. Department of Commerce 1951; Bureau of Labor Statistics 2011. In addition, just about 10 percent of people employed in the "professional and business services" sector are male veterans (U.S. Department of Labor 2011).

43. The supplemental veteran interviewees, quoted in this chapter, are Keith Rogers (African American, Cincinnati), Claude Whitfield (African American, New York City), and Alan Salazar (Latino, New York metro area).

44. Alan Salazar, another former marine interviewee, defined "squared away": "There's a certain way that you [should] look in uniform, if you break out the actual manual. . . . Your emblems should be aligned perfectly, everything should be pressed. . . . If you're wearing the leather boots, you had to make sure that they were shined. . . . At any time

you should be able to stand [and undergo an] inspection if you had to. And that's what a squared-away marine should look like all the time." The manual that he referred to, the U.S. Marine Corps Uniform Regulations, puts it this way: "Marines will maintain their uniforms and equipment in a neat and serviceable condition and will, by their appearance, set an example of neatness and strict conformity."

45. Claude, who had served in the U.S. Air Force, agreed with this sentiment: "It starts out with like the simple things in terms of how you dress, how you act . . . teamwork . . . 'cause if you're leading someone into war in the military, you know, you gotta feel confident that you know what you're doing. You can do it well. So why not start with the simple things of teaching you how to dress, or how to walk right, for that matter." Learning how to "walk right" shows how the military is dedicated to (re)training its members in various aspects of embodiment.

46. Keith names here several places that marines are stationed: Camp Pendleton (just north of San Diego, California), Camp LeJeune (in Jacksonville, North Carolina, the site of my husband's first duty station after his initial training), and Quantico, Virginia.

47. These regulations can be found on the Marine Corps website, http://www.marines. mil/Portals/59/Publications/MCO%20P1020.34G%20W%20CH%201–5.pdf.

48. Once in a sociology class I was teaching, I was trying to explain the concept of a social type (e.g., jock, nerd). Students gave me blank looks until I called on the one former marine in the class to provide an impromptu definition of a shitbag. He provided a detailed, paragraph-long verbal exposition on this social type, and his fellow students seemed shocked that my illustrative pedagogical stunt had worked. He did, however, tell me of a newer synonym that had come into use in the corps: "shitbird." It somehow seems a nicer way to insult someone.

49. While in their job, service members know that they are to wear the "uniform of the day," specified by the commanding officer and communicated to the troops. Commanding officers have some discretion in which uniforms to require, but general guidelines exist, as do specific instructions for which clothing items are included in a uniform and how they must be arranged or worn.

50. Using the example of the famous British military veteran-turned-fashion plate Beau Brummell (1778–1840), Peoples argues that military "techniques of the body . . . last beyond the career of a person dressed in military uniform, and continues [sic] to be absorbed into the body of one's civilian identity" (2014, 8).

51. See Delaney 2012 for an interesting discussion of the chicken-and-egg question of whether people's personalities influence their choice of career or vice versa.

52. One said, referring to his work clothing, "I'm loud in other ways, but not that way."

4. THE METROSEXUAL IS DEAD, LONG LIVE THE METROSEXUAL!

1. Simmel (1904) 1957, 549.

2. Bordo 1999; Entwistle 2009; Gill, Henwood, and McLean 2005. Scholars and industry reports have attested that "men's interest in dress and fashion has been rapidly growing and menswear sales have been increasing" (Kang, Sklar, and Johnson 2011, 413).

3. On histories of men's dress, see Cole 2000; Kuchta 2008; McNeil and Karaminas 2009; Mort 1996; and Nixon 1996.

4. As other research has shown, people present portraits of themselves that characterize their practices as not just normal but also norma*tive* in the sense that they view those with different practices negatively. For examples, see Mose Brown 2011 on West Indian nannies who criticize their employers' parenting and Reich 2014 on debates over whether parents should vaccinate their children. Many empirical studies asking people to account for their practices find that they justify their choices by contrasting them with the choices they associate with other social groups.

5. More details on the demographics of all seventy-one participants are provided in the appendix.

6. Earlier works on masculinity include Chafetz 1974 and Brannon 1976.

7. Connell and Messerschmidt 2005. Sherri Grasmuck put it this way: "Whatever we call the alternative versions of traditional masculinity, the range of actual male *behavior* is often far broader than our dominant *ideas* about how men should behave" (2005, 96).

8. Connell and Messerschmidt 2005, 849.

9. Connell 1995, 78; this certainly applies in other parts of the world too.

10. Demetriou 2001, 346.

11. Ibid., 348.

12. Anderson's (2005) concept of "orthodox masculinity," a commitment to the norms of hegemonic masculinity that is adopted by marginalized men, extends this line of reasoning.

13. Fee 2000, 44.

14. Ibid., 61.

15. Bridges 2014, 59. Popular discussions of this topic also employ humor, as in Peter Hyman's memoir, *The Reluctant Metrosexual: Dispatches from an Almost Hip Life*: "I should admit that I fall squarely in what has come to be termed the 'straight but gayish' (or previously alluded to 'metrosexual') camp. This defines men, like myself, who, while completely certain of their heterosexuality, tend toward midcentury modern design and flat-front trousers. That we even use the term 'flat-front trousers' is evidence of the sexual ambiguity we seem to emit. To the women who like this sort of style and emotional sensitivity, we are just gay enough" (2004, 9).

16. Bridges 2014, 80.

17. St. John 2003.

18. Miller 2005.

19. Simpson 1999, 207. The city context is key to the popular understandings of metrosexuality and to the views of the men I spoke with; more on this later.

20. Coad 2008, 18.

21. Rinallo 2007; Wickman 2011.

22. Wickman 2011.

23. Ibid., 117–118.

24. Coad 2008; Rinallo 2007.

25. The young, mostly Italian American men on this program embody the latest iteration of the stereotypical "Guido" aesthetic, characterized by meticulous care and grooming of the body and tight, flamboyant clothing that accentuates the male physique (Tricarico 2008).

26. The hipster and the metrosexual were perceived as distinct social types by the interviewees. (There is some tongue-in-cheek debate in pop culture about whether the category of hipster can include women; here I am speaking specifically of male hipsters.) One New York interviewee, Michel Jean, described the hipster as part of the backlash to the metrosexual: whereas metrosexuals were supposedly obsessed with grooming, hipsters were "grungy." Both Michel and Travis Jones, who also worked in New York, described the hipster image and especially the popularity of beards among youngish men as an indication of the hipster's rejection of metrosexuality. An entire book could probably be written on the relationship between these two styles of masculine embodiment and their place in larger social-cultural debates about what it means to be (or look like) a man in the contemporary United States. The newest target of parody, the "lumbersexual," combines elements of the hipster and metrosexual (gearjunkie.com 2014).

27. There have been historical precursors to the metrosexual: the "dandy," the figure that Simmel referred to as the "dude," the eighteenth-century British "macaroni" (McNeil 2009), or the famous flâneurs of nineteenth-century Paris (Baudelaire 1964; Benjamin

1983) all bear a certain resemblance to the metrosexual. The difference between these previous iterations and today's version, as I see it, comes from the heightened emphasis on the (fit) body as a vehicle for individual identity in contemporary society (Shilling 2003) and the proliferation of new commodities specifically designed to help men dress, accessorize, and groom the body (Rinallo 2007).

28. "Metrosexual" was chosen as the "Word of the Year" in 2003 by the American Dialect Society (Rinallo 2007, 79).

29. Coad 2008.

30. Reilly, Rudd, and Hillary 2008; Rinallo 2007.

31. Rinallo 2007.

32. Davis 1992, 35.

33. Mills (1951) 2002, 250.

34. This reputation is due to the concentration of fashion design firms (and in earlier eras, garment manufacturers) in New York and is propagated by fashion culture and media events such as Fashion Week and television programs including *Project Runway* and *Sex and the City*.

35. Costco is a bulk retailer of groceries, home goods, electronics, and clothing that requires an annual membership fee.

36. Outside densely packed city centers, white-collar life is more dispersed and privatized; it doesn't involve as many interactions in common areas such as lobbies or sidewalks.

37. Hearn and Parkin 1995, 159.

38. Wickman and Langeland 2013, 128.

39. Coad 2008.

40. The links between gender identity and sexual orientation are complex and somewhat messy in everyday life; see Bridges 2014 and Fee 2000. For more discussion of and evidence for what Ian referred to as "gay sensibility," or tastes associated with gay men, see Bridges 2014, Coad 2008, Cole 2000 (who specifically discusses gay men's dress), and Higgins 1998. For an enlightening if now somewhat dated account of how gay men in corporate America conceal their sexual orientation at work, see Woods 1993.

41. My only direct question about participants' sexual orientation occurred toward the end of the interview, in a straightforward list of demographic questions (e.g., "Where were you born?"). I asked the men, "Do you identify as gay, straight, or something else?" Although some men gave humorous answers to this question ("My wife hopes I'm straight!"), only two men seemed offended. The calm answering of a direct question about sexual preferences that I routinely encountered might have been harder to achieve if I had been a male interviewer, but I can't be sure.

42. Even some scholars have relied on or supported this stereotype in their research, for example, saying that fashion is a "gay consumer interest" that is "grounded in shared knowledge and value orientations," which leads to a "distinctly gay social voice" (Higgins 1998, 156; see also Edwards 2009). There is a fine line between reporting on what one has observed or been told and contributing to the maintenance of stereotypes, a fact I was acutely aware of in this study.

43. Rinallo's Italian interviewees agreed that dress was not an indication of sexual orientation, leading him to conclude that "gaydar is dead" (2007, 88). Gaydar (a portmanteau of "gay" and "radar") refers to an ability to sense whether a person is gay.

44. As in my study, some gay men in a recent U.K. study reported not being out at work or not being out to everyone at work (Rumens 2011). See also Speice (forthcoming), in which gay interviewees say they don't want to dress or look "too gay" at work, and Woods 1993.

45. By traditional masculinity I mean predominant contemporary forms of hegemonic masculinity in the United States (associated with white, middle-class, heterosexual men), which still eschew fashion or perceived excessive concern with appearance on the part of straight men.

46. My finding that some men welcome compliments from other men (gay or straight) runs counter to previous research, which suggested that a man telling a male coworker, "Hey, nice suit" would be interpreted as "Hey, wanna go out on a date?" (Edwards 1997, 119). See also Simpson 2015.

47. That is, a gay man hitting on a straight man in 2013 in a center of gay population and culture like Manhattan is less risky (Linneman 2000) than such an action would have been in, say, 1955, or in a rural area of Nebraska.

48. This reinforces a hierarchy of masculinity that places heterosexual men at the top and subordinates gay-identified men as less masculine.

49. Men of all ages told me that you cannot determine whether a man is gay just by looking at how he is dressed. Luiz Rodrigues, a middle-aged father, told me he had asked his grown children (whom he described as having many gay friends) whether gay people dressed differently than straight people. Their answer, according to Luiz: "Pop, you'd be surprised. It's totally random today" (see also Rinallo 2007).

50. Rinallo 2007, 88. Rinallo writes that gay men see straight men's new fashion consciousness as evidence that they are becoming more "civilized."

51. Bridges 2014; Fee 2000.

52. Bridges 2014, 71.

53. Connell 1995.

54. James 2011; Gates and Newport 2013.

55. Although my sample of seventy-one interviews was not random, five of the ten gay men I interviewed held manager-level positions or above, and three of these five men were based in San Francisco.

56. This may be the case in other cities as well, and even within San Francisco it may be truer for some corporate settings than others. For example, men who worked for clothing retailers talked about the prevalence of out gay men in their offices. Aiden Curry, whom I interviewed in San Francisco, claimed that his field of public relations was populated primarily by women and gay men. Some fields of white-collar work are seen as more likely to employ gay workers.

57. One study claims that San Francisco "provides a social laboratory of sorts" in which people can "explore unconventional genders and sexualities" and "sexual categories, roles, and institutions" that "are not available in other locales" (Williams, Weinberg, and Rosenberger 2013, 719).

58. Cultural capital and social capital are theorized in Bourdieu 1984.

59. Bridges 2014; Demetriou 2001.

60. Forms of male identification among gay men or nonwhite men.

61. Demetriou 2001.

62. "Although 'softer' and more 'sensitive' styles of masculinity are developing … [they do not] necessarily contribute to the emancipation of women; in fact, quite the contrary may be true" (Messner 1993, 725).

63. Bridges 2014, 23.

64. Bordo 1999; Craig 2002; Kaiser 2012; Pascoe 2007.

65. See O'Neal 1999.

66. My argument here runs counter to the assumption that establishing gay-straight alliances in the workplace will help to transform the way that sexuality and gender operate in corporate environments (Rumens 2011).

67. Bordo 1999, 17.

ZUCK'S HOODIE

1. Here Sean is referring to the fact that in a 2010 public interview, Zuckerberg apparently became uncomfortably warm and removed his trademark gray hoodie. He revealed the inside of the hoodie, which has a symbol representing the Facebook mission statement

in light and dark blue. Several blogs referred to it as mysterious and reminiscent of the occult symbols of the Illuminati in their analysis of Zuckerberg's analysis of what it meant.

2. Zuckerberg's visit to investors took place in early May 2012. In Florida, a black teen named Trayvon Martin had been shot to death while wearing a hoodie in the final days of February that same year. This provoked several "Million Hoodie March" events organized around the country by people outraged by Martin's killing, along with campaigns to have people tweet or Instagram photographs of themselves wearing hoodies as a sign of solidarity with Martin's family and the African American community. Why would the hoodie be seen as a sign of immaturity when donned by a young white man but a sign of adultifying criminal intent when covering the body of a young black man? In both cases, the hoodie is cast as a deviant form of dress, despite its widespread popularity.

3. See Dvorak 2012; Fralic 2012; Friedman 2011; Garrahan 2012; Gaudin 2012; Gross 2012; Guynn 2013; Larson 2011; Lazarowitz 2013; Lefifi 2012; Rohrer 2012; Sengupta 2012; Silverman 2012.

4. Lazarowitz 2013.

5. Fralic 2012.

6. Gaudin 2012; Dvorak 2012.

7. Sengupta 2012.

8. Gross 2012.

9. Rohrer 2012. In addition to the mission symbol in the lining, the shirt bears the logos for three categories seen on every Facebook user's page: friend requests, messages, and notifications.

10. The editor of *Esquire* is quoted in Rohrer (2012) as saying, "The hoodie is part of his [Zuckerberg's] personal brand and that is part of Facebook's brand."

11. Dvorak 2012; Lefifi 2012; Silverman 2012.

12. Guynn 2013.

13. The $168 Executive Hoodie is sold on the Beta website, http://www.betabrand.com/collections/west-coast-workwear/navy-executive-pinstripe-hoodie.html. It is available in gray or navy pinstripe and other classic suit patterns such as windowpane check and glen plaid. There is no word on whether Mark Z. has bought one.

5. WHAT ABOUT WOMEN?

1. Fashion blog readers may object to my calling *The Sartorialist* a men's blog. Though the eponymous sartorialist is a male blogger, the site includes examples of both men's and women's fashion, usually more women's than men's. Several interviewees mentioned *The Sartorialist* and *A Continuous Lean* by name. All these blogs are written by men, according to their online descriptions.

2. See, e.g., Entwistle 2000a, 2000b; Gimlin 2002; Hesse-Biber 2007; Weitz 2010.

3. In sociological terms, more aesthetic labor and emotional labor are expected or required of women than of men.

4. For scholarly accounts of the dearth and low status of women in finance, see Ho 2009 and McDowell 1997.

5. Padavic and Reskin 2002.

6. A typical interviewee comment: "[Looking at] many women here, you wouldn't think that we work in a casual workplace. But the men, you would." Another response directly connects "better" or more formal dress with caring more: "I will say that women at work, are usually dressed a lot better [than the men] . . . and maybe that's just women in general pay more attention to how they are dressed than men." Another interviewee singled out the tech employment sector: "If you go to a tech company . . . the women look appropriate or nicely dressed . . . and half the guys look like they couldn't get a job at wherever, dressed the way they are. But they have, you know, they have good brains." This

recalls the long-standing tradition in Western philosophy and popular culture of evaluating women on appearance and men on intellect.

7. Some research seems to support this conclusion: for a review, see Kaiser, Freeman, and Chandler 1993.

8. Here Brett verbalizes an anxiety that I felt acutely as I was designing this research project: Would I get one-word answers, or would men be willing to really talk with me? I found I had nothing to worry about, as interviewees generally had much to say about dressing for work.

9. Note that knowing about women's clothing and how it should fit is represented as a characteristic of gay rather than straight men.

10. Skeptical readers might argue that *of course* women workers in the *retail* sector talk about clothing (it's something their companies may sell), and they might shop more for clothing than other white-collar workers because of employee discounts. Yet men in a variety of fields claimed that women were more likely than men to include dress in their office conversations.

11. Linda McDowell also found this use of "girls" in her study of banking and finance in London, noting that "many women also refer to each other as girls" (1997, 141).

12. For more on this topic, see Berebitsky 2012; Hearn and Parkin 1995.

13. Barney is referring to the business doctrines introduced by the U.S. engineer and management expert Frederick Taylor (1856–1915), which emphasize efficiency, smooth workflow, and strict rules for employee behavior.

14. Demonstrating that this is a gendered risk, the possibility of men's showing too much skin in the corporate environment was brought up only once by a research participant, as a joke.

15. See Harvey Wingfield 2013 for discussion of black professional men's perceptions of the potential advantages to being a woman or a racial minority in their fields.

16. For social science perspectives on gossip, see Dreby 2009 and Rosnow and Fine 1976.

17. See Finlay and Coverdill 2007; Rivera 2012.

18. Of course, women who are overhearing or participating in this gossip about other women may pick up useful information about what clothes are seen as appropriate.

19. See Brewis and Sinclair 2000 and Entwistle 2000b on women's work dress dilemmas, including issues of standing out versus blending in and managing their sexuality.

20. Ann Taylor Loft is a retailer of both dressy and casual clothing for women: http://www.loft.com.

21. See Davis 1992; Entwistle 1997.

22. See Bartky 1988; Bordo 1993; Cregan 2006; DeMello 2014; Mears 2011.

23. For an excellent overview of these debates as applied to cosmetic surgery, see Pitts-Taylor 2007.

24. For more details on the self-identified relationship status and sexual orientation of the men in the sample, see the appendix.

25. In Kanter's classic study *Men and Women of the Corporation*, she claims that "many of the things a [manager's] wife does would simply go undone if she were not there to perform them; organizations would be unlikely to replace most of a wife's services with that of a paid employee" (1977, 127). This description may seem old-fashioned today, when dual-earner couples are the norm. Though I did not systematically collect data on spouses' employment, I interviewed at least half a dozen high-ranking men whose wives were not in the paid labor market and had taken on primary responsibility for their husbands' work wardrobes.

26. Men without a woman in their life can take to the Internet, where the fashion blog StyleGirlfriend.com claims to offer "the female perspective on male style."

27. I didn't interview anyone who claimed to work with his romantic partner, although of course I may not be privy to all these details.

28. See Davis 1992 on "antifashion."

29. See, e.g., Acker 1990; Britton 2000.

6. THE F WORD

1. Entwistle 2000a, 44–45.

2. The fashion industry has traditionally focused on women as consumers; this is changing rapidly (Rinallo 2007).

3. Entwistle 2000a, 40.

4. See Barry 2014 for a discussion of slim versus muscular male ideals in advertisements; muscular bodies are also crucial to a hegemonically masculine appearance.

5. Previous research addresses men's rejection of fashion, describing it as rooted in ideas such as the following: (1) there is no male fashion; (2) men are interested in fit and comfort rather than style; and (3) women dress men and shop for their clothes (Craik 1994; Goodrum 2001). The level of agreement among participants against being fashionable is all the more striking when compared with the variety of opinions men expressed about the metrosexual label, which seemed to me the more negative term (see chapter 3).

6. Kaiser, Freeman, and Chandler claim that there is "more aesthetic experimentation in shared female culture" (1993, 38).

7. For a discussion of the relationship between hip-hop and fashion, see Robinson 2008.

8. Women also differentiate between style and taste (Heti, Julavits, and Shapton 2014). Taste as a sociological concept is often traced to Pierre Bourdieu (1984), who associated it with class status and maintaining boundaries between people of different class positions.

9. Some studies find that women "dress more for social reasons, rely more on their friends to evaluate personal clothing choices, and display more awareness of, and interest in, clothing" (Kaiser, Freeman, and Chandler 1993, 29).

10. Dress scholar Susan Kaiser reminds us that the word "classic" is derived from social "class"; indeed, what makes these looks classic is their association with middle- and upper-class dress (2012, 106).

11. Pete was not the only gay participant to discuss age-related dress concerns; this finding fits with the literature on gay men's identities and the high value placed on youth and/or youthful appearance in U.S. gay communities (Slevin and Linneman 2010).

12. These findings echo those of Pascoe 2007 and Kaiser 2012.

13. Ed Hardy T-shirts feature vintage-tattoo-inspired designs: www.edhardyshop.com.

14. For more on legible or illegible masculinities within specific race and class contexts, see Neal 2013.

15. Some men—particularly gay men and men of color—explained that they were more likely to indulge in trends when dressing for leisure rather than work.

16. Dressing is a balancing act for men, who are constantly "navigating deftly between youth and age; caring but not overdoing; looking nice but not *too* nice" (Kaiser 2012, 143).

17. Men claimed this, for example, in relation to the term "metrosexual" (chapter 4).

18. Morrison 1992, 65.

19. Clothing messages are, however, often ambiguous, as Davis (1992) and others have noted.

20. Bordo 1999, 17.

21. Men's Wearhouse is a men's clothing retailer known for reasonably priced off-the-rack suits and tuxedo rentals: www.menswearhouse.com.

22. There may be social class and race connotations to these body-conforming styles. While in San Francisco I went out with a friend one night, and on our way home, we missed the last train at the nearest station. As we waited and waited for a cab, a few passed

us by. A young Latino man who was trying to hail a cab at the same corner blamed his loose-fitting pants, grumbling that a taxi would certainly stop for him if he were wearing "skinny jeans."

23. Men interviewed by Barry (2014) expressed similar views..

24. See Farrell 2011; Rothblum and Solovay 2009.

25. See Shilling 2003, esp. 4–7.

26. See Casanova and Jafar 2013; Casanova and Sutton 2013; Jafar and Casanova 2013; and Talukdar and Linders 2013 for empirical studies of how bodies and body projects relate to globalization and the increasing movement of people, money, and products across national borders.

27. Farrell 2011; Rothblum and Solovay 2009.

28. For a discussion of these attitudes see Hartley 2010.

29. The Centers for Disease Control (CDC) defines as obese people who have a body mass index (BMI) of thirty or higher (http://www.cdc.gov/obesity/adult/defining.html). BMI is calculated by dividing your weight (in kilograms) by your height squared (in meters). Information on obesity rates is available in several places on the Internet, but I drew it from the following website: http://www.governing.com/gov-data/obesity-rates-by-state-metro-area-data.html.

30. Here my findings echo research with male and female managers in New Zealand, who pointed to the importance of smaller, thinner bodies achieved through fitness practices (Longhurst 2004, chap. 5).

31. Heavier men and older men are significantly more likely to prefer looser-fitting clothing and higher waistlines (Chattaraman, Simmons, and Ulrich 2013).

32. Tim Edwards (1997) similarly argued that the men most likely to participate in fashion were trim, attractive, white, young, and well-off.

33. Barry 2014; Craig 2013; Mallyon et al. 2010.

34. See Mallyon et al. (2010) for how men redefine dieting as a masculine rather than feminine practice.

35. Bartky 1988; Grogan et al. 2013.

36. E.g., Franzoi and Shields 1984.

37. There were exceptions, however, as with the research participant who claimed, "I'm five nine and a half, 150 pounds, and I am like as average size as they come, so nine out of ten things that I would need, I wouldn't need to try on."

38. Rinallo 2007, based on Kimle and Damhorst 1997.

39. For these claims see Duggan and McCreary 2008; McArdle and Hill 2009; Rudd 2008.

7. BEING/BECOMING THE BOSS

1. On changing management practices and organizational structures, see Kastelle 2013; Moore and Hill 2011; Shaer 2013.

2. Anyone can walk into the outer waiting area of many business offices. Yet even in these offices, there may be rooms or hallways that are kept locked and require electronic badges or keys for access. Offices in large buildings often have a doorman, security guard, or concierge whose permission visitors need to venture past the lobby. The private-public fuzziness exists for employees, too. We recognize that being in the office is more public than being at home, yet we may feel comfortable there or adapt our physical space to be more homey (e.g., with decorations, rugs, etc.). These are a few of the features that make offices simultaneously public and private.

3. Those who did not have bosses in the way this relationship is usually thought of included a man who had started his own company and the number two man at a large Fortune 500 company.

4. See Bordo 1999; Craig 2013; DeMello 2014.

5. Thinking back to chapter 3, we see that the bureaucratic organizational structures and stratified personal relations of the military bear more than a passing resemblance to those of contemporary businesses.

6. See Roper 1996.

7. For in-depth discussion of the importance of homosociality (same-sex identification and interaction) for men in organizations, see Collinson and Hearn 1996; Hearn and Parkin 1995.

8. This heightened scrutiny is not specific to traditionally structured business organizations, as I show in the case of direct sales directors in Ecuador (Casanova 2011, chap. 4).

9. Brooks Brothers is a retailer many interviewees mentioned as an example of classic or traditional white-collar business attire. For some, this was a favorite brand, while others saw it as stuffy, stodgy, or unaffordable. Dress shirts are generally in the $90–100 range, with dress slacks costing anywhere from $170 to upwards of $400 (www.brooksbrothers.com).

10. Compare this influence on the part of the boss with, for example, the case of Frank Miller, who worked in finance and said that any consequences of poor dress would come from the client, not the boss: "Even when I wear my worst suit, he [my boss] doesn't say anything.... If I don't wear my jacket, he doesn't say anything."

11. While offering similar styles to Brooks Brothers, Jos. A. Bank's items tend to be a bit less expensive, especially when it comes to dress pants (www.josbank.com). According to my interviewees, this retailer often has sales that feature highly discounted prices.

12. Respondents in Kang, Sklar, and Johnson's study of men's work dress also used this phrase, with one saying, "If you want to move up the political corporate ladder you need to jump into a suit" (2011, 421).

13. See McDowell (1997), particularly part 2, on how bodies and dress matter for both men and women working in financial firms in the City of London. In Ho's (2009) study of Wall Street, one informant quickly learned that "junior people don't wear suspenders."

14. The sociologist Max Weber called this magical quality "charisma" ([1921] 1946).

15. The term "CEO" was commonly used by research participants for the top official in a publicly traded company, and "president" was used more by those who worked for private companies without shareholders. Some companies have both CEOs and presidents, and there seems to be a lively Internet debate over whether terms such as these (and others, such as COO and chair of the board) have consistent meanings across companies, sectors, and countries.

16. As an aside, the term "the man" was used in the 1960s and 1970s by black American activists and various social movements; it was a name assigned to the collective white male oppressor. (*The Man* was also an ironically titled 1972 film starring James Earl Jones as the first black president of the United States.) In more recent slang, telling someone "you're the man" has been a sign of respect and admiration. While most examples of The Man discussed by my research participants—like the majority of CEOs and upper-level executives in the United States—are white men, I do not intend for this moniker to be interpreted as overtly political.

17. Perhaps this is not hyperbole but an accurate account of what they've seen in rare glimpses of The Man. Either way, such descriptions serve to set The Man apart from other men in corporate settings.

18. Finlay and Coverdill 2007; Lane 2011.

19. Interviewees frequently pointed out how tall their CEO or president was. This brings to mind popular stereotypes of powerful men as tall and the concrete consequences of those stereotypes in the form of the higher wages and greater career success enjoyed by tall men (Judge and Cable 2004).

20. There are many places to find this information—e.g., http://www.catalyst.org/knowledge/women-ceos-fortune-1000.

21. Brody, Rubin, and Maume 2014.

22. According to a 2013 report by the Alliance for Board Diversity: http://theabd.org/2012_ABD%20Missing_Pieces_Final_8_15_13.pdf.

23. Managers, who had less status than Brad, told similar stories of climbing the corporate ladder. However embellished or inaccurate those accounts may be, it's the narrative that I'm interested in rather than the accuracy of self-reported facts.

24. See Brody, Rubin, and Maume 2014; Sánchez Voelkl 2011.

APPENDIX

1. Three interviews were not recorded, in two cases because of interviewees' preference and in one case because the recording equipment failed. At these interviews, I took detailed notes that capture the gist of what interviewees said and the exact wording of some of their statements.

2. The criteria for inclusion were that a man be over twenty-one (i.e., past college age) and employed full-time for a private company. I excluded men who worked for government agencies and nonprofit organizations or who were self-employed; the structures of these types of organizations tend to be different from that of the typical capitalist firm, and profit is not a concern for the public and nonprofit organizations. I was initially interested in speaking to lawyers but eventually decided to exclude them because of the very different audiences they have for their work dress: the courtroom was just too distinct from offices and conference rooms. Because of the unique structures of white-collar life in San Francisco, especially resulting from the influence of the dot-com and tech business sectors, I interviewed a few men there who worked from home one or more days per week. It seemed important to capture these employees engaged in somewhat nontraditional work arrangements, which are more common in the Bay Area than in the other two sites.

3. Lofland et al. 2006.

4. I was thirty-three and thirty-four years old when conducting the interviews.

5. "People who aren't that fashionable may be quite smart, nevertheless, about what they have on" (Heti, Julavits, and Shapton 2014, 5).

6. See, e.g., Mort 1996.

7. Tseëlon 2003, 245.

8. As Khan and Jerolmack note, "Verbal accounts researchers gather cannot stand in for action; rather, they are themselves a form of action often aimed at social signaling" (2013, 17).

9. On justifying interview-based research, see Damaske 2011; Gerson 2009; Ho 2009; Lane 2011.

10. Mose Brown and Casanova 2014.

11. Ibid.

12. For methodological discussions of studying up, see Nader 1972; Davison 2007; Gusterson 1997; Khan and Jerolmack 2013; Morrill 1996.

13. Cherlin 2010; Ciabattari 2004.

References

Acker, Joan. 1990. "Hierarchies, Occupations, Bodies: A Theory of Gendered Organizations." *Gender & Society* 4:139–158.

Adkins, Lisa, and Celia Lury. 2000. "Making Bodies, Making People, Making Work." In *Organizing Bodies: Policy, Institutions, and Work*, edited by Linda McKie and Nick Watson. London: Macmillan.

American Heritage Dictionary. 2000. 4th edition. Houghton Mifflin Harcourt.

Anderson, Eric. 2005. *In the Game: Gay Athletes and the Cult of Masculinity*. Albany: SUNY Press.

Arthur, Linda Boynton. 2008. "East Meets West: The Aloha Shirt as an Instrument of Acculturation." In Reilly and Cosbey, *The Men's Fashion Reader*, 295–310.

Balestri, Andrea, and Marco Ricchetti. 2000. "Manufacturing Men's Wear: Masculine Identity in the Structure of the Fashion Industry." In *Material Man: Masculinity, Sexuality, Style*, edited by Giannino Malossi, 52–63. New York: Abrams.

Barry, Ben. 2014. "Expanding the Male Ideal: The Need for Diversity in Men's Fashion Advertisements." *Critical Studies in Men's Fashion* 1 (3): 275–293.

Barthes, Roland. (1967) 1985. *The Fashion System*. Translated by Matthew Ward and Richard Howard. London: Jonathan Cape.

——. 2006. *The Language of Fashion*. Translated by Andy Stafford. Oxford: Berg.

Bartky, Sandra Lee. 1988. "Foucault, Femininity, and the Modernization of Patriarchal Power." In *Feminism and Foucault: Reflections on Resistance*, edited by Irene Diamond and Lee Quinby, 61–86. Boston: Northeastern University Press.

Baudelaire, Charles. 1964. *The Painter of Modern Life*. New York: Da Capo Press.

Baudrillard, Jean. (1976) 1993. "Fashion, or the Enchanting Spectacle of the Code." In *Symbolic Exchange and Death*. London: Sage.

Benjamin, Walter. 1983. *Charles Baudelaire: A Lyric Poet in the Era of High Capitalism*. London: Verso Books.

Berebitsky, Julie. 2012. *Sex and the Office: A History of Gender, Power, and Desire*. New Haven: Yale University Press.

Bettie, Julie. 2003. *Women without Class: Girls, Race, and Identity*. Berkeley: University of California Press.

Blair-Loy, Mary. 2003. *Competing Devotions: Career and Family among Women Executives*. Cambridge: Harvard University Press.

Blum, Virginia L. 2005. *Flesh Wounds: The Culture of Cosmetic Surgery*. Berkeley: University of California Press.

Blumer, Herbert. 1969. "Fashion: From Class Differentiation to Collective Selection." *Sociological Quarterly* 10 (3): 275–291.

Brewis, Joanna, and John Sinclair. 2000. "Exploring Embodiment: Women, Biology, and Work." In *Body and Organization*, edited by John Hassard, Ruth Holliday, and Hugh Wilmott, 192–214. Thousand Oaks, CA: Sage.

Britton, Dana M. 2000. "The Epistemology of the Gendered Organization." *Gender & Society* 14 (3): 418–434.

Bordo, Susan. 1999. *The Male Body: A New Look at Men in Public and in Private*. New York: Farrar, Straus and Giroux.

——. 1993. *Unbearable Weight: Feminism, Western Culture, and the Body*. Berkeley: University of California Press.

Bourdieu, Pierre. 1984. *Distinction: A Social Critique of the Judgment of Taste*. Translated by Richard Nice. Cambridge: Harvard University Press.

——. 2002. *Masculine Domination*. Translated by Richard Nice. Stanford: Stanford University Press.

Bourdieu, Pierre, and Jean-Claude Passeron. 1990. *Reproduction in Education, Society, and Culture*. 2nd ed. Translated by Richard Nice. Thousand Oaks, CA: Sage.

Brannon, Robert. 1976. "The Male Sex Role—and What It's Done for Us Lately." In *The Forty-Nine Percent Majority*, edited by Deborah S. David and Robert Brannon, 1–40. Reading, MA: Addison-Wesley.

Bridges, Tristan. 2014. "A Very 'Gay' Straight? Hybrid Masculinities, Sexual Aesthetics, and the Changing Relationship between Masculinity and Homophobia." *Gender & Society* 28 (1): 58–82.

Brody, Charles J., Beth A. Rubin, and David J. Maume. 2014. "Gender Structure and the Effects of Management Citizenship Behavior." *Social Forces* 92 (4): 1373–1404.

Bureau of Labor Statistics (U.S. Department of Labor). 2011. *Veterans in the Civilian Labor Force, 2011*. http://www.bls.gov/opub/ted/2012/ted_20121109.htm.

Carter, J. A. 2014. "'Let's Bang': Constructing, Reinforcing, and Embodying Orthodox Masculinity in Women's Full-Contact, Tackle Football." PhD diss., University of Cincinnati.

Casanova, Erynn Masi. 2011. *Making Up the Difference: Women, Beauty, and Direct Selling in Ecuador*. Austin: University of Texas Press.

——. 2013. "Embodied Inequality: The Experience of Domestic Work in Urban Ecuador." *Gender & Society* 27 (4): 561–585.

Casanova, Erynn Masi, and Afshan Jafar, eds. 2013. *Bodies without Borders*. New York: Palgrave Macmillan.

Casanova, Erynn Masi, and Barbara Sutton. 2013. "Transnational Body Projects: Media Representations of Cosmetic Surgery Tourism in the U.S. and Argentina." *Journal of World-Systems Research* 19 (1): 57–81.

Chafetz, Janet Saltzman. 1974. *Masculine/Feminine or Human?* Itasca: F.E. Peacock.

Chattaraman, Veena, Karla P. Simmons, and Pamela V. Ulrich. 2013. "Age, Body Size, Body Image, and Fit Preferences of Male Consumers." *Clothing and Textiles Research Journal* 31 (4): 291–305.

Cherlin, Andrew J. 2010. *The Marriage-Go-Round: The State of Marriage and the Family in America Today*. New York: Knopf Doubleday.

Ciabattari, Teresa. 2004. "Cohabitation and Housework: The Effects of Marital Intentions." *Journal of Marriage and the Family* 66:118–125.

Coad, David. 2008. *The Metrosexual: Gender, Sexuality, and Sport*. Albany: SUNY Press.

Cole, Shaun. 2000. *Don We Now Our Gay Apparel: Gay Men's Dress in the Twentieth Century*. London: Bloomsbury Academic.

Collinson, David L., and Jeff Hearn. 1996. *Men as Managers, Managers as Men: Critical Perspectives on Men, Masculinities, and Managements*. London: Sage.

Connell, R. W. 1995. *Masculinities*. Berkeley: University of California Press.

Connell, R. W., and James W. Messerschmidt. 2005. "Hegemonic Masculinity: Rethinking the Concept." *Gender & Society* 19 (6): 829–859.

Connell, R. W., and Julian Wood. 2005. "Globalization and Business Masculinities." *Men and Masculinities* 7 (4): 347–364.

Corrigan, Peter. 2008. *The Dressed Society: Clothing, the Body, and Some Meanings of the World*. Thousand Oaks, CA: Sage.

Craig, Maxine Leeds. 2002. *Ain't I a Beauty Queen? Black Women, Beauty, and the Politics of Race*. New York: Oxford University Press.

——. 2013. *Sorry I Don't Dance: Why Men Refuse to Move*. New York: Oxford University Press.

Craik, Jennifer. 1994. *The Face of Fashion: Cultural Studies in Fashion*. London: Routledge.

——. 2003. "The Cultural Politics of the Uniform." *Fashion Theory* 7 (2): 127–147.

——. 2005. *Uniforms Exposed: From Conformity to Transgression*. New York: Berg.

——. 2008. "Uniforms and Men's Fashion: Tailoring Masculinity to Fit." In Reilly and Cosbey, *The Men's Fashion Reader*, 429–444.

Cregan, Kate. 2006. *The Sociology of the Body*. Thousand Oaks, CA: Sage.

Damaske, Sarah. 2011. *For the Family? How Class and Gender Shape Women's Work*. New York: Oxford University Press.

Dasgupta, Romit. 2010. "Globalisation and the Bodily Performance of 'Cool' and 'Un-cool' Masculinities in Corporate Japan." *Intersections: Gender and Sexuality in Asia and the Pacific* 23. http://intersections.anu.edu.au/issue23/dasgupta.htm.

Davis, Fred. 1992. *Fashion, Culture, and Identity*. Chicago: University of Chicago Press.

Davison, Kevin G. 2007. "Methodological Instability and the Disruption of Masculinities." *Men and Masculinities* 9 (3): 379–391.

Delaney, Kevin J. 2012. *Money at Work: On the Job with Priests, Poker Players, and Hedge Fund Traders*. New York: New York University Press.

Dellinger, Kirsten. 2002. "Wearing Gender and Sexuality 'On Your Sleeve': Dress Norms and the Importance of Occupational and Organizational Culture at Work." *Gender Issues* 20 (1): 3–25.

DeMello, Margo. 2014. *Body Studies: An Introduction*. New York: Routledge.

Demetriou, Demetrakis Z. 2001. "Connell's Concept of Hegemonic Masculinity: A Critique." *Theory and Society* 30 (3): 337–361.

Dreby, Joanna. 2009. "Transnational Gossip." *Qualitative Sociology* 32:33–52.

Duggan, Scott J., and Donald R. McCreary. 2008. "Body Image, Eating Disorders, and the Drive for Muscularity in Gay and Heterosexual Men." In Reilly and Cosbey, *The Men's Fashion Reader*, 410–421.

Dvorak, John C. 2012. "Zuckerberg Wears Hoodie, World Ends." *PC Magazine*.com, May 10. http://www.pcmag.com/article2/0,2817,2404300,00.asp.

Edwards, Tim. 2009. "Consuming Masculinities: Style, Content, and Men's Magazines." In *The Men's Fashion Reader*, edited by Peter McNeil and Vicki Karaminas, 462–471. Oxford: Berg.

——. 1997. *Men in the Mirror: Men's Fashion, Masculinity, and Consumer Society*. London: Cassell.

Eicher, Joanne B., and Mary Ellen Roach-Higgins. 1997. "Definition and Classification of Dress: Implications for Analysis of Gender Roles." In *Dress and Gender: Making and Meaning in Cultural Contexts*, edited by Ruth Barnes and Joanne B. Eicher. 8–28. Oxford: Berg.

Elias, Juanita, and Christine Beasley. 2009. "Hegemonic Masculinity and Globalization: Transnational Business Masculinities and Beyond." *Globalizations* 6 (2): 281–296.

Entwistle, Joanne. 1997. "Power Dressing and the Fashioning of the Career Woman." In *Buy This Book: Studies in Advertising and Consumption*, edited by Mica Nava, Andrew Blake, Iain MacRury, and Barry Richards, 208–219. London: Routledge.

——. 2000a. *The Fashioned Body: Fashion, Dress, and Modern Social Theory*. Cambridge: Polity Press.

——. 2000b. "Fashioning the Career Woman: Power Dressing as a Strategy of Consumption." In *All the World and her Husband: Women and Consumption in the Twentieth Century*, edited by Margaret R. Andrews and Mary M. Talbot, 224–238. New York: Cassell.

——. 2009. "From Catwalk to Catalogue: Male Fashion Models, Masculinity, and Identity." In McNeil and Karaminas, *The Men's Fashion Reader*, 197–209.

Farrell, Amy Erdman. 2011. *Fat Shame: Stigma and the Fat Body in American Culture*. New York: New York University Press.

Fee, Dwight. 2000. "'One of the Guys': Instrumentality and Intimacy in Gay Men's Friendships with Straight Men." In *Gay Masculinities*, edited by Peter M. Nardi, 44–65. Thousand Oaks, CA: Sage.

Finlay, William, and James E. Coverdill. 2007. *Headhunters: Matchmaking in the Labor Market*. Ithaca, NY: ILR Press.

Fralic, Shelley. 2012. "Facebook Fatigue Is Setting In." *Vancouver Sun*, May 26, Issues & Ideas. http://www.vancouversun.com/technology/Facebook+fatigue+sett ing/6682321/story.html.

Franzoi, Stephen L., and Stephanie A. Shields. 1984. "The Body Esteem Scale: Multidimensional Structure and Sex Differences in a College Population." *Journal of Personality Assessment* 48:173–178.

Friedman, Vanessa. 2011. "Facebook and the Hoodie." *Financial Times*, January 15, Life & Arts. http://www.ft.com/cms/s/2/dcd7c002-1f55-11e0-8c1c-00144feab49a.html.

Garrahan, Matthew. 2012. "Zuckerberg Move [Los Angeles Notebook]." *Financial Times*, July 18, 2012, Notebook, page 8. Accessed via Lexis-Nexis.

Gates, Gary J., and Frank Newport. 2013. "Gallup Special Report: New Estimates of the LGBT Population in the United States." http://www.gallup.com/poll/160517/lgbt-percentage-highest-lowest-north-dakota.aspx.

Gaudin, Sharon. 2012. "Hoodie Gate: Facebook CEO's Attire a Sign of 'Immaturity'?" *Computerworld*, May 9. http://www.computerworld.com/article/2504115/it-management/hoodie-gate--facebook-ceo-s-attire-a-sign-of--immaturity--.html.

Gearjunkie.com. 2014. "The Rise of the 'Lumbersexual.'" October 30, http://gearjunkie.com/the-rise-of-the-lumbersexual.

Gerson, Kathleen. 1986. *Hard Choices: How Women Decide about Work, Career, and Motherhood*. Berkeley: University of California Press.

——. 1994. *No Man's Land: Men's Changing Commitments to Family and Work*. New York: Basic Books.

——. 2009. *The Unfinished Revolution: How a New Generation is Reshaping Family, Work, and Gender in America*. New York: Oxford University Press.

Gill, Matthew. 2009. *Accountants' Truth: Knowledge and Ethics in the Financial World*. New York: Oxford University Press.

Gill, Rosalind, Karen Henwood, and Carl McLean. 2005. "Body Projects and the Regulation of Normative Masculinity." *Body & Society* 11 (1): 37–62.

Gimlin, Debra. 2002. *Body Work: Beauty and Self-Image in American Culture*. Berkeley: University of California Press.

Goffman, Erving. 1959. *The Presentation of Self in Everyday Life*. New York: Doubleday.

Goodrum, Alison. 2001. "Land of Hip and Glory: Fashioning the 'Classic' National Body." In *Dressed to Impress: Looking the Part*, edited by William J. F. Keenan, 85–104. Oxford: Berg.

GQ. 2013. "Dropping Knowledge: Glen Plaid." *The GQ Eye Style Blog*. http://www.gq.com/style/blogs/the-gq-eye/2013/10/dropping-knowledge-glen-plaid.html.

Grasmuck, Sherri. 2005. *Protecting Home: Class, Race, and Masculinity in Boys' Baseball*. New Brunswick: Rutgers University Press.

Grogan, Sarah, Simeon Gill, Kathryn Brownbridge, Sarah Kilgariff, and Amanda Whalley. 2013. "Dress Fit and Body Image: A Thematic Analysis of Women's Accounts during and after Trying on Dresses." *Body Image* 10:380–388.

Gross, Doug. 2012. "Zuckerberg's Hoodie Rankles Wall Street." *CNN*.com, May 9. http://www.cnn.com/2012/05/09/tech/social-media/zuckerberg-hoodie-wall-street/.

Gusterson, Hugh. 1997. "Studying Up Revisited." *PoLAR: Political and Legal Anthropology Review* 20 (1): 114–119.

Guynn, Jessica. 2013. "Twitter Goes to Wall Street." *Los Angeles Times*, October 26, B-2. http://articles.latimes.com/2013/oct/25/business/la-fi-tn-twitter-goes-to-wall-street-dick-costolo-wears-blazer-but-no-tie-20131025.

Halberstam, Judith. 1998. *Female Masculinity*. Durham: Duke University Press.

Hall, Richard H. 1994. *Sociology of Work: Perspectives, Analyses, and Issues*. Thousand Oaks, CA: Pine Forge Press.

Hartley, Cecilia. 2010. "Letting Ourselves Go: Making Room for the Fat Body in Feminist Scholarship." In *The Politics of Women's Bodies: Sexuality, Appearance, and Behavior*, edited by Rose Weitz, 245–254. 3rd ed. New York: Oxford University Press.

Harvey, David. 2005. *A Brief History of Neoliberalism*. New York: Oxford University Press.

Harvey Wingfield, Adia. 2013. *No More Invisible Man: Race and Gender in Men's Work*. Philadelphia: Temple University Press.

Hearn, Jeff, and Wendy Parkin. 1995. *Sex at Work: The Power and Paradox of Organisation Sexuality*. Basingstoke: Palgrave Macmillan.

Hesse-Biber, Sharlene. 2007. *The Cult of Thinness*. 2nd ed. New York: Oxford University Press.

Heti, Sheila, Heidi Julavits, and Leanne Shapton. 2014. *Women in Clothes*. New York: Penguin.

Higgins, Ross. 1998. "À la Mode: Fashioning Gay Community in Montreal." In *Consuming Fashion: Adorning the Transnational Body*, edited by Anne Brydon and Sandra Niessen, 129–158. Oxford: Berg.

Ho, Karen. 2009. *Liquidated: An Ethnography of Wall Street*. Durham: Duke University Press.

Hochschild, Arlie Russell. 1983. *The Managed Heart: Commercialization of Human Feeling*. Berkeley: University of California Press.

——. 1989. *The Second Shift*. With Anne Machung. New York: Penguin.

——. 1994. "The Cultural Spirit of Intimate Life and the Abduction of Feminism: Signs from Women's Advice Books." *Theory, Culture, & Society* 11:1–24.

——. 2001. *The Time Bind: When Work Becomes Home and Home Becomes Work*. New York: Metropolitan Books.

Hollander, Anne. 1994. *Sex and Suits: The Evolution of Modern Dress*. New York: Knopf.

Holliday, Ruth, and Graham Thompson. 2001. "A Body of Work." In *Contested Bodies*, edited by Ruth Holliday and John Hassard. London: Routledge.

Huun, Kathleen. 2008. "The Ubiquitous Necktie: Style, Symbolism, and Signification through Transitions of Masculinity." In Reilly and Cosbey, *The Men's Fashion Reader*, 33–51.

Hyman, Peter. 2004. *The Reluctant Metrosexual: Dispatches from an Almost Hip Life*. New York: Villard Books.

Jafar, Afshan, and Erynn Masi de Casanova. 2013. *Global Beauty, Local Bodies*. New York: Palgrave Macmillan.

James, Susan Donaldson. 2011. "Gay Americans Make Up 4 Percent of Population." ABC News. http://abcnews.go.com/Health/williams-institute-report-reveals-million-gay-bisexual-transgender/story?id=13320565.

Janus, Teresa, Susan B. Kaiser, and Gordon Gray. 1999. "Negotiations @ Work: The Casual Businesswear Trend." In *The Meanings of Dress*, edited by Mary Lynn Damhorst, Kimberly Miller, and Susan Michelman. New York: Fairchild Books.

Joseph, Nathan. 1986. *Uniforms and Nonuniforms: Communication through Clothing.* Santa Barbara: Praeger.

Judge, Timothy A., and Daniel M. Cable. 2004. "The Effect of Physical Height on Workplace Success and Income: Preliminary Test of a Theoretical Model." *Journal of Applied Psychology* 89 (3): 428–441.

Kaiser, Susan. 2012. *Fashion and Cultural Studies.* London: Bloomsbury Publishing.

Kaiser, Susan, Carla M. Freeman, and Joan L. Chandler. 1993. "Favorite Clothes and Gendered Subjectivities: Multiple Readings." *Studies in Symbolic Interaction* 15:27–50.

Kaiser Family Foundation. 2014. "Workers by Occupational Category." http://kff.org/other/state-indicator/blue-and-white-collar-workers/.

Kang, Miliann. 2010. *The Managed Hand: Race, Gender and the Body in Beauty Service Work.* Berkeley: University of California Press.

Kang, Minjeong, Monica Sklar, and Kim K. P. Johnson. 2011. "Men at Work: Using Dress to Communicate Identities." *Journal of Fashion Marketing and Management* 15 (4): 412–427.

Kanter, Rosabeth Moss. 1977. *Men and Women of the Corporation.* New York: Basic Books.

Kastelle, Tim. 2013. "Hierarchy Is Overrated." *Harvard Business Review* (blog), November 20. http://blogs.hbr.org/2013/11/hierarchy-is-overrated/.

Keenan, William J. F. 2001. *Dressed to Impress: Looking the Part.* New York: Bloomsbury Academic.

Khan, Shamus, and Colin Jerolmack. 2013. "Saying Meritocracy and Doing Privilege." *Sociological Quarterly* 54 (1): 9–19.

Kidwell, Claudia B., and Margaret C. Christman. 1974. *Suiting Everyone: The Democratization of Clothing in America.* Washington, DC: Smithsonian Institution Press.

Kimle, Patricia A., and Mary L. Damhorst. 1997. "A Grounded Theory Model of the Ideal Business Image for Women." *Symbolic Interaction* 20 (1): 45–68.

Krogstad, Jens Manuel. 2014. "Hispanics Only Group to See its Poverty Rate Decline and Incomes Rise." Pew Research Center Report. http://www.pewresearch.org/fact-tank/2014/09/19/hispanics-only-group-to-see-its-poverty-rate-decline-and-incomes-rise/.

Kuchta, David M. 2008. "'Graceful, Virile, and Useful: The Origins of the Three-Piece Suit." In Reilly and Cosbey, *The Men's Fashion Reader*, 498–511.

Lane, Carrie M. 2011. *A Company of One: Insecurity, Independence, and the New World of White-Collar Unemployment.* Ithaca, NY: ILR Press.

Lareau, Annette. 2003. *Unequal Childhoods: Class, Race, and Family Life.* Berkeley: University of California Press.

Larson, Chase. 2011. "Mark Zuckerberg Speaks at BYU." *Deseret News*, March 25.

Lazarowitz, Elizabeth. 2013. "Workers Don't Like—They Love—Zuck!" *New York Daily News*, March 16, Business, 24.

Lefifi, Thekiso Anthony. 2012. "Not What You Wear but How You Wear It." *Sunday Times* (Johannesberg, South Africa), May 20.

Linneman, Thomas J. 2000. "Risk and Masculinity in the Everyday Lives of Gay Men." In Nardi, *Gay Masculinities*, 83–100.

Lofland, John, David Snow, Leon Anderson, and Lyn H. Lofland. 2006. *Analyzing Social Settings: A Guide to Qualitative Observation and Analysis.* Belmont, CA: Wadsworth/Cengage.

Longhurst, Robyn. 2004. *Bodies: Exploring Fluid Boundaries.* London: Routledge.

Mallyon, Anna, Mary Holmes, John Coveney, and Maria Zadoroznyj. 2010. "I'm Not Dieting, 'I'm Doing It for Science': Masculinities and the Experience of Dieting." *Health Sociology Review* 19 (3): 330–342.

Marcuse, Herbert. (1964) 1991. *One-Dimensional Man*. 2nd ed. New York: Beacon.

McArdle, Keri A., and Melanie S. Hill. 2009. "Understanding Body Dissatisfaction in Gay and Heterosexual Men: The Roles of Self-Esteem, Media, and Peer Influence." *Men and Masculinities* 11 (5): 511–532.

McDowell, Linda. 1997. *Capital Culture: Gender at Work in the City*. Oxford: Blackwell.

McElhinny, Bonnie. 1994. "An Economy of Affect: Objectivity, Masculinity, and the Gendering of Police Work." In *Dislocating Masculinity: Comparative Ethnographies*, edited by Andrea Cornwall and Nancy Lindisfarne, 159–171. London: Routledge.

McLeod, Harriet. 1996. "Business Casual Dress: An African American Male Perspective." In *The Meanings of Dress*, edited by Mary Lynn Damhorst, Kimberly A. Miller, and Susan O. Michelman, 272–274. New York: Fairchild Publications.

McNeil, Peter. 2009. "Macaroni Masculinities." In McNeil and Karaminas, *The Men's Fashion Reader*, 54–71.

McNeil, Peter, and Vicki Karaminas. 2009. *The Men's Fashion Reader*. Oxford: Berg.

Mead, George H. (1934) 1967. *Mind, Self, and Society*. Chicago: University of Chicago Press.

Mears, Ashley. 2011. *Pricing Beauty: The Making of a Fashion Model*. Berkeley: University of California Press.

Merton, Robert. 1961. "Bureaucratic Structure and Personality." In *Complex Organizations: A Sociological Reader*, edited by Amitai Etzioni, 48–61. New York: Holt, Rinehart & Winston.

Messner, Michael A. 1993. "'Changing Men' and Feminist Politics in the United States." *Theory and Society* 22:723–737.

Miller, Toby. 2005. "A Metrosexual Eye on Queer Guy." *GLQ: A Journal of Lesbian and Gay Studies* 11 (1): 112–117.

Mills, C. Wright. (1951) 2002. *White Collar: The American Middle Classes*. 50th anniversary ed. New York: Oxford University Press.

Monaghan, Lee F. 2002a. "Embodying Gender, Work and Organization: Solidarity, Cool Loyalties and Contested Hierarchy in a Masculinist Occupation." *Gender, Work and Organization* 9 (5): 504–536.

——. 2002b. "Hard Men, Shop Boys, and Others: Embodying Competence in a Masculinised Occupation." *Sociological Review* 50 (3): 334–355.

Moore, Karl, and Kyle Hill. 2011. "The Decline but Not Fall of Hierarchy—What Young People Really Want." Forbes.com. http://www.forbes.com/sites/karlmoore/2011/06/14/the-decline-but-not-fall-of-hierarchy-what-young-people-really-want/.

Morrill, Calvin. 1996. *The Executive Way: Conflict Management in Corporations*. Chicago: University of Chicago Press.

Morrison, Toni. 1992. *Jazz*. New York: Knopf.

Mort, Frank. 1996. *Cultures of Consumption: Masculinities and Social Space in Late Twentieth-Century Britain*. London: Routledge.

Mose Brown, Tamara. 2011. *Raising Brooklyn: Nannies, Childcare, and Caribbeans Creating Community*. New York: New York University Press.

Mose Brown, Tamara, and Erynn Masi de Casanova. 2014. "Representing the Language of the 'Other': African American Vernacular English in Ethnography." *Ethnography* 15 (2): 208–231.

Moss, Mark. 2011. *The Media and the Models of Masculinity*. New York: Lexington Books.

Nader, Laura. 1972. "Up the Anthropologist—Perspectives Gained from Studying Up." In *Reinventing Anthropology*, edited by Dell H. Hymes, 284–311. New York: Pantheon Books.

Nardi, Peter M. 2000. *Gay Masculinities*. Thousand Oaks, CA: Sage.

Neal, Mark Anthony. 2013. *Looking for Leroy: Illegible Black Masculinities*. New York: New York University Press.

Nixon, Sean. 1996. *Hard Looks: Masculinities, Spectatorship and Contemporary Consumption*. New York: St. Martin's.

O'Neal, Gwendolyn. 1999. "The Power of Style: On Rejection of the Accepted." In *Appearance and Power*, edited by Kim K. P. Johnson and Sharron J. Lennon, 127–139. Oxford: Berg.

Padavic, Irene, and Barbara F. Reskin. 2002. *Women and Men at Work*. 2nd ed. Thousand Oaks, CA: Sage.

Pascoe, C. J. 2007. *Dude, You're a Fag: Masculinity and Sexuality in High School*. Berkeley: University of California Press.

Peoples, Sharon. 2014. "Embodying the Military: Uniforms." *Critical Studies in Men's Fashion* 1 (1): 7–21.

Pitts-Taylor, Victoria. 2007. *Surgery Junkies: Wellness and Pathology in Cosmetic Culture*. New Brunswick: Rutgers University Press.

Pugh, Allison. 2009. *Longing and Belonging: Parents, Children, and Consumer Culture*. Berkeley: University of California Press.

Rau, Cordula. 2008. *Why Do Architects Wear Black?* New York: SpringerWein.

Reich, Jennifer. 2014. "Neoliberal Mothering and Vaccine Refusal: Imagined Gated Communities and the Privilege of Choice." *Gender & Society* 28 (5): 679–704.

Reilly, Andrew, and Sarah Cosbey, eds. 2008. *The Men's Fashion Reader*. New York: Fairchild Books.

Reilly, Andrew, Nancy A. Rudd, and Julie Hillery. 2008. "Shopping Behavior among Gay Men: Issues of Body Image." *Clothing and Textiles Research Journal* 26 (4): 313–326.

Rinallo, Diego. 2007. "Metro/Fashion/Tribes of Men: Negotiating the Boundaries of Men's Legitimate Consumption." In *Consumer Tribes*, edited by Bernard Cova, Robert V. Kozinets, and Avi Shankar, 76–92. New York: Butterworth-Heinemann.

Rivera, Lauren A. 2012. "Hiring as Cultural Matching: The Case of Elite Professional Service Firms." *American Sociological Review* 77 (6): 999–1022.

Robinson, Rebecca J. 2008. "It Won't Stop: The Evolution of Men's Hip-Hop Gear." In Reilly and Cosbey, *The Men's Fashion Reader*, 253–264.

Roche, Daniel. 1996. *The Culture of Clothing: Dress and Fashion in the Ancient Regime*. Cambridge: Cambridge University Press.

Rohrer, Finlo. 2012. "Facebook's Mark Zuckerberg: Does It Matter That He Wears a Hoodie?" *BBC News Magazine*, May 11. http://www.bbc.com/news/magazine-18032190.

Roper, Michael. 1994. *Masculinity and the British Organization Man since 1945*. Oxford: Oxford University Press.

Rosnow, Ralph L., and Gary Alan Fine. 1976. *Rumor and Gossip: The Social Psychology of Hearsay*. New York: Elsevier.

Rothblum, Esther, and Sondra Solovay, eds. 2009. *The Fat Studies Reader*. New York: New York University Press.

Rucker, Margaret, Elizabeth Anderson, and April Kangas. 1999. "Clothing, Power, and the Workplace." In *Appearance and Power*, edited by Kim K. P. Johnson and Sharron J. Lennon. Oxford: Berg.

Rudd, Nancy Ann. 2008. "Body Image and Self-Presentation among Gay Men." In Reilly and Cosbey, *The Men's Fashion Reader*, 355–374.

Rumens, Nick. 2011. *Queer Company: The Role and Meaning of Friendship in Gay Men's Work Lives*. London: Ashgate.

Rutherford, Jonathan. 1987. "Who's That Man?" In *Male Order: Unwrapping Masculinity*, edited by Rowena Chapman and Jonathan Rutherford, 21–67. London: Lawrence and Wishart.

Sánchez Voelkl, Pilar. 2011. *La construcción del gerente: Masculinidades en élites corporativas de Colombia y Ecuador* [The construction of the manager: Masculinities among corporate elites in Colombia and Ecuador]. Quito, Ecuador: FLACSO Ecuador.

Sandberg, Sheryl. 2013. *Lean In: Women, Work, and the Will to Lead*. New York: Knopf.

Sapir, Edward. (1931) 2007. "Fashion." In *Fashion Theory: A Reader*, edited by Malcolm Barnard. London, U.K.: Routledge.

Schilt, Kristen. 2011. *Just One of the Guys? Transgender Men and the Persistence of Gender Inequality*. Chicago: University of Chicago Press.

Sengupta, Somini. 2012. "Zuckerberg's Hoodie Sets Off Hand-Wringing." *New York Times*, May 14, B-10. http://query.nytimes.com/gst/fullpage.html?res=9A0CE1D 8173DF937A25756C0A9649D8B63.

Shaer, Matthew. 2013. "The Boss Stops Here." *New York Magazine*, June 16. http://nymag.com/news/features/bossless-jobs-2013-6/.

Shilling, Chris. 2003. *The Body and Social Theory*. 2nd ed. Thousand Oaks, CA: Sage.

———. 2007. "Sociology and the Body: Classical Traditions and New Agendas." *Sociological Review* 55 (1): 1–18.

Silverman, Gary. 2012. "When It's Time to Dress the Part." New York Notebook. *Financial Times*, May 11. http://www.ft.com/intl/cms/s/0/9ce5ccd2-99ca-11e1-aa6d-00144feabdc0.html#axzz3WAjjiuwI. 8.

Simmel, Georg. (1904) 1957. "Fashion." *American Journal of Sociology* 62 (6): 541–558.

Simpson, Mark. 1999. "Metrosexuals: Male Vanity Steps Out of the Closet." In *It's a Queer World: Deviant Adventures in Pop Culture*. New York: Harrington Park Press, 207–210.

———. 2015. "Objectify Yourself: Why Straight Young Men Crave Gay Adulation." *OUT Magazine*, January 6. http://www.out.com/entertainment/2015/01/06/objectify-yourself-why-straight-young-men-crave-gay-adulation.

Slevin, Kathleen F., and Thomas J. Linneman. 2010. "Old Gay Men's Bodies and Masculinities." *Men and Masculinities* 12 (4): 483–507.

Speice, Travis D. Forthcoming. "Managing Gendered and Sexual Identities in Everyday Life: A Study of Gay Men." PhD diss., University of Cincinnati.

St. John, Warren. 2003. "Metrosexuals Come Out." *New York Times*, June 22.

Stone, Pamela. 2007. *Opting Out? Why Women Really Quit Careers and Head Home*. Berkeley: University of California Press.

Suttles, Gerald D. 1984. "The Cumulative Texture of Local Urban Culture." *American Journal of Sociology* 90 (2): 283–304.

Talukdar, Jaita, and Annulla Linders. 2013. "Gender, Class Aspirations, and Emerging Fields of Bodywork in Urban India." *Qualitative Sociology* 36 (1): 101–123.

Tricarico, Donald. 2008. "Dressing Up Italian Americans for the Youth Spectacle: What Difference Does Guido Perform?" In Reilly and Cosbey, *The Men's Fashion Reader*, 265–278.

Tseëlon, Efrat. 2003. "Ontological, Epistemological and Methodological Clarifications in Fashion Research: From Critique to Empirical Suggestions." In *Through the Wardrobe: Women's Relationships with Their Clothes*, edited by Ali Guy, Eileen Green, and Maura Banim, 237–254. Oxford: Berg.

U.S. Department of Commerce. 1951. *Annual Report on the Labor Force, 1950*. Series P-50, no. 31:26. Obtained via personal communication with Bureau of Labor Statistics staff.

U.S. Department of Labor. 2011. *The Veteran Labor Force in the Recovery*. Special report. http://www.dol.gov/_sec/media/reports/VeteransLaborForce/VeteransLaborForce.pdf.

Warhurst, Chris, and Dennis Nickson. 2001. *Looking Good, Sounding Right*. London: Industrial Society.

Weber, Max. (1905) 2001. *The Protestant Ethic and the Spirit of Capitalism*. 3rd ed. Edited by Stephen Kalberg. Cary, NC: Roxbury Publishing.

——. (1921) 1946. "The Sociology of Charismatic Authority." In *From Max Weber: Essays in Sociology*, edited by H. H. Gerth and C. Wright Mills. New York: Oxford University Press, 245–252.

Weitz, Rose. 2010. *The Politics of Women's Bodies: Sexuality, Appearance, and Behavior*. 3rd ed.. New York: Oxford University Press.

Whyte, William H. 1956. *The Organization Man*. Philadelphia: University of Pennsylvania Press.

Wickman, Jan. 2011. Review of *The Metrosexual: Gender, Sexuality and Sport*, by David Coad. *Men and Masculinities* 14 (1): 117–119.

Wickman, Jan, and Fredrik Langeland. 2013. "Metrosexuality as a Body Discourse: Masculinity and Sports Stars in Global and Local Contexts." In *Global Beauty, Local Bodies*, edited by Afshan Jafar and Erynn Masi de Casanova, 125–150. New York: Palgrave Macmillan.

Williams, Colin J., Martin S. Weinberg, and Joshua G. Rosenberger. 2013. "Trans Men: Embodiments, Identities, and Sexualities." *Sociological Forum* 28 (4): 719–741.

Willis, Paul. 1981. *Learning to Labor: How Working Class Kids Get Working Class Jobs*. New York: Columbia University Press.

Wilson, Sloan. (1955) 2002. *The Man in the Gray Flannel Suit*. Cambridge: Da Capo Press.

Witz, Anne, Chris Warhurst, and Dennis Nickson. 2003. "The Labour of Aesthetics and the Aesthetics of Organization." *Organization* 10 (1): 33–54.

Wolkowitz, Carol. 2006. *Bodies at Work*. London: Sage.

Woods, James D. 1993. *The Corporate Closet: The Professional Lives of Gay Men in America*. With Jay H. Lucas. New York: Free Press.

Index